the

Signature

of

God

Astonishing Biblical Discoveries

the

Signature

of

God

Grant R. Jeffrey

WORD PUBLISHIN
Nashville • London • Vancouver • M

Word Publishing, Nashville, Tennessee

The Signature of God—Astonishing Biblical Discoveries

Book design by Kandi Shepherd

Library of Congress Cataloging-in-Publication Data

Jeffrey, Grant R.
    The signature of God: astonishing biblical discoveries / by Grant
R. Jeffrey.
        p. cm.
    Originally published: Toronto, Ont. : Frontier Research
Publications, 1996.
    Includes bibliographical references.
    ISBN 0-8499-4094-X
    1. Bible—Evidences, authority, etc. 2. Bible—Inspiration.
I. Title.
    BS480.J44 1998
220.1—dc21

                                                        97-44087
                                                           CIP

Printed in the United States of America
8 9 0 1 2 3 4 OPM 9 8 7 6 5 4 3 2 1

Table of Contents

The Signature of God is affectionately dedicated to my lovely wife, Kaye, who is my partner in ministry and the joy of my life. She accompanies me in my research tours around the world, and shares my love of the Scriptures.

Many of the greatest scholars in the last two thousand years have explored the Scriptures and concluded that they are truly inspired by God. During the last few decades, I completed many research trips and communicated with bookstores throughout the world acquiring numerous old and often rare books written by these great men of God from past generations. These volumes contain tremendous archeological, historical, and scientific evidence that confirms the inspiration and authority of the Word of God. I am greatly indebted to the work of countless Bible scholars who have labored to find the wealth of evidence that proves the inspiration of the Scriptures.

I have truly enjoyed completing the research and writing *The Signature of God*. My hope is that every reader will be as thrilled by this evidence proving the inspiration of the Bible as I was to uncover it as a researcher. Finally, if my book renews in the hearts of my readers a new love and appreciation for the Word of God, I will be well rewarded.

"The Bible is the greatest of all the books ever penned by men; to study it diligently is the most worthy of all possible pursuits; to clearly understand what the Lord is saying to us through its pages is truly the most noble and the highest of my goals. The application to my heart, mind and spirit of the truths of the Word of God through the Holy Spirit's gift of understanding and my subsequent obedience to that revelation is my supreme purpose and duty."

Found in an old Bible in England

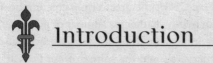# Introduction

Is there a God? Does my life have any meaning or does everything happen solely by chance? How can I find the truth about life and death? What will happen when I die? Is the Bible truly the "inspired" Word of God or is it just the philosophical writings of a group of ancient men? These questions occur to all of us at some point in our life. Our answers to these questions are vitally important because they affect our goals, our relationships, our peace of mind, and, ultimately, our eternal destiny. The Bible claims to be the inspired Word of God and declares that its message is absolutely true. Therefore, it is of utmost importance that all of us determine for ourselves whether the Bible is truly the Word of God or not.

If the Bible is literally true and God does exist, then every one of us will someday stand before God to be judged by Him as to our eternal destiny—heaven or hell. The Scriptures tell us that, following our death, we will give an account to God about how we have responded to Jesus Christ and His offer of personal salvation. On the other hand, if the Bible is untrue and God does not exist, then men are free to live as they please and experience the consequences of their choices only in this world. The philosophy of "Eat, drink, and be merry, for tomorrow we die" is one logical response if man lives in a universe that has no God and no purpose. The answer to this question, "Is the Bible truly the Word of God?" is of the greatest possible importance to every human being whether we admit it or not. Our beliefs are the most important thing in our lives because they determine the decisions and the course of our lives. If we change our deeply held beliefs, we will change our actions, our decisions, and the direction of our lives.

Is there some way to determine the truth about God and the Bible? This book, *The Signature of God*, will examine incredible scientific discoveries that prove that the Bible is authoritative and inspired by God. Some people are content to follow a blind faith based on the religious convictions of their forefathers. However, many of us want to examine these matters for ourselves to determine the answer to this vital question.

How Would God Reveal Himself to Mankind?

Let's conduct an experiment to examine the question of how God would reveal Himself to mankind if He truly exists. After creating this universe and mankind, how would God reveal Himself and His instructions to His creatures? He could choose to speak to every single one of the billions of humans in every generation, but that would be somewhat impractical. On the other hand, God could choose a number of men over a period of years and inspire them to record faithfully in writing His instructions for the rest of mankind. Obviously, the second option is the most practical.

However, there is another problem that God would face in revealing His will to mankind. How would God prove that the Bible was His legitimate revelation to mankind? The challenge would be how best to differentiate the true inspired Scriptures of God from the many other religious books produced by religious philosophers over the centuries. I believe the solution is quite obvious: God would authenticate His own true revelation by writing His signature on the pages of His Scriptures. This signature of God would consist of <u>evidence, knowledge, and phenomena in the text of the Bible that no unaided human could possibly have written.</u> In other words, the genuine Scriptures should contain supernatural evidence within their texts that no one apart from a divine intelligence could create. Interestingly, the Scriptures do contain a direct statement from God that He had provided precisely this type of supernatural evidence as unmistakable proof of the Bible's inspiration and His divine powers to foretell future events through His prophets. Twenty-five centuries ago, the prophet Isaiah recorded this amazing declaration from God: "Remember the former things of old: for I am God, and there is none else; I am God, and there is none like me, declaring the end from the beginning, and from ancient times the things that are not yet done, saying, My counsel shall stand, and I will do all my pleasure" (Isaiah 46:9–10). In this passage God declared that <u>fulfilled prophecy is an absolute proof that the Scriptures are inspired by the Lord because no one but God,</u> whether human or Satan, can possibly predict precise events in the future. It is significant that not one of the hundreds of religious books outside of the Bible contains detailed predictions about future events. The reason is simple. Any attempt by humans to predict the future precisely always ends in abject failure. The writers of other religious books knew that they did not know what would occur in the future. They wisely refrained from exposing themselves to ridicule by creating what would have inevitably proved to be false predictions. God is the only One who knows the future as well as the past.

My thesis in *The Signature of God* is that the Bible contains a number of fascinating proofs that absolutely authenticate the Scriptures as the inspired and authoritative Word of God. The evidence from hundreds of fulfilled prophecies forms one of the strongest and most obvious proofs of divine inspiration. However, there are a number of other intriguing and undeniable proofs that only God could have inspired the ancient writers to record His message in the Scriptures.

The Bible Contains the Characteristics of a Genuine Revelation from God

How would God authenticate His message so that naturally skeptical men and women could be assured that the Scriptures were truly from God and not simply the speculations of religious philosophers? How would the Lord identify His presence, His divine nature, and His commands to mankind and provide proof that this communication was truly from God?

1. The written revelation of God's nature and commands was progressively revealed step-by-step to a series of carefully chosen men over a period of sixteen centuries. The recipients were closely connected by race and faith to facilitate their gathering, assembling, preserving, and distributing God's written revelation throughout this time. The Lord chose the Jewish people, a small, defined group that has

maintained its identity over the centuries as the faithful guardian of His written revelations.

2. Although His divine communications were transmitted by inspiration to individual Jews, they were recorded in a permanent written form capable of being examined and read by the writer's contemporaries as well as generations to follow.

3. These divine communications were sometimes accompanied by supernatural miracles to prove their origin from God.

4. This revelation contains internal evidence that proves that God is the ultimate author. The Bible includes information that could not have been written by men without divine inspiration.

5. The Bible contains thousands of detailed prophecies concerning events that were precisely fulfilled many years after the predictions were made. Their fulfillment proves that God inspired the Bible. No one but God can prophesy accurately.

6. God inspired biblical writers to record His profound wisdom and truth that transcend all of man's wisdom.

7. God's Holy Spirit supernaturally transforms the lives of millions who commit themselves to the Bible's revelation.

8. The primary purpose of the Bible is to reveal God's plan of salvation. However, whenever the Scripture deals with history, archeology, nature, or science, it reveals advanced knowledge that is true and verifiable. Such biblical statements are far in advance of the knowledge of the time of the original human writer.

9. The Bible's wisdom, knowledge, and ethics clearly proclaim its supernatural origin to anyone who is truly

seeking answers to life's profound questions. The wisest people of all cultures and times are committed to its truths.

10. The Scriptures contain advanced medical and sanitation knowledge that was thousands of years ahead of its time. This medical knowledge from the Bible has saved countless millions of lives of those who followed its divine precepts over the centuries since the Bible was written. In addition, its lifesaving commands still prove their worth in this century.

11. A careful examination of the names and numbers in the Bible's text reveals special mathematical designs and codes that are so complex that no human or super-computer could have produced these features. Many of these designs are not obvious and occur throughout a series of biblical books written by different biblical authors over several centuries. There is no human explanation for this phenomenon except for divine inspiration.

12. Recently, Jewish computer scientists discovered a series of incredible messages encoded at equally spaced intervals hidden beneath the Hebrew text of the first five books of the Bible, the Torah. God inspired the writers to unknowingly use specific words and letters to produce the most astonishing and incredibly complicated mathematical and letter codes ever produced. These features were carefully hidden from the eyes of everyone until this century and the development of mathematical and super-computer analysis. The discovery of these complex patterns of wheels within wheels provides compelling evidence that constitutes an unanswerable argument for the divine inspiration of the Bible. The scientists declared that these patterns are so complex that they could not have been produced by humans.

Furthermore, while these incredible patterns exist in the Hebrew text of the Torah, no apocryphal texts display these patterns, nor can they be found in any other Hebrew religious or secular texts. This incredible phenomenon provides overwhelming evidence that there is one inspired author of the Scriptures.

13. In normal human literature, authors naturally try to present themselves in the best light possible. However, the Bible presents these men "warts and all," revealing them often as weak, afraid, and lacking in wisdom. It runs contrary to human experience to find authors revealing themselves with such candor. Additionally, biblical revelation contains many intricate details and unintended coincidences in its stories that, while easily overlooked, prove the overall truthfulness of the historical accounts.

14. Although written by forty-four men over sixteen centuries, the complete text of the Bible reveals a coherent unity and progressive revelation from Genesis to Revelation that develops God's plan of redemption for mankind. The books of the Old Testament continuously point to the coming of a Messiah-King to redeem His people. The New Testament displays the fulfillment of these divine prophecies in the life, death, and resurrection of Jesus the Messiah. The unity of theology and the focus on the message of redemption throughout the Bible argues strongly that a single author created this text. The combined evidence presented in this book reveals that the single author who inspired the writers of the Bible was God.

Three thousand years ago, King David, the great king of Israel, wrote these words revealing the nature of God's inspired Word: "The law of the LORD is perfect, converting the soul: the testimony of the LORD is sure, making wise the simple. The statutes of the LORD are right, rejoicing the heart: the commandment of the LORD is pure, enlightening the eyes. The fear of the LORD is clean, enduring forever: the judgments of the LORD are true and righteous altogether. More to be desired are they than gold, yea, than much fine gold: sweeter also than honey and the honeycomb. Moreover by them is thy servant warned: and in keeping of them there is great reward" (Psalm 19:7–11).

The Inspiration of Scripture

The early Christians, Jewish scribes, and generations of Christian believers shared an unshakable conviction that the Scriptures contain the infallible, inspired, and authoritative words of God. The Bible itself claims that "All scripture is given by inspiration of God, and is profitable for doctrine, for reproof, for correction, for instruction in righteousness" (2 Timothy 3:16). The Greek word translated "inspired" literally means "God breathed," indicating the Lord's direct supervision of the writing by the biblical writer. The Bible claims that its words were not written by men in an ordinary manner but that God actually inspired men to record His direct words as His revelation to mankind for all time. Just as God created only one sun to provide light to our planet, He gave us only one book, the Bible, to enlighten our world spiritually.

Tragically, during this century many pastors, professors, and laymen have lost their faith and confidence that the Bible is truly the inspired and reliable Word of God. Dr. Kennedy, a Regius Professor of Classics at Cambridge University in the early decades of this century, warned of the relentless battle that was about to begin over the authority of the Bible. "The inspiration of Scriptures will be the last battle ground between the Church and the world." Unfortunately, many in our churches and seminaries today have abandoned this battlefield too easily and accepted defeat at the hands of skeptics who hate the authority of the Word of God. This widespread rejection of the truthfulness of the Scriptures reveals the folly of men who "have forsaken me the fountain of living waters, and hewed them out cisterns, broken cisterns" of vain philosophy (see Jeremiah 2:13). Jeremiah the prophet spoke these words twenty-five centuries ago.

The Bible itself declares in numerous passages that it is the inspired Word of God. The prophet Jeremiah declared, "Then the LORD put forth His hand and touched my mouth, and the LORD said to me: 'Behold, I have put My words in your mouth'" (Jeremiah 1:9, NKJV). God confirmed that He directly inspired His servants, the prophets, to record His words and instructions "word for word." In the New Testament the apostle Peter declared that "knowing this first, that no prophecy of Scripture is of any private interpretation, for prophecy never came by the will of man, but holy men of God spoke as they were moved by the Holy Spirit" (2 Peter 1:20–21, NKJV). One of the strongest statements found in the Bible records the inspired words of Jesus Himself who declared, "The Scripture cannot be broken" (John 10:35).

We will examine the overwhelming scientific evidence that proves the inspiration and authenticity of the Bible as the Word of God. The evidence provided in *The Signature of*

God will establish the credibility and authority of the Scriptures for both non-believers and Christians as a foundation for faith in God's inspired revelation. The book is divided into sections that will examine the various areas in which the Scriptures can be tested as to their authenticity and authority. The evidence we will explore includes the following areas:

1. Fascinating ancient inscriptions and manuscripts that prove the historical accuracy of the Scriptures.

2. Little-known archeological discoveries that provide overwhelming confirmation of the biblical accounts, including the Tower of Babel and the Exodus.

3. The tremendously accurate scientific statements in the Bible that cannot be explained apart from God's inspiration.

4. The incredible fulfillment of prophecies in our generation that authenticate the Scriptures.

5. The staggering phenomenon of hidden codes and mathematical patterns found in the text of the Bible that could not have been produced by human intelligence.

6. Scriptural "coincidences" that confirm the divine inspiration of the Scriptures.

7. The phenomenon of the transformed character and lives of the writers of the Bible.

8. The unprecedented influence of the Bible on the lives of individuals and the culture and history of the Western world.

While many of the topics we will explore in this book are fascinating in and of themselves, their true value for a Christian lies in their ability to confirm and illustrate the events, personalities, and statements of the Word of God. Alexander Knox once wrote about the relationship between human and sacred knowledge as follows: "If in the rills which trickle down amidst these intellectual Alps and Apennines, I could discern no connection with that river which maketh glad the city of God, I own that I should look upon them with as little interest as upon the rocky fragments through which they passed" (quoted by Rev. Charles Forster in *Sinai Photographed*, [London: Richard Bentley, 1862]). As a researcher and writer I feel a tremendous responsibility to check carefully the accuracy of every statement because of the incredible importance of prophecy and scriptural truths. Those who write about the truths of the Scriptures are like the scribes of ancient Israel. The Scriptures declare that "every scribe which is instructed unto the kingdom of heaven is like unto a man that is an householder, which bringeth forth out of his treasure things new and old" (Matthew 13:52). When we seek as writers to explore the wonderful truths of the Bible we also "bringeth forth out of his treasure things new and old" in our attempt to reveal the deeper truths of the Word of God.

The Accuracy of the Bible Manuscripts

Over the last four thousand years, Jewish scribes, and later, Christian scribes, were very careful to copy and transmit the original manuscripts of sacred Scriptures without any significant error. The Jewish scribes who carefully copied out by hand the manuscripts of the Old Testament were called "Masoretic" from the Hebrew word for "wall" or "fence." Their extreme care in meticulously counting the letters of the Bible created a "fence around the Law" to defend its absolute accuracy. For example, out of the 78,064

Hebrew letters in the Book of Genesis, they counted precisely 4,152 ה letters and 8,448 י letters. These sages were so precise in counting the exact number of letters in the Scriptures that they were able to pinpoint the middle verse of Genesis, which is: "And by thy sword shalt thou live, and shalt serve thy brother; and it shall come to pass when thou shalt have the dominion, that thou shalt break his yoke from off thy neck" (Genesis 27:40). When a scribe completed his copy, a master examiner would painstakingly count every individual letter to confirm that there were no errors in the newly copied manuscript. If an error was found, the mistaken copy was destroyed to prevent its ever being used as a master copy in the future.

As a proof of the incredible accuracy of this transmission through the centuries, consider the Masoretic and Yemenite translations of the Torah. Over a millennium ago, Yemenite Jews were separated from their brother Jews in the Middle East and Europe. Despite separate transmissions and copying of their Torah manuscripts, a thousand years later only nine Hebrew letters, out of some 304,805 letters in the Yemenite Torah manuscript, differ from the accepted Hebrew Masoretic text of the Torah. Not one of these nine variant letters in the Yemenite Torah changes the meaning of a significant word. This astonishing fact proves how exceptionally careful, over a thousand-year period, Jewish scribes were in copying their original Torah manuscripts. God has carefully preserved the original text of His sacred Scriptures throughout the last three and a half thousand years, enabling us to have confidence that we still possess the inspired Word of God. The prophet Isaiah declared that the Word of God is eternal: "The grass withereth, the flower fadeth: but the word of our God shall stand for ever" (Isaiah 40:8). In the New Testament, Jesus Himself confirmed the indestructibility of His Holy Word. "For verily I say unto you, Till heaven and earth pass, one jot or one tittle shall in no wise pass from the law, till all be fulfilled" (Matthew 5:18).

Dr. Samuel Johnson's suggestion, "Keep your friendships in repair," was excellent advice regarding our relationship to our Bible as well as for our human relationships. Our relationship with the Word of God needs to be cared for just as much as our friendships. We need to respect God's Holy Word and handle it with care and love. We can enjoy the unchanging companionship of God expressed through His divine Word even when we are separated from human friends by distance or death. Our Bibles that show signs of wear and tear reveal our love and use of them. While our experiences, our possessions, and our relationships constantly undergo change throughout the years, we can return again and again to the unchanging Word of God as a solid foundation for our faith that will never change. Unlike human friends who sometimes misunderstand or fail to communicate when we need them, our Bible will always be there to speak to our hearts with God's words of wisdom, comfort, and love.

The Oldest Biblical Inscription Ever Found

Several years ago archeologists found more than one thousand items of jewelry and pottery in nine burial caves across the Hinnom Valley opposite the southern walls of the Old City of Jerusalem. The treasures from the past included two silver charms with remarkable biblical inscriptions. The cave where these charms were found was about nine hundred yards south of where Solomon's Temple stood three thousand years ago. While most of the burial caves had previously been cleaned out by grave robbers, these fascinating silver inscriptions were still there in 1979, as confirmed to the Associated Press by Tel Aviv archeologist Gabriel Barkay. The items of jewelry were composed of thin pieces of pure silver that were rolled up like tiny scrolls to be worn as charms around the neck. While part of the text was lost, the remaining portion revealed that these silver charms contained the oldest biblical inscription ever found. The remaining text recorded the priestly blessing from the Book of Numbers. It reads, "The LORD bless thee, and keep thee: The LORD make his face shine upon thee, and be gracious unto thee: The LORD lift up his countenance upon thee, and give thee peace" (Numbers 6:24–26). I had the privilege of examining this inscription in the Israel Museum. Incredibly, the archeologists found that this ancient biblical text was inscribed by some Jewish craftsman over 2,600 years ago in the seventh century before Christ, over four hundred years before the writing of most of the Dead Sea Scrolls.

It is fascinating to note that the Bible records only one statement made by God to the atheist or agnostic who declares, "There is no God." This sole declaration and verdict of God in response to those who deny His existence is, "The fool hath said in his heart, There is no God" (Psalm 14:1). When I attended school, I used to engage in debates with atheists and agnostics about the existence of God. However, as I began to analyze the underlying attitude of those I debated, I began to realize that debates of this kind were futile. Now when I get into a discussion with an atheist or agnostic, I simply respond as follows: I will not debate you about whether or not God exists for the same reason that I would not debate someone about whether or not the world is round. <u>I believe that those who claim "There is no God," in the face of overwhelming evidence of design found throughout nature, are either fools or liars</u>. Any person who honestly believes that all of the marvelous complexity of this universe simply happened by chance is a fool. If he is not a fool, yet still claims to believe that this incredibly complex universe is a result of random chance, then I must conclude that he is not being honest. In either case, it is clearly a waste of time to argue the obvious.

The wonders of creation reveal God's awesome creative power to anyone whose eyes are open to see the truth. God's marvelous providence reveals His wisdom; God's Law revealed in the Old Testament shows us His great justice; the Gospels reveal His overwhelming love for mankind through the person of Jesus Christ.

The Supreme Value of the Bible

Sir Walter Scott, the brilliant author of more than sixty popular books, was finally approaching his moment of death. As he lay on his deathbed, Scott asked his son-in-law, Lockhart, to bring him "the book" from his huge library. When Lockhart naturally asked, "Which book, Sir Walter?" Scott answered, "There is only one book," pointing to the Holy Bible. In this final deathbed conversation, Sir Walter Scott, one of the greatest writers of his day, correctly assessed the supreme value of the Holy Scriptures far above the other great books in his large library, including his own classics.

The most important event in the history of man is the life, death, and resurrection of Jesus Christ. The most important fact in the life of mankind is the reality of God and His divine revelation to us through His Holy Word. The most important decision in the life of any human is the choice they must make in regard to their personal faith in Jesus Christ. Another great man, Abraham Lincoln, wrote: "I believe that the Bible is the best gift God has ever given to man. All the good from the Savior of the world is communicated to us through the book."

The Pony Express Bible

The history of the Pony Express forms a fascinating part of the history of the American West. These dedicated and resourceful riders carried the mail from St. Joseph, Missouri, over nineteen hundred miles through dangerous Indian country, to Sacramento, California. The Pony Express acquired five hundred of the strongest and fastest horses the company could find. Incredibly, forty brave men rode these magnificent horses in relays with each man riding fifty miles to the next station. Using four relays per day, the Pony Express riders traveled up to two hundred miles a day. A letter could be delivered in relays covering the complete nineteen hundred miles in only ten days.

In order to cut down on any unnecessary weight, the riders would use the lightest saddles made, with very small, flat leather bags holding the mail. Amazingly, to cut down on the weight, the riders carried no rifles. Mail carried by the Pony Express was written on very thin paper. However, the postage rate was $5 an ounce (equal to $200 per letter in today's currency). The managers of the Pony Express believed that the Holy Scriptures were so important that they presented a special full-size Pony Express Bible to each rider when he signed up to join this unusual company. Surprisingly, despite their overwhelming concern for reducing the weight of their riders' equipment, every one of the riders carried a full-size Pony Express Bible as part of his regular gear.

Stanley and Livingstone

The famous Christian missionary and explorer David Livingstone had disappeared without a trace on a trip into the unknown regions of Central Africa. The last reliable news of his expedition reported that Livingstone was sick, without supplies, and deserted by his guides. Many in Europe gave him up as lost forever after more than a year with no news from Africa. However, a small group of supporters in London believed that they must launch a rescue mission in an attempt to save Scotland's finest son. This group outfitted the brilliant explorer Henry M. Stanley to mount an expedition to find Livingstone. Stanley embarked on an arduous journey across the jungles and rivers of the unknown continent of Africa in his valiant attempt to locate David Livingstone. When he commenced his journey, Stanley carried extensive baggage that included several cases containing seventy-three of his favorite hardbound books weighing one hundred and eighty pounds. As he and his group of African carriers began to succumb to fatigue after three hundred miles of arduous travel through the jungle, Stanley reluctantly began to abandon his precious books or burn them to light fires each night. As they continued through the jungle, Stanley's library dwindled in size until there was only one book left, his precious Bible. With God's supernatural assistance, Stanley finally found the great man of God and greeted him with the famous words, "Dr. Livingstone, I presume?" The two explorers shared their deep personal faith in Jesus Christ. Livingstone told Stanley about the wonderful conversions of many tribes to faith in Christ although they had previously engaged in cannibalism. When he returned from his incredible journey, Stanley reported that he had read his beloved Bible through from Genesis to Revelation three times during his long journey.

As you read *The Signature of God,* I hope you will experience the same thrill of discovery and wonder that I have felt as the Lord led me to research the incredible evidence for the inspiration of the Scriptures that I share in this book. I hope this book will be a great resource for pastors and families to help them provide those who are seeking the truth about the Bible with the latest exciting research proving the authority of the Word of God. My prayer is that the information I share in these chapters will enable many readers to restore their confidence in the Bible as God's inspired Word. Then, they can confidently study the Scriptures knowing that God has provided the proof that the Bible is truly the Word of God because the evidence of His signature appears throughout its pages. The apostle Paul wrote to all Christians as follows: "All scripture is given by inspiration of God, and is profitable for doctrine, for reproof, for correction, for instruction in righteousness" (2 Timothy 3:16).

One

The Battle for the Bible

Our modern world has departed so far from the religious faith that governed the founding fathers of both the United States and Canada that it is almost impossible for the average citizen to recognize the vast gulf that exists between the beliefs of our modern world and the beliefs of those who founded our nations. The colonists who came to North America centuries ago were determined to escape the religious oppression of Europe. They wanted to create a free nation on this continent where men and women could worship God freely without restriction. The founders of the United States of America determined to create an educational system based on Christianity and the inspired Word of God. A close examination of the lives and the writings of the framers of the American Constitution clearly reveals that their intent was to create in America a "freedom for religious expression; not a freedom from religious expression."

The writer Frederick Rudolph wrote in his book, *The American College and University,* that within a generation of their landing on Plymouth Rock the original Puritan settlers laid the foundations of an educational system dedicated to training "a learned clergy and a lettered people." These Christians created Harvard College in 1636 as a Christian college dedicated to upholding the truths of the Bible. In fact, during the first century of Harvard University's existence, every single one of its professors was a minister of the Gospel. The initial Charter of Harvard College declares unashamedly, "Everyone shall consider the main end of his life and studies to know Jesus Christ which is eternal life." It has been calculated that 87 percent of the first one hundred and nineteen colleges built in America were established by Christians to educate young people in their faith. Most major universities in the eastern United States were created as Christian institutions of learning—including Harvard, Princeton, Yale, and Columbia. More than 25 percent of the 1855 graduating class of these universities became ministers of the Gospel.

Although our society is increasingly agnostic, millions still seek the truth by studying the Word of God. The *Dallas Times Herald* on October 24, 1983, found in one study that over forty-three million Americans are involved in regular Bible study groups (Roy Abraham Varghese, *The Intellectuals Speak Out About God* [Chicago: Regnery Gateway, 1984], pp. xxii-xxiii).

The Attempt to Destroy the Bible

Throughout history there has been a continual and relentless conflict between acceptance of God and an open rebellion against His rule. This continuing struggle can be correctly described as a tale of two cities: the ongoing war between the City of God and the City of Man. For two thousand years, the battleground has revolved around the Bible. Satan hates the Word of God because it reveals the truth about Jesus Christ, our hope of salvation, and the eternal destiny facing each of us between heaven and hell. A close examination of the history of Christianity over the last two thousand years reveals that the greatest attacks that occurred during the first centuries following Christ came from the pagans outside the Church. However, during the last one hundred and fifty years, the most effective enemies of the Cross arose from those false Christians who professed to follow Christ while denying the authority of the Bible and His identity as the Son of God.

The Roman emperors did everything in their power to destroy the new faith of Christianity by burning both Christians and the manuscripts of the Bible throughout their vast empire. As an example, in A.D. 303, the emperor Diocletian issued an official command to kill Christians and burn their sacred books. Professor S. L. Greenslade, the editor of the *Cambridge History of the Bible*, recorded the history of this persecution: "An imperial letter was everywhere promulgated, ordering the razing of the churches to the ground and the destruction by fire of the Scriptures, and proclaiming that those who held high positions would lose all civil rights, while those in households, if they persisted in their profession of Christianity, would be deprived of their liberty" (Professor Stanley L. Greenslade, *Cambridge History of the Bible* [Cambridge University Press, 1963]).

However, the Christians' enthusiasm and dedication to the Scriptures in those first centuries following Christ motivated them to produce numerous manuscripts that were widely copied, distributed, and translated throughout the empire. The New Testament is the most widely quoted book in history from the moment of its writing by the apostles until today. Ignatius, the Bishop of Antioch in A.D. 70, the minister responsible for several churches in Syria, quoted extensively from the New Testament in his writings. Clement, the Bishop of Rome in A.D. 70 (mentioned by Paul in Philippians 4:3), also quoted extensively from the New Testament only forty years after Christ's resurrection. Historians have recovered almost one hundred thousand manuscripts and letters from the first few centuries of this era that were composed by Christian writers. Their love and devotion to the inspired Scriptures were so overwhelming that these letters contain an enormous number of direct quotations from the New Testament. This was the primary way that the truths of Scripture were transmitted throughout the Roman Empire, despite the rampant persecution and burning of Bibles by the Roman emperors. If the Roman government had been successful in totally destroying every New Testament throughout the Roman Empire, the survival of these one hundred thousand letters from early Christians guaranteed the survival of the Word of God. These numerous letters by the early Christians contain an astonishing 98 percent of the New Testament. In other words, even if the Romans had succeeded in destroying the New Testament, we could still reliably reconstruct 98 percent of the New Testament text from these numerous quotations. This fact shows the absolute integrity of the text of the New Testament as it exists today as well as demonstrating the passion the early Christians possessed for the Holy Word of God.

Despite the efforts of the pagan emperors to burn every copy of the Bible during the first three centuries after Christ, Christianity became the official state religion of the Roman

Empire following the conversion of the emperor Constantine in A.D. 325. Eventually, however, the medieval church fell into apostasy from biblical truth and compromised with the kings and aristocracy of Europe. Over the centuries, laws were issued that made possession of the Bible illegal for any Christian layman. During those centuries of the Inquisition in Europe, there were appalling penalties, including burning at the stake, for anyone found to possess a copy of the Scriptures. During the Dark Ages, even priests in the medieval church of Rome were usually unable to read the Latin manuscripts of the Bible for themselves. As a result of their ignorance of the Bible, they were unable to compare the false doctrines that were widespread in the medieval Roman church against the doctrines of the Word of God. Few Christians today realize that, in Italy, it was illegal to possess a Bible until 1870 due to the hatred of apostate church officials for the truth of the Scriptures.

John Lea reported in his book, *The Greatest Book in the World,* that a French king once proposed to his court that they should launch a new wave of persecution against the Christians within his realm. However, a wise counselor and general replied to the king's proposal in these words, "Sire, the Church of God is an anvil that has worn out many hammers" (John Lea, *The Greatest Book in the World,* [Philadelphia: 1929]). The enemies of the Bible have attacked the Scriptures without respite for almost two thousand years. However, the Bible still stands unshaken as the most widely read and published book in history, while the philosophies of the enemies of the Scriptures are buried with their spokesmen. The survival of the Scriptures against these unrelenting attacks by Satan provides irrefutable evidence that it is truly inspired by God.

Finally, after almost a thousand years of virtual spiritual darkness, the Protestant Reformation under the leadership of Martin Luther opened the floodgates of biblical truth to the European population through the translation and printing of the Bible in contemporary languages such as German, French, and English. The revolution in religion and spiritual freedom surpassed anything ever seen in the history of mankind. The spiritual rallying cry of the Reformation was *Sola Scripture* meaning "solely Scripture." In opposition to the medieval Roman church's position that church councils, tradition, and papal decrees could supersede the teaching of Scripture, the Reformers insisted that every doctrine taught in the Church must be drawn from the clear teaching of the Bible. This absolute reliance on the actual words of the inspired Word of God placed the Reformation on the strongest possible spiritual foundation. The stronghold of Scripture motivated the Reformers to preach the Gospel of Jesus Christ everywhere, leading to the greatest influx of souls into the kingdom of God in the history of the Church.

While most people in our Western culture in past centuries accepted the truth of God's existence and His creation of the universe, a growing number of people in our modern world deny the existence of God and His creative role. Those who accept evolution as the answer to how human life was formed have rejected the concept of a divine Creator who created this earth in all of its awesome complexity. In addition, large numbers of people today totally reject the inspiration and authority of the Scriptures in the false belief that the Bible has somehow been proven to be "full of errors and contradictions." The unrelenting attack by agnostic scholars and the media on the authority of the Bible during the last century is unprecedented in Western history. The attack launched on the accuracy and reliability of the Scriptures and the resurrection of Jesus Christ has come not only from academics outside the Church, but also from countless pastors and theologians who have lost their personal confidence and faith in the authority of the Word of God.

Professor E. B. Pusey, in his brilliant defense of the authenticity of the Book of Daniel against the higher critics of his day, wrote about the continual attacks on the inspiration of Scripture from those who claimed to be ministers of the Gospel: "The faith can receive no real injury except from its defenders. Against its assailants, those who wish to be safe, God protects. If the faith shall be (God forbid!) destroyed in England, it will not be by open assailants, but by those who think that they defend it, while they have themselves lost it. So it was in Germany. Rationalism was the product, not of the attacks on the Gospel but of its weak defenders. Each generation, in its controversies with unbelief, conceded more of the faith, until at last it was difficult to see what difference there was between assailants and defenders. Theology was one great graveyard; and men were disputing over a corpse, as if it had life. The salt had 'lost its savour.' The life was fled" (Dr. E. B. Pusey, *The Prophet Daniel* [Plymouth: Devonport Society, 1864], pp. xxv–xxvi).

There are few things in life so spiritually ineffective or ridiculous as a preacher or seminary professor who has lost his faith in the authority and inspiration of the Scriptures, yet continues to preach or teach about the Bible. People who refuse to accept the authority of the Word of God will never learn the truths of life and death from such unbelieving teachers. Jesus Christ Himself declared: "If they hear not Moses and the prophets, neither will they be persuaded, though one rose from the dead" (Luke 16:31).

The Loss of Faith by Religious Leaders

After a century and a half of continuous assault on the authority and reliability of the Scriptures, many pastors and seminary professors have lost their confidence in the inspiration of the Word of God. The sociologist Jeffrey Hadden completed a survey of the beliefs of over ten thousand Protestant ministers in 1965 for the Danforth Foundation. These ten thousand mainline Protestant pastors from six major denominations were asked these questions:

1. Was Jesus born of a virgin?
2. Was Jesus the Son of God?
3. Is the Bible the inspired Word of God?

More than half of these pastors could not answer "Totally Agree" to these questions. A majority of the pastors surveyed qualified their answers to these questions indicating either partial agreement or disagreement. Significantly, a century ago, the vast majority of pastors would have answered "Totally Agree" to these questions.

Is there any doubt as to why many church leaders and denominations are spiritually weak and without conviction?

When pastors and teachers lose their faith in the Word of God, they would be more honest if they openly left the ministry rather than lead a whole generation of laymen in their congregations to an eternity without Christ and without hope of salvation based on the Word of God.

The widespread agnosticism and atheism in our modern government, media, universities, and seminaries have resulted in the moral collapse of our society. The philosopher Thomas Hobbes wisely described the inevitable effects on our society of the growing agnosticism and the gradual abandonment of the authority of Scriptures in the life of our nations. Hobbes described the terrible results that would follow the loss of a national religious faith in Christ in these insightful words: "No arts, no letters, no society, and which is worst of all, continual fear and danger of violent death, and the life of man solitary, poor, nasty, brutish and short." Tragically, the results of our national apostasy were accurately predicted in his writings. In 1831, the government of France sent a well-respected judge, Alexis de Tocqueville, to study the society, the beliefs, and the prisons of the United States of America to find out why there were so little crime and so few prisons. After several years of study, he wrote a celebrated book called *Democracy in America* in 1840. Alexis de Tocqueville wrote about the reason for America's greatness as a nation and the real reason for her low crime rate at that time. "I sought for the greatness of the United States in her commodious harbors, her ample rivers, her fertile fields, and boundless forests—and it was not there. I sought for it in her rich mines, her vast world commerce, her public schools system and in her institutions of higher learning—and it was not there. I looked for it in her democratic Congress and her matchless Constitution—and it was not there. Not until I went into the churches of America and heard her pulpits flame with righteousness did I understand the secret of her genius and power. America is great because America is good, and if America ever ceases to be good, America will cease to be great!"

A century and a half later, America has publicly abandoned the Bible as the moral anchor of our society and education. It should surprise no one that, after decades of teaching our children that there are no absolute rights and wrongs, we face an appalling breakdown in public morality and rising levels of crime. President Andrew Jackson shared the same opinion as Alexis de Tocqueville about the central position of the Scriptures to the life of his nation. As he lay on his deathbed, President Jackson pointed to the Bible on the table by his bed and said to his companion, "That Book, Sir, is the rock on which our Republic rests."

The Authenticity of the Old Testament

Dr. Robert Dick Wilson was the professor of Semitic Philology at Princeton Seminary for many decades. He was an expert in forty-five languages and dialects. He was considered the greatest expert alive in the Hebrew Old Testament. Dr. Wilson contributed numerous scholarly works confirming the accuracy of the Old Testament throughout his career of fifty years. His brilliant criticisms of errors and weaknesses in the positions of the higher critical school were so powerful they were never answered. The liberal critics simply ignored his devastating arguments against their dismissal of the Bible's accuracy. Over the years, a series of authorities, including R. D. Wilson, James Orr, Oswald Allis, and Edward J. Young, thoroughly refuted the anti-Bible claims of the higher critics. Dr. Wilson summarizes the situation as follows: "In conclusion, we claim that the assaults upon the integrity and trustworthiness of the Old Testament along the line of language have utterly failed. The critics have not succeeded in a single line of attack in showing that the diction and style of any part of the Old Testament are not in harmony with the ideas and aims of writers who lived at, or near, the time when the events occurred that are recorded in the various documents. . . . We boldly challenge these Goliaths of ex-cathedra theories to come down into the field of ordinary concordances, dictionaries, and literature, and fight a fight to the finish on the level ground of the facts and the evidence" (Dr. Robert Dick Wilson, *A Scientific Investigation of the Old Testament* [Chicago: Moody Press, 1959], p. 130).

Old Testament Statements Regarding Its Inspiration

The Scriptures themselves clearly and repeatedly declare that the Bible is inspired by God. Moses closed his ministry with this command to the Children of Israel affirming inspiration: "Set your hearts unto all the words which I testify among you this day, which ye shall command your children to observe to do, all the words of this law" (Deuteronomy 32:46). The Book of Proverbs also states: "Every word of God is pure: he is a shield unto them that put their trust in him. Add thou not unto his words, lest he reprove thee, and thou be found a liar" (Proverbs 30:5–6).

The Authority of the Old Testament
Confirmed by Jesus Christ

One of the most important evidences regarding the accuracy and inspiration of the Old Testament Scriptures is that both Jesus Christ and the apostles absolutely confirm the authority of these writings as being inspired directly by God. Jesus Christ declared that "the scripture cannot be broken" (John 10:35). In another passage Jesus stated, "And it is easier for heaven and earth to pass, than one tittle of the law to fail" (Luke 16:17). In addition, the Lord confirmed that Moses was the writer of the first five books of the Law (Luke 24:27; John 5:46–47). Christ also stated that Isaiah was the author of the Book of Isaiah (Matthew 13:14, citing Isaiah 6:9–10). One of Jesus' most significant statements was His declaration that Daniel had written the Book of Daniel (Matthew 24:15), thereby contradicting those critics who claim that Daniel was written by someone pretending to prophesy in 165 B.C. Jesus spoke of Adam, Eve, and their son Abel as real personalities (Matthew 19:4–5; 23:35). In Luke 17:26, 28, Jesus referred to both Noah and Lot. According to John 8:56–58, the Lord confirmed the Bible's narrative about Abraham. Perhaps, most important, Jesus confirmed the accuracy of the Genesis account about the Creation (Mark 10:6–9) and the worldwide Flood (Matthew 24:37–39).

Christ affirmed His belief in the Old Testament miracles when He talked about the supernatural judgment on Sodom and Gomorrah (Luke 17:29), including the death of Lot's wife (v. 32). In other passages, Jesus described the feeding of manna to the Israelites during the Exodus (John 6:32) and the miraculous healing of the serpent's bites (John 3:14). The Gospels record Christ's confirmation of the miraculous events in the lives of Elijah and Elisha (Luke 4:25–27) and the supernatural swallowing of Jonah by a great fish (Matthew 12:39–40). Jesus settled all doubts of Christians in His declaration: "For verily I say unto you, Till heaven and earth pass, one jot or one tittle shall in no wise pass from the law, till all be fulfilled" (Matthew 5:18). Jesus Christ rebuked Satan by quoting Deuteronomy 8:3: "Man doth not live by bread only, but by every word that proceedeth out of the mouth of the LORD doth man live" (see Matthew 4:4; also Luke 4:4). In His discussion with the Pharisees, Jesus won His argument based on the presence of a single word in the Scriptures. The Lord asked the Jewish scholars, "If David then call him Lord, how is he his son?" (Matthew 22:45).

In light of these absolute confirmations by Jesus Christ of historical events and miraculous occurrences in the Old Testament, it is astonishing that some preachers and Christians dare to deny the truthfulness of these biblical events. Those who accept Jesus Christ as truly God should find it quite easy to accept His divine verdict that the Old Testament is absolutely truthful and inspired directly by God. If I accept Jesus as my God and Savior, then I will accept His confirmation that I can safely trust in the authority of the Old Testament.

Statements from the Apostles

The apostles constantly affirmed verbal inspiration. The apostle Paul described the Scriptures as the very "oracles of

God" (Romans 3:2; Hebrews 5:12). Later, in Galatians 3:16, Paul said: "Now to Abraham and his seed were the promises made. He saith not, And to seeds, as of many; but as of one, And to thy seed, which is Christ." Notice that in this passage, Paul based his entire argument to his readers on the presence of a single word and noted the fact that the word was the singular word *seed* and not the plural word *seeds*. Paul's doctrine regarding the inspiration of Scripture is absolutely clear: "All scripture is given by inspiration of God, and is profitable for doctrine, for reproof, for correction, for instruction in righteousness: That the man of God may be perfect, thoroughly furnished unto all good works" (2 Timothy 3:16–17).

The Early Date of the Writing of the New Testament

It is now acknowledged, even by many liberal scholars, that the New Testament Gospels and Epistles were written and widely circulated throughout the Christian communities of the Roman Empire within forty or fifty years of the events they describe. This fact is of overwhelming importance in verifying the absolute historical accuracy of these documents. Thousands of people who witnessed the events of Jesus Christ's life, teaching, death, and resurrection were still alive when the disciples composed and distributed the Gospels and Paul's Epistles to the various churches. These carefully copied manuscripts were read in hundreds of Christian assemblies every Sunday, by millions of Gentile and Jewish believers, from the cold northern shores of Britain to the hot deserts of Syria and North Africa. In addition to Christian testimony about the enormous number of new believers, even the enemies of Christ, such as the Roman historians Tacitus and Pliny, acknowledged that there were vast multitudes of Christians throughout the Roman Empire.

If the New Testament actually contained factual errors regarding the events of Christ's life, His teaching, or the miracles He performed, there would have been an enormous split within the early Church as witnesses to these historical events would have debated and contested any inaccurate historical records. Although the Christians were subject to the most terrifying tortures and martyrdom conceivable, not one of them ever declared that the Gospel account of Jesus Christ was in error. If they had denied the reality of the life, death, and resurrection of Jesus, the Roman judges would have been delighted to set them free. Rome would have widely published such a denial of the Gospels' statements about Jesus Christ's death and resurrection. However, despite the fact that a large number of Roman official records and a much larger number of Christian writings have survived till today, we cannot find evidence of a single eyewitness to these Gospel events ever denying their truthfulness. This fact is of outstanding importance in assessing the reliability and truthfulness of the Gospel records as any judge or lawyer would confirm.

The early Church had many enemies among the pagans. During the second and third centuries of this era, some pagans and gnostics infiltrated the Church. In response to the warnings of our Lord and the apostle Paul about false teachers and "teachers having itching ears," the Church leadership was vigilant in detecting and rejecting any spurious writings that counterfeited the genuine New Testament inspired writings. As an example, two important early Church writers, Tertullian and Jerome, tell us that a presbyter from Asia [Turkey] published a counterfeit epistle that he claimed the apostle Paul had written. Church leaders instantly instigated an ecclesiastical trial to examine this claim. They subsequently convicted this counterfeiter and repudiated his spurious forgery. Their rejection of this forgery was widely published to other churches throughout the empire. Is it probable that people who were so vigilant to establish the truth of the Gospel and to preserve the genuine Scriptures would blindly accept the New Testament record of Christ's miracles and resurrection unless they had overwhelming proof of its truthfulness? When you consider that millions of these converts died horribly as martyrs rather than deny their Lord, it stands to reason that they were convinced with all their mind, soul, and spirit that the Gospels spoke the truth about Jesus Christ as the Son of God.

The Universal Distribution of the New Testament

All scholars acknowledge that the New Testament was widely copied and translated into many other languages during the first few decades following the resurrection of Christ. Numerous ancient manuscripts of the New Testament have survived in different languages. These manuscripts confirm that there were no differences in the text regarding doctrine or factual matters. The libraries of Europe and North America contain many ancient copies and translations of the Greek New Testament, including the Syriac, Egyptian, Arabic, Ethiopian, Armenian, Persian, Gothic, Slavonic, and

Latin translations. This widespread publication assisted greatly in the effective distribution of the Gospels and Epistles into "Judea, and Samaria and the uttermost parts of the earth." In addition, the widespread copying and translation of the Scriptures made it absolutely impossible for anyone to corrupt the legitimate text of the New Testament by introducing an invented story of a miracle or a false doctrine into a counterfeit copy. Due to their overwhelming love of the Scriptures, the early Christians constantly quoted from these texts.

If anyone were so foolish as to attempt to introduce a spurious text with an invented story, miracle, or doctrine, this counterfeit alteration would have been instantly detected and denounced throughout the hundreds of churches. Once the original Greek manuscript of the New Testament was translated faithfully into Hebrew, Syriac, Egyptian, Coptic, Latin, and other languages between A.D. 60 and A.D. 70, it would have been impossible for anyone, even a corrupt high Church official, to impose a counterfeit text on the Christians. A counterfeit text's alterations would be compared against the countless other widely available genuine Greek manuscripts and the additional translations in other languages. Any textual differences would instantly identify a counterfeit text as a forgery. The profound love of the saints for the New Testament during the first centuries of the Church age assures us that they were vigilant in their defense and preservation of the integrity of the Scriptures. This fact allows us to have total confidence that we possess today the same New Testament that was given to the Church by the inspired writers.

The Survival of the Bible

The famous French writer Voltaire, a skeptic, often wrote expressing his contempt for the Bible and Christianity. He had an intense hatred of the Word of God because it reminded him that he would someday stand before the Great White Throne to be judged by Almighty God. His sinful arrogance expressed itself in his utter contempt for the Scriptures and Christians who followed the words of Jesus Christ. Voltaire wrote a prediction about the future of the Bible more than two centuries ago from his library in Paris: "I will go through the forest of the Scriptures and girdle all the trees, so that in one hundred years Christianity will be but a vanishing memory." Despite Voltaire's prediction, there are more Christians alive today than at any other time in history. Those who study the statistics have found that more than 85,000 people accept Jesus Christ as their personal Savior every day around the world. Ironically, despite Voltaire's confident prediction about the imminent death of Christianity, his library, in which he wrote his false prediction, was acquired years later by the British and Foreign Bible Society. His library was soon filled from floor to ceiling with thousands of copies of the Bible he hated, but could not destroy (David John Donnan, *Treasury of the Christian World* [New York: Harper Brothers, 1953]).

Despite the opposition of Satan and his followers to the Scriptures, the Bible remains triumphant as the most widely read, published, and influential book in the history of man. The truths found in its pages have changed the lives and destinies of untold billions. The Scriptures have profoundly influenced the course of history for nations and empires. When an ambassador of an African prince was introduced to Queen Victoria, the greatest queen of England, he asked her the question his monarch had requested he present to her. "What is the secret of your country's power and success throughout the world?" Queen Victoria picked up the Bible on her table and answered, "Tell your prince that this book is the secret of England's greatness."

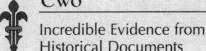

Two

Incredible Evidence from Historical Documents

The Incredible Accuracy of the Old Testament

Although the Bible has been relentlessly attacked by unbelieving scholars for more than a century, it still stands as the most accurate and authoritative book ever written. Despite the continuing media assaults on the Bible's claim to be a supernatural revelation from God, evidence from historical inscriptions and manuscripts discovered in the last century proves that the Word of God is inspired. Although we will never be able to verify every one of the thousands of historical personalities, events, and places recorded in the Bible, the overwhelming evidence presented in this chapter will provide any intelligent reader with the confidence that we have established the credibility of the greatest book ever written.

My library has hundreds of books containing accounts from numerous historians of the ancient world, including Herodotus, the so-called "Father of History." However, a Roman historian titled Herodotus "the Father of Lies" in recognition of the factual inaccuracy of his fanciful accounts of the past. Any examination of these secular histories reveals a multitude of gross errors regarding details such as dates, locations, people, and sequence and duration of events. To state that ancient secular historians were casual in their approach to accuracy is an understatement. An example of this casual attitude regarding factual accuracy is revealed in Herodotus's own history where he wrote, "My business is to record what people say. But I am by no means bound to believe it—and that may be taken to apply to this book as a whole" (*Mysteries of the Bible* [New York: The Reader's Digest Association, Inc., 1988], p. 107). However, when we closely examine the evidence found in the Bible, we discover that the writers are extremely careful and accurate in their recording of historical facts. The writers of the Bible were contemporaries of the times and events they recorded. A comparison of the discoveries during the last century of historical and archeological research with the statements of the Bible reveals forty-one different kings of Israel and surrounding nations that are confirmed by contemporary inscriptions and documents. The whole body of ancient literature does not reveal a single report from secular historians that can be confirmed by archeology with the same degree of confidence by which we can prove thousands of biblical statements, personalities, and events.

In the last one hundred and fifty years many critics of the Bible upheld the so-called Documentary Hypothesis that denied the biblical claim that Moses was the author of Genesis and the rest of the first five books of the Bible. They claimed that the different names for God that appeared in Genesis (Elohim, Jehovah, Adonai, etc.) indicated that five different authors composed portions of this book. They believed that an editor later recompiled the five records into one book approximately six hundred years before Christ. However, this widely taught theory is absurd when you carefully consider the history of the Jewish people. Remember that in a court of law, a judge and jury place great weight on evidence that is acknowledged to be factual by both sides, the prosecution and the defense, for the simple reason that if both sides agree, it is extremely likely that it is true.

The Jewish people are known for their brilliance and their willingness to debate at great length any issue involving their religion and history. Ask yourself if it is credible that the Jews would universally adopt the complicated and onerous religious regulations of Passover, Pentecost, and the Feast of Tabernacles unless their forefathers had begun celebrating these feasts to commemorate the miraculous events of the Exodus. Obviously, such national festivals were transmitted from generation to generation through the ages. How could this happen if the original miraculous deliverance from Egypt had never occurred? Moses, the great Lawgiver of Israel, reminded the Jews that they had personally witnessed with their own eyes these miracles and supernatural acts by God to deliver them from the bondage of Egypt. "Know today that I do not speak with your children, who have not known and who have not seen the chastening of the LORD your God, His greatness and His mighty hand and His out-stretched arm—His signs and His acts which He did in the midst of Egypt, to Pharaoh king of Egypt, and to all his land; what He did to the army of Egypt, to their horses and their chariots: how He made the waters of the Red Sea overflow them as they pursued you, and how the LORD has destroyed them to this day; what He did for you in the wilderness until you came to this place; . . . but your eyes have seen every great act of the LORD which He did" (Deuteronomy 11:2–7, NKJV).

If an unknown editor had created the five books of the Torah a thousand years later and tried to get the Jewish people, scattered in diverse communities from Iran to Spain, to universally adopt these festivals of Passover, etc., when no one had ever celebrated them before, he would have been denounced as an impostor. At the very least, Jewish rabbis and sages would have conducted strong debates opposing the introduction of such a book that no one had ever seen before. However, there is no record whatsoever that such debates or discussions ever occurred. The critics' theory of an unknown editor creating the Torah is absurd. The Samaritans were a group of colonists imported into the West Bank of Israel around 700 B.C. by the Assyrians to repopulate the area after they took the Israelite population of the ten northern tribes in chains back to Assyria (modern Iraq-Iran). One of the oldest manuscripts in the world is the Samaritan Pentateuch, an ancient copy of the first five books of the Law, which contains virtually every single word found in the Hebrew text of the Torah. From the moment the Samaritan colonists moved into the center of Israel, they found themselves in opposition to the Jewish people who returned from the Babylonian Captivity, which continued into the time of Christ's ministry. Although the Samaritans accepted the five books of the Torah as genuine, their own version was jealously guarded and preserved for thousands of years until today. Why would the Samaritans, who hated the Jews, accept the historical accuracy and authority of the Torah of the Jews if they knew these books were not authoritative and true? The fact that the Samaritans, the enemies of the Jews, agree with them in accepting the genuineness of

An Illustration of the Israelites Leaving Egypt

the five books of Moses should prove to any unbiased mind that we have the original, unaltered writings of Moses, the great Lawgiver of Israel.

In addition, critics denied that Moses could have written his account in the fifteenth century before Christ because they claimed that writing was not yet invented. However, the discovery by archeologists of numerous ancient written inscriptions, including the famous black stele containing the Laws of Hammurabi written before 2000 B.C., has conclusively proven that writing was widespread for many centuries before the time of Moses.

The Greek historian Herodotus discussed the Exodus in his book *Polymnia,* section c. 89: "This people [the Israelites], by their own account, inhabited the coasts of the Red Sea, but migrated thence to the maritime parts of Syria, all which district, as far as Egypt, is denominated Palestine."

It is interesting to note that Strabo, a pagan historian and geographer who was born in 54 B.C., also confirmed the history of the Jews and their escape from Egypt under the leadership of Moses. He wrote, "Among many things believed respecting the temple and inhabitants of Jerusalem, the report most credited is that the Egyptians were the ancestors of the present Jews. An Egyptian priest named Moses, who possessed a portion of the country called lower Egypt, being dissatisfied with the institutions there, left it and came to Judea with a large body of people who worshipped the Divinity" (Strabo, *Geography*, lib. xvi., c.2).

Food and Water in Sinai

Many critics have suggested that such a dry desert area as Sinai could never have supported the huge flocks of sheep of the Israelites as recorded in Exodus. In 1860, W. Holland explored most of the Sinai Peninsula. Despite the present desolate and dry condition of the barren land, he found that some areas would still support large flocks of sheep. If the temperature or level of rainfall was only slightly changed, the amount of available pasturage would have been much greater than today's conditions would indicate. In his book Holland wrote, "Large tracts of the northern portion of the plateau of the Tih, which are now desert, were evidently formerly under cultivation. The Gulf of Suez (probably by means of an artificial canal connecting it with the Bitter Lakes) once extended nearly fifty miles further north than it does at present, and the mountains of Palestine were well clothed with trees. Thus there formerly existed a rain-making area of considerable extent, which must have added largely to the dews and rains of Sinai. Probably, also, the peninsula itself was formerly much more thickly wooded. The amount of vegetation and herbage in the Peninsula, even at the present time, has been very much underrated; and a slight increase in the present rainfall would produce an enormous addition to the amount of pasturage. I have several times seen the whole face of the country, especially the wadies, marvelously changed in appearance by a single shower" (W. Holland, *Recent Explorations in the Peninsula of Sinai,* 1869).

It is fascinating to note that numerous biblical personalities (including Nebuchadnezzar, Belshazzar, and Darius), who were totally repudiated by higher critics in past decades, have now been reliably verified by recent historical and archeological discoveries. In the past, critics of the Bible's accuracy contemptuously rejected the story of the defeat of the confederation of five kings from the East by the small army of Abraham as found in Genesis 14. These critics claimed that there was no evidence to support this biblical account, and therefore denied the story. However, the continuing archeological research in the Middle East has found ample evidence proving that the story is credible in all its particular details.

Dr. Nelson Glueck, considered by many to be the leading Palestinian archeologist in this century, was the president of the Hebrew Union College. Reporting on the newly discovered evidence about this invasion, Glueck wrote the following report: "Centuries earlier, another civilization of high achievement had flourished between the 21st and 19th centuries B.C., till it was savagely liquidated by the Kings of the East. According to the Biblical statements, which have been borne out by the archaeological evidence, they gutted every city and village at the end of that period from Ashtaroth Karnaim, in southern Syria through all of Trans-Jordan and the Negev to Kadesh-Barnea in Sinai (Genesis 14:1-7)" (Nelson Glueck, *Rivers in the Desert* [New York: Farrar, Straus, and Cudahy, 1959], p. 11).

Dr. Glueck spent many years of his life exploring the land of Israel in his search for archaeological records. As a result of his many discoveries, he concluded that the Bible was totally reliable in every area where he could examine the evidence. Summarizing the results of the numerous archeological discoveries during the last century, Dr. Glueck concluded: "As a matter of fact, however, it may be stated categorically that no archeological discovery has ever controverted a Biblical reference. Scores of archaeological findings have been made which confirm in clear outline or in exact detail historical statements in the Bible. And, by the same token, proper evaluation of Biblical descriptions has often led to amazing discoveries. They form tesserae in the vast mosaic of the Bible's almost incredible correct historical memory" (Nelson Glueck, *Rivers in the Desert* [New York: Farrar, Straus, and Cudahy, 1959], p. 31).

The explorations and excavations in the Middle East during the last century and a half have thrown remarkable light on the accuracy and reliability of the words of the Holy Scriptures. With each additional discovery we find new exciting confirmations of the most remarkable statements from the Word of God. In this chapter I will share some of the most fascinating of these discoveries and their implications for the authority of the Bible.

An Illustration of the Tower of Babel

King Nebuchadnezzar's Inscription
About the Tower of Babel

From the time of Adam and Eve, "The whole earth had one language and one speech" (Genesis 11:1, NKJV) before the dispersion of the population following God's supernatural act causing the confusion of their languages at the Tower of Babel. God purposely confounded the language of all the people on the earth (Genesis 11:9) so they could not understand the speech of their neighbors, to force them to disperse throughout the earth. The people had gathered together in sinful pride against God in their attempt to build a tower

that would reach to the heavens. Moses recorded God's subsequent judgment and destruction of the Tower of Babel
and the city of Babylon. The remains of the Tower of Babel
are vitrified (melted to form a kind of rough glass), which
indicates that God used a huge amount of heat to destroy
this tower that was erected at the dawn of time by men in
their sinful pride to reach up to the heavens in defiance of
God. Scientists who study the origin of languages, known as
philologists, have concluded that it is probable that the
thousands of dialects and languages throughout the planet
can be traced back to an original language in man's ancient
past. Professor Alfredo Trombetti claims that he can prove
the common origin of all languages. Max Mueller, one of the
greatest oriental language scholars, declared that all human
languages can be traced back to one single original language. Professor Otto Jespersen stated that the first language
was given to man by God (Joseph Free, *Archeology and Bible
History* [Wheaton: Scripture Press Publications, 1969]).

The French government sent Professor Oppert to
report on the cuneiform inscriptions discovered in the ruins
of Babylon. Oppert translated a long inscription by King
Nebuchadnezzar in which the king referred to the tower in
the Chaldean language as *Barzippa,* which means "tongue-
tower." The Greeks used the word *Borsippa,* with the same
meaning of "tongue-tower," to describe the ruins of the
Tower of Babel. This inscription of Nebuchadnezzar clearly
identified the original tower of Borsippa with the Tower of
Babel described by Moses in Genesis. King Nebuchadnezzar
decided to rebuild the base of the ancient Tower of Babel,
built over sixteen centuries earlier by Nimrod, the first king

of Babylon. He also called it the Temple of the Spheres. During the millennium after God destroyed it, the tower was reduced from its original height and magnificence until only the huge base of the tower (four hundred and sixty feet by six hundred and ninety feet), standing some two hundred and seventy-five feet high, remained within the outskirts of the city of Babylon. Today the ruins have been reduced to about one hundred and fifty feet above the plain with a circumference of 2,300 feet. Nebuchadnezzar rebuilt the city of Babylon in great magnificence with gold and silver, and then decided to rebuild the lowest platform of the Tower of Babel in honor of the Chaldean gods. King Nebuchadnezzar resurfaced the base of the Tower of Babel with gold, silver, cedar, and fir, at great cost on top of a hard surface of baked clay bricks. These bricks were engraved with the seal of Nebuchadnezzar. (A photograph of one of these Babylonian bricks created by Nebuchadnezzar is included in the photo section.) In this inscription found on the base of the ruins of the Tower of Babel, King Nebuchadnezzar speaks in his own words from thousands of years ago confirming one of the most interesting events of the ancient past.

King Nebuchadnezzar's Inscription Found on the Tower of Babel

> The tower, the eternal house, which I founded and
>   built.
> I have completed its magnificence with silver, gold,
>   other metals, stone, enamelled bricks, fir and pine.
> The first which is the house of the earth's base,

the most ancient monument of Babylon; I built and
finished it.

I have highly exalted its head with bricks covered with
copper.

We say for the other, that is, this edifice, the house of
the seven lights of the earth,

the most ancient monument of Borsippa.

A former king built it, (they reckon 42 ages) *but he did
not complete its head.*

*Since a remote time, people had abandoned it, without
order expressing their words.*

Since that time the earthquake and the thunder had
dispersed the sun-dried clay.

The bricks of the casing had been split, and the earth of
the interior had been scattered in heaps. Merodach,
the great god, excited my mind to repair this building.

I did not change the site nor did I take away the foundation.

In a fortunate month, in an auspicious day,

I undertook to build porticoes around the crude brick
masses, and the casing of burnt bricks.

I adapted the circuits, I put the inscription of my name
in the Kitir of the portico.

I set my hand to finish it. And to exalt its head.

As it had been in ancient days, so I exalted its summit.

(Italics added)

This inscription was translated by Professor Oppert.
In addition, Mr. William Loftus translated this fascinating
inscription in his book, *Travels and Researches in Chaldea*

and Sinai (London: James Nisbet, 1857, p. 29). This incredible inscription confirms the biblical accuracy of one of the most fascinating stories in the Book of Genesis. The pagan king Nebuchadnezzar confirms in his own words the incredible details that "a former king built it, but he did not complete its head," confirming the truthfulness of the Genesis account that God stopped the original builders from completing the top of the Tower of Babel. Most significant, King Nebuchadnezzar's inscription declares that the reason the original king could not complete the tower was because, "Since a remote time, people had abandoned it, without order expressing their words." In other words, they had lost the ability to control their language and communication!

The Bible's Account of the Tower of Babel

"And it came to pass, as they journeyed from the east, that they found a plain in the land of Shinar, and they dwelt there. Then they said to one another, 'Come, let us make bricks and bake them thoroughly.' They had brick for stone, and they had asphalt for mortar. And they said, 'Come, let us build ourselves a city, and a tower whose top is in the heavens; let us make a name for ourselves, lest we be scattered abroad over the face of the whole earth.' But the LORD came down to see the city and the tower which the sons of men had built. And the LORD said, 'Indeed the people are one and they all have one language, and this is what they begin to do; now nothing that they propose to do will be withheld from them. Come, let Us go down and there confuse their language, that they may not understand one another's speech.'

So the LORD scattered them abroad from there over the face of all the earth, and they ceased building the city. Therefore its name is called Babel, because there the LORD confused the language of all the earth; and from there the LORD scattered them abroad over the face of all the earth" (Genesis 11:2–9, NKJV).

Compare the statement of Nebuchadnezzar, "A former king built it, but he did not complete its head. Since a remote time, people had abandoned it," with the words of Moses in Genesis 11:7; "So the LORD scattered them abroad from there over the face of all the earth, and they ceased building the city." Even more startling is the phrase of the pagan king where he declared that the reason they could not complete the top of the "tongue-tower" was that the "people had abandoned it, without order expressing their words." This expression by Nebuchadnezzar clearly confirms the historical event recorded in Genesis that God supernaturally "confused the language of all the earth" and He "scattered them abroad over the face of all the earth" (Genesis 11:2–9). This inscription by King Nebuchadnezzar is one of the strongest proofs possible that the Bible is an accurate record of the events it describes.

Joseph and the Seven Years of Famine

A fascinating inscription confirming the Bible's account of the "seven years of great plenty" followed by the "seven years of famine" (Genesis 41:29–30) was discovered during the nineteenth century in southern Saudi Arabia. This inscription was found on a marble tablet in a ruined fortress on the seashore of Hadramaut in present-day Democratic Yemen. An examination of the writing suggests that it was written approximately eighteen hundred years before the birth of Christ, a time that corresponds with the biblical narrative about Jacob and his twelve sons. This inscription was rendered in Arabic by Professor Schultens and was later translated into English by Rev. Charles Forster.

This is his translation of this ancient inscription:

> We dwelt at ease in this castle a long tract of time;
> nor had we a desire but for the region-lord of the vineyard.
> Hundreds of camels returned to us each day at evening,
> their eye pleasant to behold in their resting-places.
> And twice the number of our camels were our sheep,
> in comeliness like white does, and also the slow moving
>   kine.
> We dwelt in this castle *seven years of good life*
> —how difficult for memory its description!
> *Then came years barren and burnt up:*
> *when one evil year had passed away,*
> *Then came another to succeed it.*
> And we became as though we had never seen a glimpse of
>   good.
> They died and neither foot nor hoof remained.
> Thus fares it with him who renders not thanks to God:
> His footsteps fail not to be blotted out from his dwelling.
>
> (Italics added)

This ancient poem records the devastation of the years of famine and barrenness that followed the seven years of plenty. The language of the poem implies that the famine also lasted seven years. This account from ancient Arabia provides independent evidence confirming the accuracy of the biblical account of the seven years of plenty in the Middle East followed by seven years of famine that occurred during the rule of Joseph as prime minister of Egypt.

Moses recorded the history of the Egyptian famine and the wise preparations that Joseph made to gather up the surplus grain during the seven years of plenty to provide against the coming years of famine. "So he gathered up all the food of the seven years which were in the land of Egypt, and laid up the food in the cities; he laid up in every city the food of the fields which surrounded them" (Genesis 41:48). Again, Moses recorded: "Then the seven years of plenty which were in the land of Egypt ended, and the seven years of famine began to come, as Joseph had said. The famine was in all lands, but in all the land of Egypt there was bread. . . . The famine was over all the face of the earth, and Joseph opened all the storehouses and sold to the Egyptians. And the famine became severe in the land of Egypt. So all countries came to Joseph in Egypt to buy grain, because the famine was severe in all lands" (Genesis 41:53–57, NKJV). As the Book of Genesis recorded, the seven-year famine was so severe in Egypt that Joseph, as the chief administrator, had to be very careful in selling food from the precious grain reserves to satisfy the hunger of all the inhabitants of the surrounding countries. Joseph could not sell the grain reserves of Egypt for gold and silver to everyone because of the danger that the grain would run out. When the famine was at its peak, grain was much more valuable than gold or money.

Explorers during the last century discovered a number of other fascinating ancient inscriptions in the Middle

East that provided confirmation of facts recorded in the sacred Scriptures. Ebn Hesham, an Arab from Yemen, showed the English explorer, Mr. Cruttenden, a rich tomb of a wealthy Yemenite woman who had died during the time of the Egyptian famine recorded in Genesis 41. This Yemenite tomb was fortunately discovered around 1850 after being exposed following a flood that uncovered the grave site.

The tomb contained the body of a rich noblewoman who was covered in beautiful jewels. Seven collars of pearls surrounded her neck; her hands and feet were covered with seven bracelets, armlets, rings, and ankle-rings displaying costly jewels. In addition, her tomb contained a coffer filled with rich treasure.

However, the greatest treasure of all was a fascinating engraved stone tablet bearing her final inscription, which confirmed the biblical account of Joseph's careful management of the remaining food reserves during the seven years of famine in Egypt.

A Yemenite Inscription About a Famine During the Time of Joseph

> In thy name O God, the God of Hamyar,
> I Tajah, the daughter of Dzu Shefar, *sent my steward to Joseph,*
> And he delaying to return to me, I sent my hand maid
> With a measure of silver, to bring me back a measure of flour:
> And not being able to procure it, I sent her with a measure of gold:

And not being able to procure it, I sent her with a
　　measure of pearls:
And not being able to procure it, I commanded them to
　　be ground:
And finding no profit in them, I am shut up here.
Whosoever may hear of it, let him commiserate me;
And should any woman adorn herself with an ornament
From my ornaments, may she die with no other than
　　my death.

> (Italics added)
> (reported in Niebuhr's *Voyage en Arabie*, PL. LIX.
> Translation by Rev. Charles Forster)

This ancient inscription reveals a Yemenite Arab noble-woman's sincere complaint that she could not purchase Egypt's grain with her gold. It also reveals Joseph's determination to resist any appeal from a stranger offering gold in return for Egypt's precious grain reserves. This determination reminds us of Joseph's similar resolve earlier in his life when he resisted the attempt of Potiphar's wife to destroy his virtue. The tragic history of famines often recorded the bartering of the most precious of metals and luxuries in trade for the smallest amount of food available.

Ancient Histories Confirm the Exodus

The biblical record in the Book of Exodus about the super-natural deliverance of the Jews from their bondage in Egypt is one of the most miraculous and fascinating accounts in the Bible. Very few Christian pastors or laymen are aware that we have numerous historical records and ancient inscriptions that provide evidence and confirmation for these key events that resulted in the creation of the Jewish people as a distinct nation. Moses recorded the following statement: "And the children of Israel journeyed from Rameses to Succoth, about six hundred thousand on foot that were men, beside children. And a mixed multitude went up also with them; and flocks, and herds, even very much cattle" (Exodus 12:37–38).

It is fascinating that the Jewish historian Flavius Josephus reported that two ancient Egyptian priest-scholars, Manetho and Cheremon, specifically named both Joseph and Moses in their history of Egypt as leaders of the Jews (Flavius Josephus, *Josephus Against Apion.* I., 26, 27, 32). Josephus recorded that the Egyptians remembered a tradition of an exodus from their country by the Jews whom they hated because they believed the Israelites were unclean. It is interesting to note that Manetho and Cheremon stated that the Jews rejected Egyptian customs, including the national worship of Egyptian gods. Most important, these pagan historians acknowledged that the Jews killed the animals that they held as sacred, indicating the Israelites' practice of sacrificing lambs on that first Passover. These historians also confirmed that the Israelites immigrated into the area of "southern Syria," which was the Egyptian name for ancient Palestine. Perhaps the most important confirmation is found in the statement by Manetho that the sudden Exodus from Egypt occurred in the reign of "Amenophis, son of Rameses, and father of Sethos, who reigned toward the close of the 18th dynasty," which places this event between 1500 and 1400 B.C. This evidence confirms the chronological data found in the Old Testament that suggests the Exodus occurred approximately 1491 B.C.

A few years ago, after much searching, I was able to locate a set of volumes containing the forty books in the *Library of Diodorus Siculus,* a Greek historian from Agyrium in Sicily who lived from 80 B.C. until his death approximately twenty years before the birth of Jesus. Diodorus traveled extensively throughout the Middle East acquiring a vast knowledge of ancient events. He compiled records from various peoples that are quite valuable because they often recorded fascinating historical details that would otherwise have been lost forever. In his book, Diodorus reported: "In ancient times there happened a great plague in Egypt, and many ascribed the cause of it to God, who was offended with them because there were many strangers in the land, by whom foreign rites and ceremonies were employed in their worship of the deity. The Egyptians concluded, therefore, that unless all strangers were driven out of the country, they should never be freed from their miseries. Upon this, as some writers tell us, the most eminent and enterprising of those foreigners who were in Egypt, and obliged to leave the country . . . who retired into the province now called Judea, which was not far from Egypt, and in those times uninhabited. These emigrants were led by Moses, who was superior to all in wisdom and prowess. He gave them laws, and ordained that they should have no images of the gods, because there was only one deity, the heaven, which surrounds all things, and is Lord of the whole" (Diodorus Siculus, *Library of History,* lib. 1., ap Phot.).

The historical records and inscriptions I have included in this chapter are only a small sample of the evidence confirming the historical accuracy of the Old Testament. However, these discoveries provide ample evidence that we can trust the Old Testament writers as accurate historians, even when they describe miraculous events such as the Tower of Babel and the seven-year famine in Egypt.

Chapter

Three

Ancient Sinai Inscriptions and the Exodus

During the last century a number of explorers rediscovered a group of ancient inscriptions in the Wadi Mukatteb (the Valley of the Writing) in the Sinai Peninsula. When they were deciphered the researchers concluded that they contained detailed descriptions of the events of the Exodus from Egypt by the Children of Israel under the leadership of Moses. Naturally, the finding of these inscriptions attracted a great deal of attention and led to serious debate between scholars regarding their origin and meaning. Most of the scholars immediately rejected any possibility that these inscriptions could be an independent record of the events of the Exodus made by the ancient Israelites. Significantly, many of those who automatically rejected the authenticity of these inscriptions also rejected the literal interpretation of the Exodus biblical record altogether. However, a number of biblical scholars concluded that these mysterious inscriptions may actually have been written in the distant past by Jews who either took part in these momentous events or by people who were alive at the time of the Exodus.

We know these inscriptions are truly ancient because they were first described by the historian Diodorus Siculus before the birth of Christ (10 B.C.) in his *Library of History*. In describing the Sinai Peninsula, Diodorus wrote: "Moreover, an altar is there built of hard stone and very old in years, bearing an inscription in ancient letters of an unknown tongue. The oversight of the sacred precinct is in the care of a man and a woman who hold the sacred office for life" (Diodorus Siculus, *Library of History,* bk. 3, sect. 42, Loeb Classical Library, C. H. Oldfather, trans. [Cambridge: Harvard University Press, 1993], p. 211). This passage by Diodorus and a parallel description by the Greek writer Strabo (A.D. 24) in his seventeen-volume *Geography* confirm that these inscriptions were so ancient in their own day that the language was unknown to those living at the time of Christ.

Cosmas Indicopleustes, a Byzantine Christian writer, also reported that the inscriptions were ancient in his day, almost fourteen hundred years ago. In A.D. 518, Cosmas wrote that the engravings appeared "at all halting places, all the stones in that region which were broken off from the mountains, written with carved Hebrew characters." It is fascinating that his Jewish companions confirmed the Hebrew nature of the script that he translated as follows: "The departure of such and such a man of such a tribe, in such a year, in such a month" (Arthur Penrhyn Stanley, *Sinai and Palestine* [London: John Murray, 1905], p. 57). Cosmas concluded that the strange inscriptions carved in the rocks were made by the ancient Israelites fleeing their Egyptian captivity. The native Arabs claimed these inscriptions were written in a language that was lost to them and of very great antiquity. Since the Arabs of the Sinai Peninsula had not suffered under foreign conquest during the five centuries between the time of Christ and A.D. 518, when Cosmas visited the site, it is safe to conclude that these inscriptions must have been written long before the time of Christ.

Otherwise, the Arab natives would not have described them as written in a lost language and unknown character. The fact that these inscriptions survived in the hot, dry climate of Sinai from the time of Diodorus (10 B.C.) until today, gives us ample evidence that they could have survived intact a further fifteen hundred years back in time to the era of Moses.

The Language of the Inscriptions

In the last few centuries numerous explorers have noted these unusual inscriptions on the rocks and cliffs of Sinai, including Bishop Robert Clayton of Ireland (1753). He wrote a report about his discovery in the *Journal of the Franciscans of Cairo* (1753), concluding that the inscriptions were of ancient Hebrew origin. However, the most interesting exploration of these inscriptions was completed by the Rev. Charles Forster in his book published in 1862. He concluded that these writings were original records of an ancient Hebrew-Egyptian alphabet describing the Israelites' exodus from Egypt. Professor Arthur Penrhyn Stanley, in his *Sinai and Palestine*, explained that Rev. Forster and Dr. Stewart concluded that "a Sinaitic inscription has been found contemporaneous with a tablet of Egyptian hiero-glyphics." Dr. Stanley and other explorers recorded that numerous graffiti and Christian crosses located near the sites of these ancient inscriptions indicate that Christian pilgrims in subsequent ages also visited and left a record of their pilgrimage as they have in other locations in the Middle East. Professor Stanley described these ancient inscriptions in numerous locations in the Sinai in Wadi Sidri, Mugharah, Mukatteb, Feirah, Aleyat, Abu-Hamad, and in great numbers in Wadi Nukb-Hawy. However, a detailed examination of seven hundred of the genuine Sinai inscriptions revealed that there were only ten cross-forms found in the whole group of ancient writings. The Egyptian cross-form is their form of the letter *T* or *Tau* that appears in most languages. To put this in context, another well-known Egyptian inscription, the Rosetta Stone, contained seventy cross-forms of *T*s and no one would ever suggest that these cross marks on the Rosetta Stone were placed there by Christian pilgrims.

One of the strongest reasons for believing that some of these inscriptions may have been composed by Israelites in the time of the Exodus is that the language appears to be an original account of the Exodus events rather than an attempt to copy Exodus passages from the inspired pages of the Torah. Although these incredible rock inscriptions describe in great detail many of the supernatural events that occurred during the Exodus from Egypt, the writers did not use any of the words or characteristic language of Moses as recorded in the Torah. In other words, there is no indication that the writers of these Sinai inscriptions derived their information about the Exodus from reading Moses' words in the Torah. An examination of the evidence suggests that the writers may have been independent witnesses who described these supernatural events in their own original language. If this conclusion is correct, then these inscriptions would be an important independent confirmation of the truth of the biblical account.

Although numerous additional inscriptions were obviously created by medieval Christian pilgrims, experts were able to distinguish the genuine ancient writings from the medieval writings. Professor Stanley rejected an Israelite origin for the inscriptions because the ones he saw personally were obviously written by pilgrims in Greek, Arabic, or Latin. The presence of casually etched crosses proved that this group of inscriptions was put there by Christian visitors to Sinai over the centuries. However, Dr. Stanley confessed that he did not have the training in ancient languages to interpret these inscriptions. Other scholars, such as Niebuhr and Forster, concluded that the graffiti and crosses were made by pilgrims much later than the original Sinai inscriptions. Scholars who examined the older Sinai inscriptions concluded that they may have been recorded by the Israelites who participated in the Exodus. All of the sites where these original inscriptions are located are on the western side of the Sinai closest to Egypt, suggesting that the writers came from that direction. Since none of these older inscriptions contain Christian or Jewish names, it is unlikely that pilgrims created them. No Christian populations ever lived in the western part of the Sinai, where these inscriptions were found, in the early centuries of our era.

One of the interesting aspects of these ancient inscriptions is that Rev. Forster notes that they were written in a twenty-three-letter combination Egyptian-Hebrew alphabet that included twelve Hebrew letters. The other eleven letters are similar to those found in the alphabets of the Phoenicians, the Greeks, and the Ethiopians and Hamyarites (ancient Arabs living before the time of Mohammed). While the letters in the Sinai inscriptions are primarily Hebrew, the language pattern is clearly Egyptian. Forster found that five out of every six words used in these inscriptions are related to the Hamyarite (ancient Arabic) language, the vernacular language of Egypt and Yemen. He claimed that the Sinai inscriptions cannot be deciphered from the Hebrew lexicon. After several centuries of captivity as slaves in Egypt, the Israelites would naturally speak and write a language that, while containing the initial evidence of Hebrew, would be heavily influenced by the Egyptian language. It is probable that God inspired Moses to modify, expand, and purify the Hebrew language when he wrote the first five books of the Bible, the Torah. These Sinai inscriptions and the Torah are the earliest known examples of the use of Hebrew in writing.

One of the fascinating features of these inscriptions is that the writer would draw a picture of a quail side by side with the inscription describing God's miraculous provision of the quails to feed the Israelites (as shown in the photo section). Another curious feature is that numerous images of animals appear in the writing, but only of animals that live in the Sinai Peninsula, not those that live only in Egypt. If a native Egyptian wrote these inscriptions you would expect to find Egyptian animals, also images of pagan gods. However, although numerous Sinai inscriptions contain Egyptian hieroglyphics as well as the Sinai writings, we find no evidence of pagan gods or symbols. This provides very strong evidence that these were created by Jews.

We know from Stephen's sermon in the Book of Acts that Moses and his followers were perfectly capable of producing written inscriptions in the style of the Egyptians. "Moses was learned in all the wisdom of the Egyptians, and was mighty in words and deeds" (Acts 7:22). Clement of

Alexandria confirms this in his book, *The Stromata,* as follows: "Having reached the proper age, he [Moses] was taught arithmetic, geometry, poetry, harmony, and besides, medicine and music, by those that excelled in these arts among the Egyptians; and besides the philosophy which is conveyed by symbols, which they point out in the hieroglyphical inscriptions. The rest of the usual course of instructions, Greeks taught him in Egypt as a royal child, as Philo says in his life of Moses. He learned, besides, the literature of the Egyptians, and the knowledge of the heavenly bodies from the Chaldeans and the Egyptians; whence in the Acts he is said 'to have been instructed in all the wisdom of the Egyptians.' And Eupolemus, in his book *On the Kings in Judea,* says that 'Moses was the first man, and the first that imparted grammar to the Jews' " (Clement of Alexandria, *The Stromata,* bk. 1, chap. XXIII).

The writings in Sinai are of two distinct kinds. One is enchorial or common writing while the other is in the hieroglyphic style of Egypt as used by the priests and royalty. The fact that several inscriptions contain lines that alternate from the enchorial writing to hieroglyphic style is the strongest evidence that the people who created these inscriptions spent time in Egypt. However, we have no historical evidence of any group of Egyptians living in Sinai at any time. On the other hand, the Bible tells us that the Israelites did live in the Sinai for forty years. The Bible reveals that the Israelites had the necessary skills to create such inscriptions with metal tools because they created the golden calf, the metal work in the Tabernacle, and their weapons. A historical precedent exists for such inscriptions at that time. The Book of

Deuteronomy declares the command of God to record His Law on stone: "And it shall be, on the day when you cross over the Jordan to the land which the LORD your God is giving you, that you shall set up for yourselves large stones, and white-wash them with lime. You shall write on them all the words of this law, when you have crossed over, that you may enter the land which the LORD your God is giving you, 'a land flowing with milk and honey,' just as the LORD God of your fathers has promised you. . . . And you shall write very plainly on the stones all the words of this law" (Deuteronomy 27:2–3, 8, NKJV). The Children of Israel fulfilled this command according to Joshua 8:30.

The Sinai Inscriptions Describe the Exodus

The Minister of Public Instruction and Worship of France sent one of their top scholars, Professor Lottin de Laval, in February 1851, to examine these inscriptions to determine whether or not they were genuine descriptions of the Exodus. After crossing the Gulf of Suez from Egypt to land on the shore of the Sinai where Moses had crossed thousands of years ago, Professor de Laval discovered the first of these incredible inscriptions near the place the Arabs call "the wells of Moses." His extensive experience in examining ancient inscriptions enabled Professor de Laval to distinguish the original ancient inscriptions from the later medieval graffiti written by Armenian Christian pilgrims. He was able to make three hundred plaster casts or squeezes of the most important of these ancient inscriptions. He recorded his discoveries in his book *Voyage dans la Peninsule Arabique du Sinai et l'Egypt emoyenne* (Paris:

S.E.M. le Ministre de l'Instruction publique et des Cultes, 1855–1859).

Rev. Charles Forster translated and recorded photographs of these inscriptions from the distant past in his 1862 book *Sinai Photographed.* This book is quite rare, but fortunately, I was able to obtain from England the only copy still available. As a language expert, Rev. Forster translated these ancient engravings and found they described many of the events of the Jews' Exodus from Egypt under Moses' leadership. While these accounts confirm the accuracy of the biblical account of the miraculous passage of the Israelites through the Red Sea, the inscriptions describe these Exodus events in original language. This fact suggests that the inscribers were not copying from the biblical account of the Exodus from Egypt as found in the Book of Exodus; rather, they were describing the events from their own experience or from the eyewitness descriptions of others. One of the most fascinating of these inscriptions was described in Rev. D. A. Randall's book *The Handwriting of God in Egypt and Sinai* (Philadelphia: John E. Potter, 1862, p. 264). This long inscription was one hundred feet high and contained forty-one successive lines in hieroglyphic characters beneath the title, which was engraved in letters six feet high.

Inscriptions Describing the Red Sea Crossing

Consider the words of this ancient inscription about the Israelites' escape from Egypt. Six ancient inscriptions were found on different cliffs in the Wadi Sidri, located on one of the natural routes the Jews would have chosen when entering the interior of the Sinai Peninsula from Egypt. In his book, *Sinai and Palestine,* Dr. A. P. Stanley wrote about his 1853 visit to Wadi Sidri as the natural place leading up from the Red Sea: "A stair of rock, the Nukb Badera, brought us into a glorious Wadi (Sidri) enclosed between red granite mountains. . . . In the midst of the Wadi Sidri, just where the granite was exchanged for sandstone, I caught sight of the first inscription" (A. P. Stanley, *Sinai and Palestine,* [London: John Murray, 1905], p. 70). Another writer, Golius, revealed that the Arabic word *Sidri* can be interpreted as "a way that leads up from the water as at a landing place." Consider the message found in the following eight separate inscriptions about the Israelites' crossing of the Red Sea. (Moses described the events of their escape from Egypt in Exodus, chapter 14.) The numbers in brackets following the translated inscription refer to their original numbering identification as recorded in Rev. Forster's book, *Sinai Photographed.* Rare photographs

"The wind blowing, the sea dividing into parts, they pass over."
Sinai Inscription No. 1
Translated by Charles Forster

of several of these precious inscriptions are located in the photo section in the center of this book, *The Signature of God*. Note that the inscription Number 41 actually names Moses as the leader of the Israelites.

The Sinai Inscriptions

> The wind blowing, the sea dividing into parts, they pass over. (1)

> The Hebrews flee through the sea; the sea is turned into dry land. (4)

> The waters permitted and dismissed to flow,
> burst rushing unawares upon the astonished men,
> congregated from all quarters banded together
> to slay treacherously being lifted up with pride. (5)

> The leader divideth asunder the sea, its waves roaring.
> The people enter, and pass through the midst of the waters. (10)

> Moses causeth the people to haste like a fleet-winged she-ostrich crying aloud;
> the cloud shining bright,
> a mighty army propelled into the Red sea is gathered into one;
> they go jumping and skipping.
> Journeying through the open channel,
> taking flight from the face of the enemy.
> The surge of the sea is divided. (41)

The people flee, the tribes descend into the deep.
The people enter the waters.
The people enter and penetrate through the midst.
The people are filled with stupor and perturbation.
Jehovah is their keeper and companion. (23)

Their enemies weep for the dead, the virgins are wailing.
The sea flowing down overwhelmed them.
The waters were let loose to flow again. (8)

The people depart fugitive.
A mighty army is submerged in the deep sea,
the only way of escape for the congregated people. (21)

The Bible's Account of the Red Sea Crossing

Contrast the wording and details of the Sinai inscriptions and Moses' words as recorded in Exodus 14:21–29. "And Moses stretched out his hand over the sea; and the LORD caused the sea to go back by a strong east wind all that night, and made the sea dry land, and the waters were divided. And the children of Israel went into the midst of the sea upon the dry ground: and the waters were a wall unto them on their right hand, and on their left. And the Egyptians pursued, and went in after them to the midst of the sea, even all Pharaoh's horses, his chariots, and his horsemen. And it came to pass, that in the morning watch the LORD looked unto the host of the Egyptians through the pillar of fire and of the cloud, and troubled the host of the Egyptians, And took off their chariot wheels, that they drave them heavily: so that the Egyptians said, Let us flee

An Illustration of the Israelites Coming Out of the Red Sea

from the face of Israel; for the LORD fighteth for them against the Egyptians. And the LORD said unto Moses,

Stretch out thine hand over the sea, that the waters may come again upon the Egyptians, upon their chariots, and upon their horsemen. And Moses stretched forth his hand over the sea, and the sea returned to his strength when the morning appeared; and the Egyptians fled against it; and the LORD overthrew the Egyptians in the midst of the sea. And the waters returned, and covered the chariots, and the horsemen, and all the host of Pharaoh that came into the sea after them; there remained not so much as one of them. But the children of Israel walked upon dry land in the midst of the sea; and the waters were a wall unto them on their right hand, and on their left" (Exodus 14:21–29).

The ancient inscriptions precisely describe the Exodus, the role of Moses, and the Jews' miraculous crossing of the Red Sea. The obvious questions are: Who inscribed these messages? And when? Another obvious question is: What could have motivated someone in the past to inscribe this record with such enormous effort when the desolate nature of the terrain would guarantee that very few people would ever see and admire the writer's handiwork? A close examination of the inscriptions reveals that the manner and style of expression are quite different from the language Moses used in the Book of Exodus. If a religious pilgrim or traveler in the distant past wanted to inscribe the biblical story from the Book of Exodus in stone, we would expect him to either quote Exodus exactly or at least use many of the same words as written by Moses. In addition, we would expect such a person to follow the biblical narrative quite closely. However, the inscriptions are quite different from the biblical text of

Exodus. While the Sinai inscriptions detail many of the key events described in Exodus, the original language suggests that the writer was either an independent observer of these events or was recording events told to him by someone who had personally observed the Exodus.

The ancient Greek historian Diodorus Siculus wrote an extraordinary ancient report about the tribes in Egypt and the miraculous drying up of the Red Sea: "It is an ancient report among the Ichtheophagi, who inhabit the shores of the Red Sea, that by a mighty reflux of the sea which happened in former days, the whole gulf became dry land, and appeared green all over; and that the water overflowed the opposite shore, and that all the ground continued bare to the very lowest depth of the gulf, until the water, by an extraordinary high tide, returned to its former channel" (Diodorus Siculus, *Library of History,* lib. iii., c. 40). The parallels between Diodorus's report and the Exodus account of the Red Sea crossing are fascinating.

The Murmuring Against Moses

The explorers found two inscriptions in Wadi Sidri that referred to the murmuring of the Jewish people against Moses about their great thirst, their hunger, and the terror they experienced during their flight from the Egyptians as they entered the great desert of the Sinai Peninsula.

> Pilgrims fugitive through the sea find a place of refuge
>   at Sidri.
> Lighting upon plain ground they proceed on their
>   pilgrimage full of terror. (77)

> The Hebrews pass over the sea into the wide waterless
>   desert,
> famishing with hunger and thirst. (17)

The prophet Moses recorded the experience in the wilderness when the Israelites complained bitterly against God and their leader because they were hungry and thirsty. It is interesting to note that while it took only one day for God to get Israel out of Egypt, it took forty years in the desert to get Egypt out of Israel. Consider how closely the Sinai inscriptions parallel the biblical account as recorded by Moses: "And all the congregation of the children of Israel journeyed from the wilderness of Sin, after their journeys, according to the commandment of the LORD, and pitched in Rephidim: and there was no water for the people to drink. Wherefore the people did chide with Moses, and said, Give us water that we may drink. And Moses said unto them, Why chide ye with me? wherefore do ye tempt the LORD? And the people thirsted there for water; and the people murmured against Moses, and said, Wherefore is this that thou hast brought us up out of Egypt, to kill us and our children and our cattle with thirst?" (Exodus 17:1–3).

The Miraculous Provision of Water

Another Sinai inscription describes God's miraculous provision of water to the Children of Israel through God's commanding Moses to cause the pure water to flow from the rock miraculously. It is worth noting that only seventy-two hours after the Israelites miraculously escaped from Egypt through the Red Sea, they came to the bitter waters of

Marah. God often tested Israel just as He tests us as individuals by bringing us to a difficult experience shortly after a great spiritual victory. The Lord wants to teach us to rely always upon His leading and deliverance instead of our natural tendency to trust in ourselves and our own resources and gifts.

> The people clamour vociferously. The people anger
>   Moses.
> Swerving from the right way, they thirst for water
>   insatiably.
> The water flows, gently gushing out of the stony rock.
> Out of the rock a murmur of abundant waters.
> Out of the hard stone a springing well.
> Like the wild asses braying,
> the Hebrews swallow down enormously and greedily.
> Greedy of food like infants,
> they plunge into sin against Jehovah. (46)

> The people drink, winding on their way,
> drinking with prone mouth,
> Jehovah gives them drink again and again. (39)

> The people sore athirst, drink vehemently.
> They quaff the water-spring without pause, ever drinking.
> Reprobate beside the gushing well-spring. (58)

The Book of Exodus also records that God supernaturally provided water in the desert for His chosen people: "Behold, I will stand before thee there upon the rock in

Horeb; and thou shalt smite the rock, and there shall come water out of it, that the people may drink. And Moses did so in the sight of the elders of Israel" (Exodus 17:6). Despite God's ample and miraculous provision for the Israelites, the Jews remained reprobate in their attitude, drinking the water but refusing either to thank God for His provision of water or trust in His continuing provision for their daily needs. Moses described their thanklessness: "And he called the name of the place Massah, and Meribah, because of the chiding of the children of Israel, and because they tempted the LORD, saying, Is the LORD among us, or not?" (Exodus 17:7).

God's Judgment on Israel's Gluttony

The inscriptions in Sinai record that the Israelites succumbed to gluttony in eating the quails that God miraculously provided at a place called Kibroth Hattaavah. Despite God's daily provision of manna, the Israelites rebelled against the Lord and against Moses by complaining about the sameness of food. This rebellion unleashed the wrath of God on their sinfulness. He sent a massive flock of quail to provide meat for the Israelites. Rather than gratefully accepting this quail meat as a gift from God, the Israelites greedily ̶̶ ̶ their mouths with the quail. Many of the Israelites ̶̶ ̶ in the plague of gluttony at Kibroth Hattaavah.

> The people have drink to satiety. In crowds they swill.
> Flesh they strip from the bone, mangling it.
> Replete with food, they are obstreperous.
> Surfeited, they cram themselves; clamouring, they vomit.
> The people are drinking water to repletion.

The tribes, weeping for the dead, cry aloud with down-
cast eyes.
The dove mourns, devoured by grief.
The hungry ass kicketh: the tempted men, brought to
destruction, perish.
Apostasy from the faith leads them to the tomb. (28)

Devouring flesh ravenously, drinking wine greedily,
Dancing, shouting, they play. (34)

Congregating on all sides to ensnare them,
the people voraciously devour the quails.
Binding the bow against them, bringing them down.
Eagerly and enormously eating the half raw flesh,
the pilgrims become plague-stricken.

Compare the message of the inscriptions with Moses'
account in the Book of Numbers: "And say thou unto the
people, Sanctify yourselves against tomorrow, and ye shall
eat flesh: for ye have wept in the ears of the LORD, saying,
Who shall give us flesh to eat? for it was well with us in
Egypt: therefore the LORD will give you flesh, and ye shall
eat. Ye shall not eat one day, nor two days, nor five days, neither ten days, nor twenty days; but even a whole month,
until it come out at your nostrils, and it be loathsome unto
you: because that ye have despised the LORD which is among
you, and have wept before him, saying, Why came we forth
out of Egypt?" (Numbers 11:18–20). In the balance of the
chapter, Moses describes God's supernatural provision of
meat: "And there went forth a wind from the LORD, and

brought quails from the sea, and let them fall by the camp, as it were a day's journey on this side, and as it were a day's journey on the other side, round about the camp, and as it were two cubits high upon the face of the earth. And the people stood up all that day, and all that night, and all the next day, and they gathered the quails: he that gathered least gathered ten homers: and they spread them all abroad for themselves round about the camp. And while the flesh was yet between their teeth, ere it was chewed, the wrath of the LORD was kindled against the people, and the LORD smote the people with a very great plague" (Numbers 11:31-33). The next statement by Moses records the location where this event occurred: the very same place where this Sinai inscription was discovered over fifteen centuries later. "And he called the name of that place Kibroth Hattaavah: because there they buried the people that lusted" (Numbers 11:34).

In a confirmation of Exodus 32:6 where Moses declares that "the people sat down to eat and to drink, and rose up to play," the Sinai inscription Number 34 describes the activities of the Israelites as, "Dancing, shouting, they play." Moses records that God destroyed the ungrateful Israelites who indulged in this sinful gluttony: "And there went forth a wind from the LORD, and brought quails from the sea, and let them fall by the camp, as it were a day's journey on this side, and as it were a day's journey on the other side, round about the camp, and as it were two cubits high upon the face of the earth" (Numbers 11:31).

William Houghton described the abundance of quails in the Middle East in an article in *Smith's Dictionary of the Bible:* "The quail migrates in immense numbers. (See Pliny,

H. N. X. 23.) Tourneyfort says that all the islands of the Archipelago at certain seasons of the year are covered with these birds. Col. Sykes states . . . 'that 160,000 quails have been netted in one season on this little island; according to Temminck, 100,000 have been taken near Nettuno in one day.' The Israelites would have had little difficulty in capturing large quantities of these birds, as they are known to arrive at places sometimes so completely exhausted by their flight as to be readily taken, not in nets only, but by the hand. Sykes says, 'They arrive in spring on the shores of Provence so fatigued that for the first few days they allow themselves to be taken by the hand.' It is interesting to note the time specified by Moses; 'it was at even' that they began to arrive, and they no doubt continued to come all the night" (William Houghton, *Smith's Dictionary of the Bible* [Boston: D. Lothrop & Co., 1878] p. 2,650).

Another authority on the wildlife in the Sinai, Professor H. B. Tristram, reported in his book, *Natural History of the Bible:* "The quail migrates in vast flocks and regularly crosses the Arabian desert, flying for the most part at night; and when the birds settle they are so utterly exhausted that they may be captured in any numbers by the hand. . . . Thus in spring and autumn they are slaughtered in numbers on Malta and many of the Greek islands. . . . The period when they were brought to the camp of Israel was in spring, when on their northward migration from Africa . . . they would follow up the coast of the Red Sea till . . . they fell, thick as rain, about the camp in month of April, according to our calculation. Thus the miracle consisted in the supply being brought to the tents of Israel by the special guidance of the Lord, in exact harmony with the known habits of the bird. . . . I have myself found the ground in Algeria, in the month of April, covered with quails for an extent of many acres at daybreak, where on the preceding afternoon there had not been one. They were so fatigued that they scarcely moved till almost trodden upon; and although hundreds were slaughtered, for two days they did not leave the district" (Professor H. B. Tristram, *Natural History of the Bible,* pp. 231, 232).

Sarbut-el-Khadem—An Ancient Mountain Graveyard at Kibroth Hattaavah

One of the most remarkable of the discoveries found in the Sinai in recent centuries was that of the graves of those Jews who had died from a supernatural plague. The Book of Numbers records: "And the LORD smote the people with a very great plague. And he called the name of that place Kibroth Hattaavah: because there they buried the people that lusted" (Numbers 11:33–34).

In 1761, the German explorer Barthold Niebuhr discovered an extensive ruined cemetery with carved inscriptions on the tombs and within a sepulcher on top of an inaccessible mountain in Sinai called Sarbut-el-Khadem (*Voyage en Arabie,* tom. i, p. 191). Niebuhr noted that these inscriptions could not have been made by native Egyptians because there are no carved stone inscriptions found in Egypt; rather the Egyptians painted their inscriptions on plaster surfaces. He found numerous gravestones with legible inscriptions in addition to a small temple carved out of the rock that also contained numerous inscriptions in the same language as appeared at other Exodus sites. Niebuhr remarked on "the

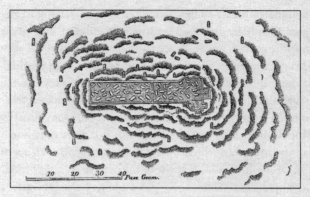

Turbet es Yahoud—"The Graves of the Jews"
An Illustration of Graveyard at Kibroth-hattaavah

wonderful preservation of the inscriptions upon this soft sandstone, exposed as they have been to the air and weather during the lapse of so many ages. On some of the stones they are quite perfect" (Niebuhr, *Biblical Researches*, vol. i, pp. 113, 114). The Byzantine monk Cosmas Indicopleustes had previously recorded his discovery of these graves in A.D. 535.

Niebuhr also found numerous engravings of quails in the cemetery. The tombstones actually depict these birds "standing, flying and apparently, even trussed and cooked" (Rev. Charles Forster, *Sinai Photographed* [London: Richard Bentley, 1862], p. 62). Niebuhr noted that the native Bedouin Arabs from the deserts of Sinai call these tombs "the Jews' graves." He said that these hieroglyphics on the tombstones were quite different from the inscriptions he had found in Egyptian tombs. The Sinai tomb inscriptions contained no mention of any of the Egyptian gods that are found in virtually all Egyptian tombs. When Dr. Stewart visited the site he described the tombs as follows: "The whole of this part of the Wadi seems to have been covered with graves, the stones of which are scattered abroad in all directions. . . . The Bedouins still maintain that they are the *Turbet es Yahoud* (the graves of the Jews)." Another graveyard at the mouth of the Wadi is called *Bounli Abou Israel* by the Arabs, indicating their belief that it contains the bones of the ancient Israelites. Significantly, there is no evidence of any other human settlement in the Sinai area, either modern or ancient. While the Egyptians always buried their dead in the plain or in a valley, this extensive graveyard sits on the top of a seven-hundred-foot-high mountain. The work involved in bringing the bodies here for burial would have been immense. However, this practice of mountain burial is normal for the Jews. Both Moses and Aaron were buried in the mountains by God. Even today, Jews in Israel often choose to be buried on the Mount of Olives and other mountains surrounding Jerusalem. Who else would be buried here on a desolate mountain in Sinai except for those ancient Israelites killed by the wrath of God?

Tombstone Inscriptions in the Sinai

The detailed molds and photographs that Dr. Stewart made when he explored this huge graveyard were translated by Rev. Charles Forster and appeared in Forster's 1862 book *Sinai Photographed* (p. 84).

> The apostates smitten with disease by God,
> by means of feathered fowls.

Smitten by God with disease in the sandy plain,
(when) exceeding the bounds of moderation.
Sickening, smitten by God with disease;
their marrow corrupted by God by means of the
    feathered fowls.
The people, given over to destruction, cry aloud.
God pours down deep sleep,
messenger of death, upon the pilgrims.
The tomb is the end of life to the sick,
smitten with disease by God.

Moses described the Jews' constant rebellion against his leadership. Despite repeated miracles that proved God's support, the Bible described the Israelites' failure to trust in His power to protect them from hunger and thirst.

Miriam's Rebellion Against Moses

One of the most interesting stories recorded in the Torah is that of Miriam's attack on Moses' leadership because she rejected his Ethiopian wife. Among the inscriptions discovered in Sinai was one that may have been engraved on the rocks of Sinai even before Moses recorded the event in the Book of Numbers. A translation of this inscription from Rev. Forster reads as follows:

Miriam, Prophetess of lying lips and deceitful tongue.
She causes the tribes to conspire against the pillar and
    prince of the people.
Convoked for tumult, perverted, full of strife,
the people revile the meek and generous man.
They lead with reproaches the blessed one of God. (48)

Moses also recorded the tragic history of his family's rebellion against his leadership: "And Miriam and Aaron spake against Moses because of the Ethiopian woman whom he had married: for he had married an Ethiopian woman. And they said, Hath the LORD indeed spoken only by Moses? hath he not spoken also by us? And the LORD heard it. (Now the man Moses was very meek, above all the men which were upon the face of the earth)" (Numbers 12:1–3). The parallels between the biblical record and the Sinai inscriptions are remarkable. The Bible records that God judged Miriam's sinful challenge to Moses' leadership by causing her to succumb to the dreaded disease of leprosy. However, when Moses appealed to God that she would be healed, the Lord graciously healed her after an imposed period of seven days isolation from the camp of the Israelites.

The Plague of Fiery Serpents

The final Sinai inscription that we will examine is one that deals with the incident of the fiery serpents recorded in the Book of Numbers.

> Bitten and destroyed by fiery, hissing serpents,
> the Hebrews are wounded for their crimes.
> Jehovah makes a stream flow from the stony rock. (47)

In Numbers 21, Moses described the Israelites' ungrateful rebellion when they complained against God's supernatural provision of manna and water in the desert: "And the people spake against God, and against Moses, Wherefore have ye brought us up out of Egypt to die in the wilderness? for there is no bread, neither is there any water; and our soul loatheth this light bread. And the LORD sent fiery serpents among the people, and they bit the people; and much people of Israel died" (Numbers 21:5–6).

The profound silence of the deserts of the Sinai Peninsula has hidden and preserved these fascinating inscriptions for three and a half thousand years. These ancient monuments and inscriptions have been inaccessible to mankind for three millennia, but they were preserved by the providence of God. A careful comparison of these ancient inscriptions from the deserts of Sinai reveals an astonishing degree of confirmation of the facts recorded in the original accounts in Genesis, Exodus, and Numbers.

The French government commissioned Professor Lottin de Laval to explore the Sinai in 1851 and to create plaster casts of the inscriptions directly from the rocks. Later, the government of England instructed its agents to take exact photographs of these inscriptions to enable scientists to examine them. Following the publication of Rev. Charles Forster's photographs of these engravings, Professor A. P. Stanley, who had disputed their antiquity in his earlier editions of his book, suggested in the fourth edition of his book, *Sinai and Palestine* (1857), that language experts should carefully reconsider the evidence of their antiquity.

An Astonishing Discovery—A Trilingual Inscription

Some critics naturally reject out of hand the possibility that these Sinai inscriptions could actually be genuine contemporary records of the Exodus. They finally challenged Rev. Forster by stating that they would not be convinced of the accuracy and authenticity of his detailed translations unless someone discovered a bilingual inscription containing the Sinai inscriptions on one side and another known language on the other side for comparison. In other words, they demanded that someone find another inscription similar to the marvelous trilingual inscription known as the Rosetta Stone, which was found in 1799 near Rosetta, Egypt, that enabled the scholars Young and Champollion to finally decipher the Egyptian hieroglyphics. Incredibly, another Sinai explorer, Pierce Butler, made a phenomenal discovery in 1860 of a trilingual inscription in a cave on the Djebel Maghara mountain. This incredible inscription contained three descriptions of the same event engraved in three languages including the alphabet used in the Sinai inscriptions. (A photograph of this incredible trilingual inscription appears in the photo section.) The importance of this final trilingual inscription discovery cannot be overestimated because it confirmed that Rev. Forster's translation of the Exodus inscriptions was accurate.

Professor Lottin de Laval declared in his 1859 book, *Voyage dans la Peninsule Arabique du Sinai et l'Egypt emoyenne,* that the miscellaneous graffiti were obviously quite different from the ancient inscriptions because the graffiti were scratched with sword points or similar rough tools on the soft rocks, often only four feet from the ground (M. Lottin de Laval, *Voyage dans la Peninsule Arabique du Sinai et l'Egypt emoyenne* [S.E.M. le Ministre de l'Instruction publique et des Cultes, 1859]). He noted that the older Sinai inscriptions were carefully engraved in the granite with proper tools after the rock surface was prepared by hard labor due to the great height and difficulty of access for the engraver. Laval reported that Christian crosses appear infrequently and bear no connection to the original older inscriptions. Precise impressions from plaster castings of these Sinai engravings created by Professor de Laval were brought to Paris for detailed examination and verification. Most important, Rev. Charles Forster published his photographs for the examination of other scientists in his 1862 book, *Sinai Photographed,* which made it possible for other scholars and laypeople to examine these marvelous inscriptions for themselves.

Professor de Laval wrote, "As for the connection existing between the Sinaitic writing and that of Egypt, we are perfectly of Mr. Forster's opinion, and shall support him with proofs. Twenty-two letters of the demotic Egyptian alphabet are constantly found in the Sinaitic inscriptions. With the exception of two or three variants, it is the same alphabet." Professor de Laval ended his remarks by concluding that it was virtually impossible that ". . . a people so intelligent, so persevering as the Hebrew people, have not left in the indelible granite of the Peninsula of Sinai a single monument of their Exode, to thank God for being able, in the midst of so much misery and danger, to recover safety and liberty."

Three scholars, Professor de Laval, Niebuhr, and Forster, have independently translated these fascinating rock inscriptions. Each of them concluded that the inscriptions were made by the ancient Israelites during the Exodus. While other scholars have dismissed their conclusion, to my knowledge, no one has produced any alternative translation of the inscriptions as evidence that anyone else produced them.

The weight of the evidence supports the conclusion that these ancient inscriptions proclaim a message from the distant past confirming the accuracy of the account of the Exodus recorded in the Word of God.

Four

Startling Archeological Discoveries

Can we trust the Bible? The answer is an overwhelming *YES!* The reason for this confident statement is that, for the past one hundred and fifty years, many brilliant scholars have conducted detailed archeological examinations at thousands of sites throughout the Middle East. The results of their discoveries have proven that the Bible is reliable and accurate in every single area where its statements could be tested. In the balance of this chapter I will share some of the wonderful archeological discoveries that provide tremendous proof that the Bible is a true and accurate record of past events in ancient Israel.

Throughout most of the last two thousand years, the majority of men living in the Western world have accepted the statements of the Scriptures as genuine. Respected biblical scholars including Brown, Adam Clarke, and Faussett, among others, wrote numerous Bible commentaries in the early part of the 1800s. However, despite their best efforts, their knowledge of the history and archeology of the ancient world was limited solely to the Bible and excerpts from classical writings from Greek and Latin writers. Unfortunately, most writers of the classics either exaggerated or failed to differentiate between mythology and historical events. As a result, most Bible commentators in past centuries were unable to add much additional knowledge to confirm the

Bible's accounts of events. Fortunately, the field of biblical archeology has exploded in the past century and a half. The discoveries have provided tremendous insight into the life, culture, and history of the ancient biblical world. Most important, these discoveries have confirmed thousands of biblical statements as true.

Beginning with the higher critical school of biblical critics in Germany and England in the nineteenth century we have witnessed a progressive abandonment of the historic faith in the Word of God. While European seminaries gradually abandoned the authority of the Scriptures, North American seminaries and Bible colleges still upheld the accuracy of the Bible to some degree. In the 1960s most North American seminaries still accepted the basic records of the Old and New Testaments as being historically true. However, in the following decades there occurred a wholesale abandonment of belief in the historical accuracy of the Bible. The attitudes behind these attacks on biblical accuracy and authority were those of complete rejection of God's inspiration of the Scriptures. In addition, many critics approach the Bible with an attitude of outright denial of supernatural events, such as miracles, and biblical prophecy. To these unbelieving critics, the presence of a miracle or prophecy in a biblical text was absolute proof that it was not genuine. Critics rejected the possibility of inspiration, miracles, and prophecy before they began their examination of the evidence.

Despite the overwhelming success unbelieving critics have had in establishing their unbelieving attitudes within the seminaries, textbooks, and popular media, something strange began to occur. The new discoveries by archeologists digging at sites in the Middle East continued to produce fascinating finds that contradicted their attitudes. Every new discovery in Israel and the surrounding nations provided tremendous confirmation of the accuracy of the Word of God in incredible ways. As a result of these continuing discoveries, Dr. Nelson Glueck, the most outstanding Jewish archeologist of this century, wrote in his book, *Rivers in the Desert,* this fascinating statement. "It may be stated categorically that no archaeological discovery has ever controverted a Biblical reference. Scores of archaeological findings have been made which confirm in clear outline or in exact detail historical statements in the Bible. And by the same token, proper evaluation of Biblical descriptions has often led to amazing discoveries. They form tesserae in the vast mosaic of the Bible's almost incredibly correct historical memory" (Dr. Nelson Glueck, *Rivers in the Desert* [New York: Grove, 1960], p. 31).

In confirmation of Dr. Glueck's statement, another respected scholar, Dr. J. O. Kinnaman, declared: "Of the hundreds of thousands of artifacts found by the archeologists, not one has ever been discovered that contradicts or denies one word, phrase, clause, or sentence of the Bible, but always confirms and verifies the facts of the biblical record." The well-known language scholar Dr. Robert Dick Wilson, formerly professor of Semitic philology at Princeton Theological Seminary, made the following comment: "After forty-five years of scholarly research in biblical textual studies and in language study, I have come now to the conviction that no man knows enough to assail the truthfulness of the Old Testament. When there is sufficient documentary evidence to make an investigation, the statement of the Bible, in the original text, has stood the test" (Dr. Robert Dick Wilson, *Speaker's Source Book,* p. 391).

The Bible claims that it is the inspired and accurate Word of God. Therefore, it is vital that we compare the scriptural records against the archeological discoveries uncovered at actual sites where many of the thrilling events of the Bible actually occurred. The results of these detailed investigations are available for anyone to examine. The archeological record provides overwhelming confirmation of thousands of detailed statements and facts recorded in the sacred Scriptures. Scholars have not found one single confirmed archeological discovery that absolutely disproves a statement of the Scriptures. To the contrary, as the evidence in *The Signature of God* reveals, the scholars have discovered literally hundreds of objects, inscriptions, and sites that confirm the accuracy of biblical statements in even unimportant areas. The most important thing for believers in God is that these archeological proofs of scriptural accuracy confirm the accuracy, the inspiration, and the authority of the Word of God. No one should expect that archeology will be able to provide detailed proof of such personal events like the sacrifice of Isaac by Abraham. By their nature, it is unlikely that such events in the lives of private individuals would ever leave any archeological evidence. Most personal events recorded in the Bible would never have left evidence that could be discovered thousands of years later. However, whenever the Bible dealt with the rise and fall of kingdoms, cities, buildings, etc., the spade of the archeologist has been able to discover wonderful confirmation of the truth of Holy Scripture.

Only fifty years ago many disbelieving scholars totally rejected the historical accuracy of the Bible because they claimed that the Scriptures talked about numerous kings and individuals that could not be confirmed from any other historical or archeological records. Recent discoveries, however, have shown that they should not have abandoned their faith in the Word of God so easily. If they had only trusted in the truthfulness of the Bible or waited a little longer, they would have been rewarded with the recent archeological discoveries that confirm many biblical details, events, and personalities. For example, many scholars contemptuously reject the Bible's statements about King David. Many textbooks used in universities and seminaries openly reject any historical statements in the Scriptures about King David or Solomon. They believe that David is a myth or literary fiction. Examples of this approach include the books *In Search of Ancient Israel,* by Philip R. Davis, and the *Early History of the Israelite People,* by Thomas L. Thompson. He wrote, "The existence of the Bible's 'United Monarchy' during the tenth-century [B.C.] is . . . impossible" (Thomas L. Thompson, *Early History of the Israelite People* [Brill: 1992]). These so-called "minimalist" scholars accept only the minimum about the Bible, rejecting every biblical statement unless it can be established by other non-biblical evidence.

This is a totally biased position and would be ridiculed in any other area of study. Imagine a student of Plato's Greek philosophy who rejected outright any statement by Plato himself, his followers, or any Greek philosophical writer in later years who quoted him favorably. This is an absurd way to approach the study of any subject. Yet many biblical scholars in the secular universities take this "minimalist" approach today. The rational way to study ancient history is to carefully examine every bit of evidence regarding a personality or event from both those who support and those who oppose the particular subject. The true scholar will then carefully weigh the evidence of all sources and come to a balanced conclusion based on the facts.

The House of David

Recent archeological investigations have demolished the position of those who rejected the biblical account of Israel's kings such as King David. In 1993, archeologists digging at Tel Dan in the Galilee in northern Israel found a fragment of a stone inscription that clearly refers to the "house of David" and identifies David as the "king of Israel." This is the first inscription outside the Bible that confirms the Bible's statement that David was the king of Israel in the ninth century before Christ. Many Bible critics who had rejected King David as a myth were upset to discover their position could no longer be defended. Some critics suggested that the fragment was a "fake." The following summer, two additional fragments of the original inscription were found that provided scholars with the whole inscription, confirming that it referred to David as king of Israel. Furthermore, another scholar, Andre Lemaire from the College de France, discovered another ninth century B.C. stone inscription created by King Mesha of Moab that also referred to "the House of David." These incredible inscriptions, recorded a century after David's death, confirm that David was king of Israel at the time the

Bible stated and that he established a dynasty, the "House of David," as the Scriptures said.

A stone inscription from Egypt confirms that Israel was established as a nation in Canaan centuries before the reign of King David, just as the Bible claims. The Merneptah Stela is a seven-and-a-half-foot-high stone inscription discovered in the temple of Pharaoh Merneptah at Thebes in Egypt. Scholars determined that Pharaoh Merneptah ruled Egypt from 1213 to 1203 B.C. and confirmed that he launched an invasion into the area of the modern-day West Bank in Canaan, defeating the Jewish inhabitants of the land. The second line from the bottom of this inscription boasts, "Israel is laid waste; his seed is not."

Critics of the Bible have claimed for decades that the Bible's statements in Joshua about the conquest of the Promised Land in the centuries before the monarchy of King David were pure fiction. Obviously, the king of Egypt would not need to invade Canaan with an army unless the Jews had established a significant presence on the frontiers of the Egyptian Empire. In light of this new archeological evidence, critics will be forced to relinquish their rejection of the Bible's record of Israel's conquest as stated by Joshua. Critics claimed that the books of Samuel, Kings, and Chronicles were recorded by Jews living in Persia centuries after the events occurred. They suggest that such records contain numerous errors and myths. However, the Bible claims these books were written at the time of the events and that God's Holy Spirit inspired the writers to record the events correctly. When you compare the Word of God to the accuracy of the ancient historians such as Herodotus, you can quickly see that most ancient histories were nothing more than creative fiction and records of hearsay evidence without careful research or checking of facts. In stark contrast, the Bible is extremely careful and accurate as to events, chronology, sequence, and personalities.

In addition to the archeological evidence for King David, we now have confirmation of other kings of Israel. The name of Omri, king of Israel, is recorded on an inscription known as the Stela of King Mesha of Moab. In addition, Omri's name appears on the rock inscriptions of three kings of Assyria, the annals of both Tiglath-Pileser III and Sargon II, and the Black Obelisk of King Shalmaneser III, who wrote, "I conquered . . . all of the Land of Omri (Israel)." Other Assyrian inscriptions found in Nineveh confirm the Bible's records about these kings of Israel: Ahab, Jehu, Joash, Menehem, Pekah, and Hoshea. In addition, the names of many of the kings of the southern kingdom of Judah are also recorded on inscriptions of the nations that fought against the Jews. The inscriptions found by archeologists also confirm the names of these kings of Judah: Ahaziah, Uzziah, Ahaz, Hezekiah, Manasseh, and Jehoiachin. Scholars found ration records of the army of Nebuchadnezzar, king of Babylon (606 to 562 B.C.) that state, "ten sila of oil to Jehoiachin, king of Judah. . . ." Obviously, the fact that these foreign nations listed the kings of Israel and Judah provides the strongest evidence confirming the accuracy of the Word of God.

In 1846, the explorer Austen Henry Layard discovered an incredible Black Obelisk in the ruins of Nimrud (present-day Iraq), the ancient capital of the great Assyrian Empire that conquered the northern kingdom of Israel. This six-and-a-half-foot-high Black Obelisk, a four-sided stone inscription, recorded the conquest of the Assyrian king Shalmaneser II over numerous foreign kingdoms, including King Jehu of Israel (approximately 841 to 814 B.C.). A detailed examination of the obelisk reveals King Jehu bowing down in obedience to the Assyrian king. The obelisk refers to Jehu as the "son of Omri," indicating their awareness that his dynasty traced back to Omri in confirmation of the Book of Kings.

The Walls of Jericho

During excavations of Jericho between 1930 and 1936, Professor John Garstang found one of the most incredible confirmations of the biblical record about the conquest of the Promised Land. The results were so amazing that he took the precaution of preparing a written declaration of the archeological discovery, signed by himself and two other members of his team. "As to the main fact, then, there remains no doubt: the walls fell outwards so completely that the attackers would be able to clamber up and over their ruins into the city." This fact is important because the evidence from all other archeological digs around ancient cities in the Middle East reveals that walls of cities always fall inward as invading armies push their way into a city. However, in the account in Joshua 6:20, we read, "The wall fell down flat, so that the people went up into the city, every man straight before him, and they took the city." Only the supernatural power of God could have caused the walls to fall outward as described in Joshua's account of the conquest of Jericho (John Garstang, *Joshua Judges* [London: Constable, 1931]).

Following the fall of East Jerusalem to the Jordanians in the 1948 War of Independence, the Jordanian army dynamited Jewish synagogues and other buildings in the Jewish Quarter of Jerusalem in the years following their conquering of the Old City. Nevertheless, this wanton destruction over a twenty-year period, until Jerusalem was liberated during the 1967 Six Day War, created a unique archeological opportunity. When the Jews recaptured the Jewish Quarter in 1967, they had to rebuild every building because of the Jordanian destruction. However, this made it possible for Israeli archeologists to remove the rubble built up over the last two thousand years and explore the bedrock of this fascinating biblical city. This was a unique opportunity because the existing modern buildings in most ancient cities prevent large archeological exploration. In addition to numerous discoveries confirming the accuracy of many passages in the Bible, the scholars, under the leadership of the archeologist Nahman Avigad of Hebrew University, found the remains of the wall of King Hezekiah built when the Assyrian army attacked Israel in 701 B.C. The Bible tells us that King Hezekiah built the walls of Jerusalem to resist the Assyrian armies: "And when Hezekiah saw that Sennacherib was come, and that he was purposed to fight against Jerusalem, he took counsel with his princes . . . they did help him. . . . Also he strengthened himself, and built up all the wall that was broken, and raised it up to the towers, and another wall without" (2 Chronicles 32:2–5). The archeologists found that portions of the wall actually cut through walls of recently built houses, indicating the urgency of the defensive actions and the authority of the king. This is confirmed in the Bible's own account, "And ye have numbered the houses of Jerusalem, and the houses have ye broken down to fortify the wall" (Isaiah 22:10).

Dr. Millar Burrows, a professor at Yale University, studied the evidence that indicates the historicity of Abraham and the other patriarchs of Israel as recorded in Genesis. "Everything indicates that here we have an historical individual. As noted above, he is not mentioned in any known archaeological source, but his name appears in Babylonia as a personal name in the very period to which he belongs" (Millar Burrows, *What Mean These Stones?* [New York: Meridian Books, 1956], pp. 258-259). Burrows wrote about the underlying reason most scholars reject the authority of the Bible, "The excessive skepticism of many liberal theologians stems not from a careful evaluation of the available data, but from an enormous predisposition against the supernatural. . . . On the whole, however, archaeological work has unquestionably strengthened confidence in the reliability of the scriptural record."

The Discovery of the Seals of Biblical Personalities

One of the most interesting discoveries in recent years was the finding of two bullæ, or clay seals, that bear the impression of the actual seal used by Baruch, the scribe of Jeremiah the prophet who transcribed the Book of Jeremiah. Both bullæ bear the inscription, "Belonging to Berekhyahu, son of Neriyahu, the Scribe." One of these clay seals is on view in the Israel Museum in Jerusalem. However, the second bullæ was found in Jerusalem earlier in this century and purchased by collector Shlomo Moussaieff of London who owns the greatest private collection of ancient Jewish inscriptions in the world. This second clay seal, bearing the same inscription, also reveals a fingerprint that probably belonged to Baruch.

At the beginning of this century, a fascinating seal was discovered in Israel that bore an inscription of a beautiful lion and the words, "Belonging to Shema servant of Jeroboam." This amazing find indicates that it belonged to an official of King Jeroboam of Israel. Other seals have been discovered confirming the biblical records about King Uzziah (777 to 736 B.C.) and King Hezekiah (726 to 697 B.C.).

Another important seal found in Jerusalem dates from the seventh century before Christ and is inscribed as follows: "Belonging to Abdi Servant of Hoshea." This seal made of orange chalcedony, used to authenticate royal documents for security, belonged to Abdi, a high official of King Hosea, the last king of the northern kingdom of Israel before it was conquered by the Assyrian Empire in 721 B.C. Another large seal on red limestone was found bearing the inscription "Belonging to Asayahu, servant of the king" together with a galloping horse. The name "Asaiah" is a short form of the name "Asayahu." This name occurs twice in the Old Testament in connection with the title "servant of the king." In 2 Chronicles 34:20 we find the name, "Asaiah a servant of the king's" and again in 2 Kings 22:12, "Asahiah a servant of the king's." It is possible that this seal was owned by "Asaiah, the servant of the king" a high court official who was sent by King Josiah to examine carefully the scroll of the lost Book of Deuteronomy that was found in the Temple by the high priest Hilkiah in approximately 622 B.C.

Dr. Henry M. Morris concluded his in-depth study of the archeological evidence concerning the Bible with these words. "Problems still exist, of course, in the complete harmonization of archaeological material with the Bible, but none so serious as not to bear real promise of imminent solution through further investigation. It must be extremely significant that, in view of the great mass of corroborative evidence regarding the Biblical history of these periods, there exists today not one unquestionable find of archaeology that proves the Bible to be in error at any point" (Henry M. Morris, *The Bible and Modern Science* [Chicago: Moody Press, 1956]).

Explorers in Iraq in the last century found the ancient inscribed clay cylinder bearing the actual decree of King Cyrus of Persia allowing the various captured natives of many different nations to return freely to their ancient homelands. It was the government policy of the preceding Babylonian Empire of King Nebuchadnezzar to displace whole peoples such as the Jews and resettle them in the far reaches of their empire. However, King Cyrus of Persia, a moderate and God-fearing monarch, reversed the cruel Babylonian policy. Immediately after conquering the Babylonian Empire, King Cyrus issued a decree allowing the Jews to return freely to their homeland in Israel ending the seventy-year-long captivity. The decree of King Cyrus began with these words, "I am Cyrus, king of the world, great king." After describing his conquests and deeds, the cylinder inscription reads, "I gathered all their former inhabitants and returned to them their habitations." In this incredible discovery we find the confirmation of one of the most astonishing events in the pages of Scripture. "Now in the first year of Cyrus king of Persia, that the word of the LORD by the mouth of Jeremiah might be fulfilled, the LORD stirred up the spirit of Cyrus king of Persia, that he made a proclamation throughout all his kingdom, and put it also in writing, saying, Thus saith Cyrus king of Persia, The LORD God of heaven hath given me all the kingdoms of the earth; and he hath charged me to build him an house at Jerusalem, which is in Judah. Who is there among you of all his people? his God be with him, and let him go up to Jerusalem, which is in Judah, and build the house of the LORD God of Israel, (he is the God,) which is in Jerusalem" (Ezra 1:1–3).

The Archeological Evidence of the New Testament

Obviously, the entire basis for the faith and hope of Christians depends on the truthfulness of the historical records of the New Testament. Our hope for heaven and salvation itself depends on the accuracy of the words of Jesus of Nazareth and the apostles as recorded in the pages of the New Testament manuscripts. It is significant that there is a relentless attack on the reliability of the Gospels and the Epistles because those who hate the Bible understand that if they can cause men to doubt the New Testament, then their faith will be immeasurably weakened. Fortunately, the continued archeological discoveries during the last century have provided an awesome amount of further evidence that confirms the total reliability of the written documents that form the foundation of the Christian faith.

The English scholar William Ramsay traveled as a young man to Asia Minor over a century ago for the sole purpose of disproving the Bible's history as described by Luke in his Gospel and in the Book of Acts. Ramsay and his professors were convinced that the New Testament record must be terribly inaccurate. He believed that Luke could not be correct in his history of Christ or in his account about the growth of the Church during the first decades following Christ. Dr. Ramsay began to dig in the ancient ruins of sites throughout Greece and Asia Minor, searching for ancient names, boundary markers, and other archeological finds that would conclusively prove that Luke had invented his history of Christ and His Church. To his amazement and dismay, William Ramsay discovered that the statements of the New Testament Scriptures were accurate in the smallest detail. Finally, Dr. Ramsay was convinced by the overwhelming evidence proving the Bible's accuracy. As a result, he accepted Jesus Christ as His personal Savior. He became both a Christian and a great biblical scholar. As a result of his conversion to belief in Jesus Christ, Sir William Ramsay's books became classics in the study of the history of the New Testament. Another great scholar, A. N. Sherwin-White, was a great classical historical scholar at Oxford University who studied the extensive evidence for and against the historical accuracy of the Book of Acts. Sherwin-White wrote his conclusion after studying the evidence, "For Acts the confirmation of historicity is overwhelming . . . any attempt to reject its basic historicity even in matters of detail must now appear absurd" (quoted by Rubel Shelley, *Prepare to Answer* [Grand Rapids: Baker Book House, 1990]).

Dr. William F. Albright was unquestionably one of the world's most brilliant biblical archeologists. In 1955 he wrote: "We can already say emphatically that there is no longer any solid basis for dating any book of the New Testament after circa A.D. 80." However, additional discoveries over the next decade convinced him that all the books in the New Testament were written "probably sometime between circa A.D. 50 and 75." Significantly, Albright concluded that the writing of the New Testament within a few years of the events it described made it almost impossible that errors or exaggeration could have entered the text. He wrote that the duration between the events of Christ's life and the writing was "too slight to permit any appreciable corruption of the essential center and even of the specific wording of the sayings of Jesus." In other words, Professor Albright, one of the greatest minds in the field of archeology and ancient texts, concluded that the New Testament records the truth about Jesus Christ and His statements.

Dr. John A. T. Robinson was a distinguished lecturer at Trinity College, Cambridge, and developed a reputation as a great scholar. Naturally, he accepted the academic consensus, universally held since 1900, which denied that the disciples and Paul wrote the New Testament and concluded that it was written up to a hundred years after Christ. However, an article in *Time* magazine, March 21, 1977, reported that Robinson decided to personally investigate for himself the arguments behind this scholarly consensus against the New Testament's reliability because he realized that very little original research had been completed in this field in this century. He was shocked to discover that much of past scholarship against the New Testament was untenable because it was based on a "tyranny of unexamined assumptions" and what he felt must have been an "almost willful blindness." To the amazement of his university colleagues, Robinson concluded that the apostles must have been the genuine writers of the New Testament books in the years prior to A.D. 64. He challenged other scholars to complete original research necessary to truly examine the question fairly. As a result of such a new analysis, Robinson believed that it would necessitate "the rewriting of many introductions to—and ultimately, theologies of—the New Testament." Robinson's book, *Redating the New Testament,* published in 1976, suggests that Matthew's Gospel was written as early as A.D. 40, within eight years of Christ.

Five

The Historical Evidence About Jesus Christ

Many modern scholars dispute the historical accuracy of the Bible. They especially reject the Gospel accounts of the life, death, and resurrection of Jesus Christ. As an example of this rejection of biblical authority, the Jesus Seminar, a group of seventy-five New Testament liberal scholars, meets semi-annually to determine whether or not any of the Gospel quotations of Jesus' words meet with their scholarly approval. Incredibly, these liberal scholars examine individual "sayings" of Jesus recorded by the four Gospels and each academic votes to accept or reject these statements of Christ. The Jesus Seminar is sponsored by the Westor Institute, a private California study center, founded by Robert Funk, a liberal New Testament scholar. This group arrogantly pretends to sit in judgment of whether or not a particular biblical statement meets with their approval and is "genuine."

One indication of the underlying attitudes of these seminarians regarding the authenticity of Jesus' words is found in the comments of Arthur Dewey of Xavier University, a member of the infamous Jesus Seminar. As reported in an article in *Time* magazine in April 1994, he stated that, while rejecting most of Christ's words, they believed Jesus was occasionally humorous: "There is more of David Letterman in the historical Jesus than Pat Robertson."

These particular liberal scholars are openly contemptuous in their rejection of the authority of the Bible based on their own exalted opinions. However, they merely represent the tip of the iceberg of academic scholarship that rejects, in whole or in part, most of Scripture as being the genuine inspired Word of God. These agnostic and unbelieving attitudes have permeated not only the academic world but also modern media. It is virtually the universal opinion today among secular academics that the Bible is without historical accuracy and cannot be relied upon by serious students.

Beginning in 1985, the Jesus Seminar has used a system of colored beads to indicate their vote or determination of the validity of particular statements that Jesus made. If, in their exalted opinion, these scholars think that Jesus would "certainly" have made such a statement, they vote by dropping a red bead in the box. If they believe that Jesus "might" have made a statement close to what the Gospel writer recorded, then they vote by dropping a pink bead. When they believe that the statement may be close to what Jesus thought, but not what He actually stated, they drop a gray bead in the box. Finally, when they reject a given statement in the Gospels as something they believe that Jesus would never have said, the scholars drop a black bead into the box, showing that they totally reject the authenticity of the Gospel's statement.

During their last meeting in Santa Rosa, California, *Time* magazine reported in its April 6, 1996, issue that the scholars had decided that the Gospels of Matthew, Mark, Luke, and John were "notoriously unreliable: the judges . . . had to throw out the Evangelists' testimony on the Nativity, the Resurrection, the Sermon on the Mount." The article in *Time* repeats "the assertion, published by the 75-person, self-appointed Seminar three years ago, that close historical analysis of the Gospels exposes most of them as inauthentic." The criteria used by these liberal scholars to judge the Gospel records reveal clearly why they reject almost everything that Christians have believed during the last two thousand years. The criteria used to reject statements included: any prophetic statements, statements by Jesus on the cross, descriptions of His trial, the Resurrection, and any claims to be the Messiah or the Son of God. Their bottom line rule: "When in sufficient doubt, leave it out." However, if the view of the Jesus Seminar is correct—that almost nothing definite can be known about the life of Jesus of Nazareth—the basis for all Christian belief is destroyed.

Incredibly, this group has chosen to publish a new version of the Gospels that displays the "words of Jesus" in various colors of ink reflecting their verdicts on the validity of His words. Not surprisingly, very little of their final Gospel text reveals Christ's words printed in red, indicating that these scholars reject many of Christ's statements. The arrogance of these self-appointed guardians of the validity of the words of Jesus Christ is almost unbelievable. As an example, when these academics examined the text containing the Lord's Prayer, they rejected every word in this prayer as spurious except for two single words, "Our Father." In reality, these liberal scholars declare by their votes whether or not they would have made these Gospel statements if they were Jesus! The cable channel Cinemax 2 ran a program in April 1996 called "The Gospel According to Jesus," which records people reading from a new version of the Bible created by the author Stephen Mitchell. In this astonishing version, Mitchell eliminated almost all of the statements and most of the miracles by Jesus as recorded in the Gospels.

The brilliant conservative evangelical scholar Professor Michael Green, of Regent College, rejects the analysis of the Jesus Seminar. Professor Green stated that the Gospels are the best authenticated of all ancient documents from that period some two thousand years ago. Green declared, "We have copies of them going back to well within the century of their composition, which is fantastic compared with the classic authors of the period. And in striking contrast to the two or three manuscripts we have attesting the text of these secular writers, we have hundreds of the New Testament. They give us the text of the New Testament with astonishing uniformity." In addition, Professor Green noted the remarkable harmony found in the Gospel records: "The artless, unplanned harmony in their accounts is impressive and convincing."

Many people see Jesus as a wonderful moral teacher, but reject the Bible's claims for His deity and that He died on the cross for our salvation. However, this opinion is totally contradicted by historical evidence and logic. The famous English theologian C. S. Lewis presented his famous trilemma argument, which makes the following statements. Any person who did the miracles and spoke the messages ascribed to Jesus could not be a mere human teacher or an uninspired prophet, no matter how enlightened or exalted they might be. Anyone who performed the miracles ascribed to Jesus and made the statements Jesus made about

His nature and powers must be the Son of God as He claimed, or a liar, or a lunatic. Anyone who claimed the things that Jesus said must be either insane, a demon from hell, or the true Son of God. As you examine the evidence in this chapter and the overwhelming evidence found in the Gospel records, I believe that every reader will conclude that Jesus Christ could not possibly have been a liar or a lunatic. This analysis leaves us with the final remaining possibility: that Jesus of Nazareth was precisely who He claimed He was, namely, the Son of God.

Historical Documents About Jesus

In this chapter I will share a number of fascinating documents and ancient inscriptions that confirm the historical accuracy of the Gospel accounts about Jesus of Nazareth. Obviously, I can only touch on the highlights in this chapter, but the evidence shared will provide ample proof that the Gospel statements can be relied upon to stand the test of historical scrutiny. The evidence presented will prove conclusively that tremendous historical evidence exists, both within and outside of the Bible, which confirms the details of the life, death, and resurrection of Jesus Christ. Many skeptics contemptuously reject the Bible's claims that Jesus Christ is the Messiah. They reject out of hand the historical evidence that has survived from the first century, which confirms many facts about Jesus that are recounted in the Gospel records. One of the strongest pieces of evidence about Jesus comes from the well-known Jewish historian Flavius Josephus who lived at the time of the apostle Paul. Josephus mentions Jesus twice in his exhaustive history,

The Antiquities of the Jews. One of these references, known as the Testimonium Flavianum Passage, confirms a number of historical facts regarding the life, death, and resurrection of Jesus of Nazareth. This testimony will be examined later in this chapter.

After a detailed analysis of the historical evidence for the life and resurrection of Jesus of Nazareth, Professor Simon Greenleaf, the greatest authority in the Western world on the matter of legal evidence and the author of the authoritative work *The Testimony of the Evangelists,* concluded that the evidence for Jesus was overwhelming.

Sir William Ramsay began his scholarly career as a complete skeptic regarding the historical evidence about Jesus of Nazareth. William Ramsay, possibly the greatest of all New Testament archeologists, completed the most in-depth studies ever completed on the Book of Acts. He wrote, "Luke is a historian of the first rank; not merely are his statements of fact trustworthy; he is possessed of the true historic sense, . . . In short this author should be placed along with the very greatest of historians" (William Ramsay, *The Bearing of Recent Discovery on the Trustworthiness of the New Testament* [Grand Rapids: Baker Book House, 1953], p. 80). Professor Ramsay's comment on Luke's reliability as a historian is of tremendous importance in that not only was Luke the author of the Gospel account that bears his name, he also records the greatest number of details about Christ's virgin birth, career, death, and resurrection. If Luke's writing is reliable regarding the Book of Acts, then he is also a worthy historian regarding the details of Christ's life and resurrection.

President Abraham Lincoln was an agnostic until he reached the age of forty. Then he read Dr. James Smith's brilliant examination called *The Christian's Defence,* which proved the historical reality of the events in Christ's life. The overwhelming evidence from this book convinced Lincoln with the result that he became a genuine Christian for the rest of his life. "My doubts scattered to the winds and my reason became convinced by the arguments in support of the inspired and infallible authority of the Old and New Testaments" (quoted in Sir Lionel Luckhoo's book, *Evidence Irrefutable Which Can Change Your Lives*). Daniel Webster, one of the greatest lawyers of his age, declared that "I believe the Scriptures of the Old and New Testaments to be the will and word of God, and I believe Jesus Christ to be the son of God."

Throughout history many men have examined the evidence regarding the life of Jesus of Nazareth. To any unbiased observer who is willing to evaluate it without prejudice, the accumulated evidence proving the Gospel record is truly overwhelming. Otto Betz, a respected scholar, stated in his book, *What Do We Know About Jesus?* that "No serious scholar has ventured to postulate the non-historicity of Jesus."

Some writers have suggested that there is little historical evidence regarding the life of Jesus. For example, the writer Solomon Zeitlin wrote, "Even Paul's epistles have awakened the question, Does he speak of a real historical personage or of an ideal? The main sources for the historicity of Jesus, therefore, are the Gospels." However, Zeitlin dismissed the Gospel historical accounts and concluded: "So we are right to assume that even the Gospels have no value as witnesses of the historicity of Jesus. The question therefore remains: Are there any historical proofs that Jesus of Nazareth ever existed?" Scholars such as Zeitlin casually dismiss the strong historical evidence that validates the Gospel accounts about Jesus because it contradicts the opinion they tenaciously hold on to that rejects the Bible's accuracy. If liberal scholars applied the same arbitrary rejection of historical evidence to other historical personages, such as Julius Caesar or Alexander the Great, they would be forced to reject all history as myth.

However, a careful unbiased analysis of the historical sources available will convince most fair-minded readers that Jesus of Nazareth is the Messiah of both history and prophecy. In his book *The New Testament Documents: Are They Reliable?* the brilliant historian F. F. Bruce wrote, "The historicity of Christ is as axiomatic for an unbiased historian as the historicity of Julius Caesar."

The Reliability of the New Testament Confirmed by Scholars

During the earlier years of this century many liberal scholars concluded that the Gospels were unreliable as historical evidence, because they believed that they were written almost one hundred years after the events described. They concluded that the Gospel documents were based on hearsay and oral traditions rather than on eyewitness accounts. This prejudice led a whole generation of liberal scholars to reject the Gospels as competent eyewitness history.

The average Christian, believing the Bible to be the inspired Word of God, rejected the liberal argument because the Gospels and the Epistles declare that they are direct eye-witness accounts of the life of Christ. For example, Luke declared that he wrote these truths, "Even as they delivered them unto us, which from the beginning were eyewitnesses, and ministers of the word" (Luke 1:2). Later, in the Book of Acts, Luke confirmed that his reports, as written to the Roman officer Theophilus, contained "many infallible proofs," the strongest historical and legal proofs possible. Luke stated that Jesus "shewed himself alive after his passion by many infallible proofs, being seen of them forty days" (Acts 1:3).

Fortunately, the tremendous advances in historical research and biblical archeology in the last century have convinced most scholars in the last two decades that the Gospels and Epistles were written within thirty-five years or less of the events that they describe. The late William F. Albright, the greatest biblical archeologist of his day, declared, "We can already say emphatically that there is no longer any solid basis for dating any book of the New Testament after about A.D. 80." In an article for *Christianity Today,* January 18, 1963, W. F. Albright wrote: "In my opinion, every book of the New Testament was written by a baptized Jew between the forties and eighties of the first century A.D."

Sir Frederic G. Kenyon, the director of the British Museum, was possibly the most respected New Testament textual scholar in our century. He commented on the significance of the fact that the evidence is overwhelming that the Gospels were composed shortly after the events of Christ's life and that the early Church widely distributed them to its congregations within a relatively short period of time. Kenyon wrote: "The interval, then, between the dates of original composition and the earliest extant evidence becomes so small as to be in fact negligible, and the last foundation for any doubt that the Scriptures have come down to us substantially as they were written has now been removed. Both the authenticity and the general integrity of the books of the New Testament may be regarded as finally established."

After a professional lifetime of in-depth review of the New Testament manuscripts, Kenyon concluded that the present text in our Bible is absolutely reliable. He wrote: "It is reassuring at the end to find that the general result of all these discoveries and all this study is to strengthen the proof of the authenticity of the Scriptures, and our conviction that we have in our hands, in substantial integrity, the veritable Word of God" (Frederic G. Kenyon, *The Story of the Bible*, Special U.S. Edition [Grand Rapids: Eerdmans Co., 1967], p. 133).

Luke's reliability as a historian is unquestionable. Professor Merrill F. Unger declares forthrightly that the recent discoveries of archeology have proven the accuracy and authority of the Gospel accounts as reliable eyewitness accounts. Unger wrote, "The Acts of the Apostles is now generally agreed in scholarly circles to be the work of Luke, to belong to the first century and to involve the labors of a careful historian who was substantially accurate in his use of sources" (*Archeology and the New Testament* [Grand Rapids: Zondervan Publishing House, 1962]).

Modern scholars now possess more than five thousand manuscript copies of portions of the New Testament in the Greek language. In addition, there are an additional fifteen thousand manuscripts in other languages from the first few centuries of this era. No other important text, whether historical or religious, has more than a few dozen copies that have survived until our generation. The twenty thousand surviving manuscripts of the New Testament reveal numerous individual differences of spelling, etc. However, this huge number of manuscripts provides the strongest evidence possible, allowing scholars to check and trace the origin of the various readings to ascertain with certainty the original text. Most important, these discrepancies, mostly caused by careless copying, are usually trivial. Not one of these small differences affects a single important fact or doctrine of the Bible.

It is virtually impossible that anyone could have created and introduced significant changes into the authenticated New Testament manuscripts during the few years that elapsed between their original recording by the apostles, and the time they were widely distributed among the early churches in the final four decades of the first century. In addition, any significant changes would have been instantly detected and corrected. Many Christians who had personally known and listened to the words of the apostles were still alive at the time these New Testament manuscripts were being read in churches every Sunday. One of the chief followers of Christ, John the Apostle, was still the bishop in charge of seven churches in Turkey until the first few years of the second century. He would obviously have instantly detected and denounced any counterfeit passages that anyone might have attempted to insert into genuine biblical manuscripts.

The significance of these scholars' conclusions about an early date for the Gospels is overwhelming. It was impossible to widely distribute a blatantly false story about Christ while thousands of followers and observers were still alive to dispute it. Furthermore, the Greek originals of the Gospels and Epistles were widely copied, distributed, and translated immediately into Hebrew, Syriac, Latin, Coptic, and other languages. These documents were treasured by the churches and read in their Sunday services. If anyone had wanted to introduce a false miracle, event, or doctrine into the Gospels, they would have faced an impossible task. In order to introduce a false statement, the forger would have to simultaneously forge this counterfeit passage into every single copy of the Gospels in every country and language without being detected or challenged by any Christian. This would have been absolutely impossible. It is significant that the Gospel's historical account about Christ's life, death, and resurrection was not denied by the Jews or the Romans who lived in the first century. This fact provides strong evidence that the Gospel account is historically true.

To put this in proper perspective, imagine that some writer wanted to create a false story in the 1990s about President Kennedy's performing miracles and being raised from the dead for forty days after his tragic assassination in November 1963. To succeed with his plan, the writer would have to accomplish two impossible things: (1) He would have to acquire simultaneously every one of the millions of books and newspaper reports about the president and insert his counterfeit passages in this material without being detected by a single reader; (2) He would have to simultaneously convince millions of people around the world to accept his forgery as true, despite the fact that these people

who were alive when Kennedy lived have independent rec-
ollections that contradict his invented story. It is obvious to
anyone who considers the problem carefully that it is
impossible for anyone to produce successfully such a forgery
about President Kennedy's life that would convince anyone,
let alone the whole population of the world. However, the
liberal scholars who suggest that the Gospel records were
altered to introduce new doctrines and statements about
Christ's virgin birth and resurrection are proposing something that is just as ridiculous as the above example. The
only reason these scholars have been able to convince many
people is that there is a great desire in the minds of many to
reject the truth of the Bible. If they accept the reality of the
Bible's accuracy, they must admit in their own minds that
they will someday have to give accounts of their lives to God.
Their inability to accept this reality forces them to reject out
of hand the possibility that the Gospel records are true.

However, the evidence proving the historical reality
about Jesus is powerful and convincing for anyone who will
openly examine the evidence. One of the most convincing
proofs of the supernatural nature of Christ's life is found in
His absolutely unprecedented influence on the subsequent
history and books that have reflected Western philosophy,
theology, and ideas. The brilliant biblical scholar Bernard
Ramm described this incredible influence on Western literature as a result of the life, death, and resurrection of Jesus
Christ: "From the Apostolic Fathers dating from A.D. 95 to
the modern times is one great literary river inspired by the
Bible—Bible dictionaries, Bible encyclopedias, Bible lexi-
cons, Bible atlases, and Bible geographies. These may be

taken as a starter. Then at random, we may mention the vast bibliographies around theology, religious education, hymnology, missions, the biblical languages, church history, religious biography, devotional works, commentaries, philosophy of religion, evidences, apologetics, and on and on. There seems to be an endless number" (Bernard Ramm, *Protestant Christian Evidences* [Moody Press, 1957], p. 239). In his comment on the sustained and overwhelming attacks on the authority of the Bible from the academic community, Bernard Ramm wrote about the total failure of these attacks to make a serious dent in the popularity and influence of the Scriptures. "A thousand times over, the death knell of the Bible has been sounded, the funeral procession formed, the inscription cut on the tombstone, and committal read. But somehow the corpse never stays put."

Confirmation from Non-Christian Sources

Following is an overview of several Roman and pagan historical manuscript records from the early centuries of this era about the life and influence of Jesus Christ that have survived for almost two thousand years.

Cornelius Tacitus—Governor of Asia

Cornelius Tacitus was a Roman historian and governor of Asia [Turkey] in A.D. 112. He referred to the persecution of the Christians caused by Emperor Nero's false accusation that the Christians had burned Rome. "Christus [Christ], the founder of the name, was put to death by Pontius Pilate, procurator of Judea in the reign of Tiberius: but the pernicious superstition, repressed for a time broke out again, not only through Judea, where the mischief originated, but through the city of Rome also" (*Annals* XV 44). Tacitus, as a careful historian with access to the government archives of Rome, confirmed many details in the Gospels, Acts, and Romans.

Suetonius—Roman Historian

Suetonius was the official historian of Rome in A.D. 125. In his *Life of Claudius* (25.4) he referred to the Christians causing disturbances in Rome that led to their being banished from the city. He identifies the sect of Christians as being derived from "the instigation of Chrestus," which was his spelling of the name Christ.

Pliny the Younger

Plinius Secundus, known as Pliny the Younger, declared that the Christians were "in the habit of meeting on a certain fixed day before it was light, when they sang in alternate verse a hymn to Christ as to a god, and bound themselves to a solemn oath, not to any wicked deeds, but never to commit any fraud, theft, adultery, never to falsify their word, not to deny a trust when they should be called upon to deliver it up."

Pliny was governor of the Roman province of Bithynia [Turkey] in A.D. 112. He wrote to the emperor requesting instructions about the interrogation of the Christians whom he was persecuting. In his *Epistles X 96*, he states that these believers would not worship Emperor Trajan and would not curse their leader, Jesus Christ, even under extreme torture. Pliny described the Christians as people who loved the truth at any cost. It is impossible to believe that these people would willingly die for something they knew was a lie. Their martyrdom was based on the fact that they knew the truth of the statements in the Gospels about Jesus.

Lucian of Samosata

Lucian lived in Samosata a century after Christ. In his book *The Passing Peregrinus* he declared that Jesus was worshiped by His followers and was "the man who was crucified in Palestine because he introduced this new cult into the world."

Evidence About Jesus from Flavius Josephus

"Now there was about this time Jesus, a wise man, if it be lawful to call him a man, for he was a doer of wonderful works, a teacher of such men as receive the truth with pleasure. He drew over to him both many of the Jews, and many of the Gentiles. He was [the] Christ, and when Pilate, at the suggestion of the principal men among us, had condemned him to the cross, those that loved him at the first did not forsake him: for he appeared to them alive again the third day: as the divine prophets had foretold these and ten thousand other wonderful things concerning him. And the tribe of Christians so named from him are not extinct at this day" (Flavius Josephus, *Antiquities of the Jews,* bk. XVIII, chap. III, Section 3).

Flavius Josephus was a Pharisee and priest living in Jerusalem. Born in A.D. 37, following the death of Christ, he witnessed first-hand the events leading up to the destruction of Jerusalem and the Temple. He fought as a general of the Jewish rebel forces in Galilee in the war against Rome. Josephus was captured by the Romans at the fall of the city of Jotapata and became friends with the Roman general Vespasian. As a historian, with access to both Roman and Jewish governmental records, he described the events in Israel during the turbulent decades of the first century. In A.D. 94, Josephus published in Rome his definitive study of the history of the Jewish people called *Antiquities of the Jews*. One of the most fascinating passages in his important history concerned the events in the life, death, and resurrection of Jesus Christ.

Numerous liberal scholars have declared that this reference to Jesus Christ and another reference to James and John the Baptist must be interpolations or forgeries by later Christian editors. In other words they have concluded that Josephus's reference to Jesus could not possibly be genuine. However, such an assertion of forgery requires significant proof. Yet none of these scholars can produce a single ancient copy of Josephus's *Antiquities of the Jews* that does not contain this passage on Jesus. If they had found dozens of ancient copies of Josephus's book that failed to contain this passage they would have some "evidence" that this was not an original passage by the Jewish historian. However, Phillip Schaff declared in his book *History of the Christian Church* that all ancient copies of Josephus's book, including the early Slavonic [Russian] and Arabic language versions, contain the disputed passage about the life of Christ. Every one of the ancient copies from the fourth and fifth centuries in several different languages contains these passages. No one has ever explained how an editor could have altered each of these widely distributed versions during the centuries following their publication. The real reason why these liberal scholars reject the Josephus passage out of hand is their deeply ingrained prejudice that it could not be genuine because it confirms the historicity of the claims about Jesus Christ. If the events recorded in the Gospels actually occurred, it is only natural that Josephus would mention them at the appropriate place in his narrative of that turbulent century. In fact, it would be astonishing if Josephus had failed to mention anything about the ministry and resurrection of Jesus.

The biblical scholar Craig Blomberg wrote in his 1987 book *The Historical Reliability of the Gospels* that "many recent studies of Josephus however, agree that much of the passage closely resembles Josephus' style of writing elsewhere. . . . But most of the passage seems to be authentic and is certainly the most important ancient non-Christian testimony to the life of Jesus which has been preserved." Blomberg concluded his lengthy analysis of the historical evidence for and against Jesus with this statement; "The gospels may therefore be trusted as historically reliable." In addition, R. C. Stone, in his article titled "Josephus," wrote the following: "The passage concerning Jesus has been regarded by some as a Christian interpolation; but the bulk of the evidence, both external and internal, marks it as genuine. Josephus must have known the main facts about the life and death of Jesus, and his historian's curiosity certainly would lead him to investigate the movement which was gaining adherents even in high circles. Arnold Toynbee rates him among the five greatest Hellenic historians" (*ZPEG*, vol. 3:697).

Evidence About James, the Brother of Jesus

In another passage in Josephus's book *Antiquities of the Jews* (bk. XX, chap. IX, sect. 1), he described the death of James, the brother of Jesus. "As therefore Ananus (the High Priest) was of such a disposition, he thought he had now a good opportunity, as Festus (the Roman Procurator) was now dead, and Albinus (the new Procurator) was still on the road; so he assembled a council of judges, and brought before it the brother of Jesus the so-called Christ, whose name was James, together with some others, and having accused them as law-breakers, he delivered them over to be stoned." While many liberal scholars reject the historicity of the first passage about Jesus Christ, most modern scholars accept the authenticity of this second passage about James "the brother of Jesus the so-called Christ."

Evidence About John the Baptist

Josephus described the death of John the Baptist as follows: "Now, some of the Jews thought that the destruction of Herod's army came from God, and that very justly, as a punishment of what he did against John, that was called the Baptist; for Herod slew him, who was a good man, and commanded the Jews to exercise virtue, both as to righteousness towards one another, and piety towards God, and so to come to baptism; for that the washing [with water] would be acceptable to him, if they made use of it, not in order to the putting away, [or the remission] of some sins [only] but for the purification of the body: supposing still that the soul was thoroughly purified beforehand by righteousness. Now, when [many] there came to crowd about him, for they were greatly moved [or pleased] by hearing his words, Herod, who feared lest the great influence John had over the people might put it into his power and inclination to raise a rebellion [for they seemed ready to do anything he should advise], thought it best, by putting him to death, to prevent any mischief he might cause, and not bring himself into difficulties, by sparing a man who might make him repent of it when it should be too late. Accordingly he was sent a prisoner, out of Herod's suspicious temper, to Macherus (Masada), the castle I before mentioned, and was there put to death" (*Antiquities of the Jews*, bk. XVIII, chap. V, sect. 2). These historical descriptions by Josephus, together with the other sources mentioned above, provide ample evidence that Jesus of Nazareth lived in the first century of this era.

Further Confirmation—Julius Africanus and Thallus

Julius Africanus was a North African Christian teacher writing in A.D. 215. He recorded the writing of a pagan historian by the name of Thallus who lived in A.D. 52 shortly after the resurrection of Christ. Thallus recorded in his history that there was a miraculous darkness covering the face of the earth at the Passover in A.D. 32. Julius Africanus records, "Thallus, in the third book of his histories, explains away this darkness as an eclipse of the sun—unreasonably, as it seems to me." Julius explained that Thallus's theory was unreasonable because a solar eclipse could not occur at the same time as the full moon and it was at the season of the Paschal full moon that Christ died.

This historical reference by the pagan historian Thallus confirmed the Gospel account regarding the darkness that covered the earth when Jesus was dying on the cross. There are other ancient historical references to this supernatural darkness at the death of Christ. Modern astronomers confirm that Julius Africanus was right in his conclusion that a normal eclipse could not possibly occur at the time of a full moon, which was the time of the Passover. The high priest carefully calculated the position of the full moon to the smallest degree because their whole Jewish liturgical calendar, especially Passover, depended on following the lunar position exactly.

It is interesting to note that the ancient Jewish Targums, or paraphrases of the Old Testament, contain additional evidence that the Jews expected the Messiah to be born in Bethlehem as prophesied in Micah 5:2. Charles R. Condor discovered that seventy-two of the Targums on various passages of the Old Testament contain information about the coming Messiah although the biblical passage itself did not contain the name Messiah. It is fascinating to note that two of these well-respected Targums indicated clearly that the Messiah would be born at or near Bethlehem. For example, the Targum on Genesis 35:21 talks about Israel pitching its tents "beyond the tower of Eder." The Targum of Jonathan adds this comment identifying this location, "which is the place where shall be revealed the King Messias in the end of days." Charles R. Condor noted in his submission to the *Palestine Exploration Fund Report* (Quarterly Report, April 1875), that "Migdol Eder, or 'the Tower of the Flock' was known in A.D. 700 as about 1,000 paces from Bethlehem," which is the location of the ruins of the Monastery of the Holy Shepherds. Another Targum, commenting on the passage Exodus 12:42, makes a fascinating reference to the area of Nazareth where Jesus was raised by His parents in His father's carpentry shop. This Targum states that "Moses cometh forth from the desert and Messias goeth forth from Roma." This "Roma" was a village located near to the town of Nazareth (Charles R. Condor, *Palestine Exploration Fund* [Quarterly Report, January 1876], p. 98).

Following an exhaustive study of the literature regarding the archeological and historical controversies about the accuracy of the New Testament, the researcher and scientist Henry M. Morris, Ph.D., concluded that we can totally trust the manuscripts as correct records of the events described. Morris wrote, "No statement in the New Testament has to this date been refuted by an unquestioned find of science or history. This in itself is a unique testimony to the amazing accuracy and authenticity of the New Testament records."

The historian Philip Schaff outlined the overwhelming influence that the life of Jesus of Nazareth had on subsequent history and culture of the Western world. "This Jesus of Nazareth, without money and arms, conquered more millions than Alexander, Caesar, Mohammed, and Napoleon; without science and learning, He shed more light on things human and divine than all philosophers and scholars combined; without the eloquence of schools, He spoke such words of life as were never spoken before or since, and produced effects which lie beyond the reach of orator or poet; without writing a single line, He set more pens in motion, and furnished themes for more sermons, orations, discussions, learned volumes, works of art, and songs of praise than the whole army of great men of ancient and modern times" (Philip Schaff, *The Person of Christ* [American Tract Society, 1913]).

While the historical records provide overwhelming evidence to prove the absolute reliability of the Gospel records about Jesus Christ, the statements of the disciples can only reveal His earthly existence as the Messiah. We have not yet witnessed the reality of His awesome glory that will be revealed when we see Him returning in His glory to take His Church home to heaven nor when He will reveal Himself to the population of earth at the Second Coming. The Puritan writer John Owen discussed the glory of Jesus Christ in these words: "Should the Lord Jesus appear now to any of us in His majesty and glory, it would not be to our edification nor consolation. For we are not meet nor able, by the power of any light or grace that we have received, or can receive, to bear the immediate appearance and representation of them. His beloved apostle John had leaned on His bosom probably many a time in His life, in the intimate familiarities of love; but when He afterward appeared to Him in His glory, 'he fell at His feet as dead.'" The men and women living in the first century of this era, who heard the words of Jesus of Nazareth, were amazed at the tremendous wisdom shown by His words. When Jesus Christ finally appears in His revealed glory as Almighty God at the Great Day of the Lord, Matthew prophesied that "then shall all the tribes of the earth mourn, and they shall see the Son of man coming in the clouds of heaven with power and great glory" (Matthew 24:30).

Extraordinary Evidence About Jesus in the Dead Sea Scrolls

If someone had asked a minister in 1947 to prove that the original Hebrew Scriptures from the Old Testament were reliably copied without error throughout the last two thousand years, he might have had some difficulty in providing an answer. The oldest Old Testament manuscript used by the King James translators was dated approximately A.D. 1100. Obviously, that old manuscript from A.D. 1100 was a copy of a copy of a copy, etc., for over two thousand years. How could we be sure that the text in the A.D. 1100 copy of the Scriptures was identical to the original text as given to the writers by God and inspired by Him? However, an extraordinary discovery occurred in the turbulent year before Israel became a nation. A Bedouin Arab found a cave in Qumran near the Dead Sea that ultimately yielded over a thousand priceless manuscripts dating back before A.D. 68, when the Roman legions destroyed the Qumran village during the Jewish war against Rome.

An Arab shepherd boy discovered the greatest archeological find in history in 1947. When the ancient Hebrew scrolls from these caves were examined by scholars they found that this Qumran site contained a library with hundreds of precious texts of both biblical and secular manuscripts that dated back before the destruction of the Second Temple and the death of Jesus Christ. Once the Bedouins recognized the value of the scrolls they began searching for additional documents in every valley and cave near the Dead Sea. The most incredible discovery was the immense library of biblical manuscripts in Cave Four at Qumran that contained every single book of the Old Testament with the exception of the Book of Esther. Multiple copies of several biblical texts such as Genesis, Deuteronomy, and Isaiah were found in Cave Four. Scholars were able to reach back a further two thousand years in time to examine biblical texts that had lain undisturbed in the desert caves during all of the intervening centuries. The scholars discovered that the manuscript copies of the most authoritative Hebrew text, the received text, used by the King James translators in 1611, were virtually identical to these ancient Dead Sea Scrolls. After carefully comparing the manuscripts they discovered that, aside from a tiny number of spelling variations, not a single word was altered from the original scrolls in the caves from the much copied A.D. 1100 manuscripts used by the Authorized King James Version translators in 1611. How could the Bible have been copied so accurately and faithfully over the many centuries without human error entering into the text? The answer is found in the overwhelming respect and fear of God that motivated Jewish and Christian scholars whose job was to faithfully copy the text of the Bible. In a later chapter dealing with the Hebrew codes beneath the text of the Bible, I will share how the Masoretic scribes meticulously copied the text of the Scriptures over the centuries.

The Essenes were a Jewish community of ascetics that lived primarily in three communities: Qumran at the Dead Sea, the Essene Quarter of Jerusalem (Mount Zion), and Damascus. They appear to have existed from approximately 200 B.C. until the destruction of their communities in

Jerusalem and Qumran by the Roman armies in A.D. 68. During the first century there were three significant Jewish religious communities: the Pharisees, the Sadducees, and the Essenes. The Essenes established their religious community near the shores of the Dead Sea. In their love for the Word of God, they faithfully copied each Old Testament scroll in their Scriptorium in the village of Qumran. New evidence indicates that these men of God were aware of the new religious leader in Israel known as Jesus of Nazareth and the group of writings about Him known as the New Testament. The Christian historian Eusebius, who wrote around A.D. 300, believed that the Essenes were influenced in their beliefs by Christianity.

When the scrolls were first discovered, many Christian scholars naturally wondered if they might contain evidence about the new faith of Christianity. Despite overwhelming interest, the vast majority of scrolls were not translated for publication in the intervening forty-nine years. For almost fifty years, the hopes of Christian scholars were frustrated by the decision of the small group of original scroll scholars to withhold publication and release of a significant number of these precious scrolls. Some scholars speculated publicly that there might be evidence about Christ in the unpublished scrolls but the original scroll scholars vehemently denied these claims. While some scroll scholars had published part of their assigned texts, after forty-five years the team responsible for the huge number of scrolls discovered in Cave Four had published only 20 percent of the five hundred Dead Sea Scrolls in their possession.

Quotes from the New Testament in the Dead Sea Scrolls

Finally, after a public relations campaign led by *Biblical Archeology Review* magazine demanded the release of the unpublished scrolls to other scholars, the last of the unpublished scrolls were released to the academic world. To the great joy and surprise of many scholars, the scrolls contain definite references to the New Testament and, most important, to Jesus of Nazareth. In the last few years, several significant scrolls were released that shed new light on the New Testament and the life of Jesus. One of the most extraordinary of these scrolls released in 1991 actually referred directly to the crucifixion of Jesus Christ.

The Crucified Messiah Scroll

In 1991 the world was astonished to hear that one of the unpublished scrolls included incredible references to a "Messiah" who suffered crucifixion for the sins of men. The scroll was translated by Dr. Robert Eisenman, Professor of Middle East Religions of California State University. He declared, "The text is of the most far-reaching significance because it shows that whatever group was responsible for these writings was operating in the same general scriptural and Messianic framework of early Christianity." Although the original scroll team still claimed that there was no evidence about early Christianity in the unpublished scrolls, this new scroll totally contradicted their statements. This single scroll is earth-shaking in its importance. As Dr. Norman Golb, Professor of Jewish History at the University of Chicago, said, "It shows that contrary to what some of the editors said, there are lots of surprises in the scrolls, and this is one of them."

This remarkable five-line scroll contained fascinating information about the death of the Messiah. It referred to "the Prophet Isaiah" and his Messianic prophecy (Chapter 53) that identified the Messiah as One who will suffer for the sins of His people. This scroll provides an amazing parallel to the New Testament revelation that the Messiah would first suffer death before He would ultimately return to rule the nations. Many scholars believed that the Jews during the first century of our era believed that, when He finally came, the Messiah would rule forever without dying. The exciting discovery of this scroll reveals that the Essene writer of this scroll understood the dual role of the Messiah as Christians did. This scroll identified the Messiah as the "Shoot of Jesse" (King David's father), the "Branch of David," and declared that he was "pierced" and "wounded." The word *pierced* reminds us of the Messianic prophecy in Psalm 22:16: "They pierced My hands and My feet." The prophet Jeremiah said, "I will raise unto David a righteous Branch" (23:5).

The scroll also describes the Messiah as a "leader of the community" who was "put to death." This reference pointing clearly to the historical Jesus of Nazareth is creating shock waves for liberal scholarship that previously assumed that the Gospel account about Jesus was a myth. Jesus is the only One who ever claimed to be the Messiah who was crucified. The genealogies recorded in both Matthew's and Luke's Gospels reveal that Jesus was the only One who could prove by the genealogical records kept in the Temple that He was the lineage of King David as the "Son of Jesse." Since the tragic destruction of the Temple and its records in A.D. 70, it would be impossible for anyone else ever to prove their claim to be the Messiah based on their genealogical descent from King David. Additionally, the scroll identified the Messiah as "the sceptre," which probably refers to the Genesis 49:10 prophecy: "The sceptre shall not depart from Judah, nor a lawgiver from between his feet, until Shiloh come; and unto him shall the gathering of the people be." This scroll confirms the historical truthfulness of the New Testament record about Jesus and His crucifixion. The evidence from the scroll suggests that the Jewish Essene writer acknowledged that Jesus of Nazareth was the "suffering Messiah" who died for the sins of His people.

The "Son of God" Scroll

Another fascinating scroll discovered in Cave Four known as 4Q246 refers to the hope of a future Messiah figure. This is another of the scrolls that was unpublished until recently. Amazingly, the text in this scroll refers to the Messiah as "the son of God" and the "son of the Most High." These words are the exact wording recorded in the Gospel of Luke.

The Text of Scroll 4Q246—the "Son of God" Scroll

> "He shall be called the son of God,
> and they shall designate [call] him son of the Most High.
> Like the appearance of comets, so shall be their kingdom.
> For brief years they shall reign over the earth and shall
>   trample on all;

one people shall trample on another and
one province on another until the people of God shall
    rise and all shall rest from the sword."

Compare the words in the scroll 4Q246 text to the inspired words found in Luke 1:32 and 35: "He shall be great, and shall be called the Son of the Highest: and the Lord God shall give unto him the throne of his father David.... And the angel answered and said unto her, The Holy Ghost shall come upon thee, and the power of the Highest shall overshadow thee: therefore also that holy thing which shall be born of thee shall be called the Son of God."

Anyone comparing these two first-century texts will be startled by the amazing similarity of concept and wording describing the Messianic leader. One of the great differences between Christian and Jewish conceptions of the promised Messiah revolves around His relationship to God. While the Jews believe the Messiah will be a great man, such as Moses, with a divine mission, the Christians believe that the Bible teaches that the Messiah would be uniquely "the Son of God." The Jewish view usually held that the concept of a "son of God" violated the primary truth of monotheism found in Deuteronomy 6:4, "Hear, O Israel: The LORD our God is one LORD." The Christians believed that Jesus' claim to be the Son of God was not a violation of Deuteronomy 6:4. Rather, Christians believe in the Trinity, the doctrine that the Father, the Son, and the Holy Spirit are revealed in the Bible to be One God, revealed in three personalities. As Christians, we do not believe in three separate gods. Therefore, Christians understand the statements about Jesus as the Son of God to be in complete conformity to the truth of monotheism—there is only one God. It is fascinating in this regard to consider the presence of these statements in this first-century Jewish text: "He shall be called the son of God, and they shall designate [call] him son of the Most High."

The presence of these statements in the Dead Sea Scrolls suggests that some of the Essenes either accepted the Messianic claims of Jesus to be the Son of God or anticipated this concept. Either possibility opens up new areas for exploration. Another possibility that must be considered is this: Is it possible that this scroll 4Q246 is a direct quote from the writer hearing the words of the Gospel of Luke that was now widely circulating according to early Christian witnesses? Luke, the physician, claimed that he wrote the Gospel of Luke as an eyewitness of the events he personally observed. In Luke 1:1–3, he says: "Forasmuch as many have taken in hand to set forth in order a declaration of those things which are most surely believed among us, even as they delivered them unto us, which from the beginning were eye-witnesses, and ministers of the word; it seemed good to me also, having had perfect understanding of all things from the very first, to write unto thee in order, most excellent Theophilus."

The discovery of the virtually identical wording "the Son of God" from Luke 1:32 and 35 to that of the scroll found buried in a cave in A.D. 68 stands as a tremendous witness to the early existence and transmission of the Gospel records within thirty-five years of Christ. If the Gospels were written and distributed within thirty-five years of the events of the life of Jesus (as the Gospels claim) then they stand as the best eyewitness historical records we could ever hope to possess. In fact, all of these ancient historical records confirm the truth of the Gospels.

Other New Testament Quotes
Identified in the Scrolls

In 1971, a Spanish biblical scholar named Jose O'Callaghan studied some of the small fragments of scrolls discovered in Cave Seven at Qumran. He was looking for correspondences between these fragments of Greek scrolls and the Septuagint, the Greek translation of the Hebrew Old Testament that was widely used by Jesus and the apostles.

These fragments are quite small, containing only small portions of each verse. After almost two thousand years, the elements and insects have significantly damaged these manuscripts. In some cases only small fragments containing parts of a verse on three or four lines remain from an original scroll. It required considerable detective work to determine the precise text in these tiny fragments.

One day he carefully examined several small scroll fragments located in a photo page in *The Discoveries of the Judean Desert of Jordan*. To his great surprise O'Callaghan noticed that several did not fit any Old Testament text. These fragments were listed as "Fragments not identified." To his amazement, Dr. O'Callaghan found that these Greek language fragments bore an uncanny resemblance to several verses in the New Testament. He read the Greek words *beget* and a word that could be *Gennesaret,* a word for the Sea of Galilee. The fragment containing *Gennesaret* appears to be a quotation of the passage referring to the feeding of the five thousand found in Mark 6:52–53, which states: "For they considered not the miracle of the loaves: for their heart was hardened. And when they had passed over, they came into the land of Gennesaret, and drew to the shore."

If these texts are actually portions of these Christian writings they would be the earliest New Testament texts ever discovered. *The New York Times* responded, "If O'Callaghan's theory is accepted, it would prove that at least one of the Gospels, that of St. Mark, was written only a few years after the death of Jesus." The *Los Angeles Times* headlined, "Nine New Testament fragments dated A.D. 50 to A.D. 100 have been discovered in a Dead Sea Cave." It stated that "if validated, [they] constitute the most sensational biblical trove uncovered in recent times."

Other Scroll Fragments and the New Testament

Dr. Jose O'Callaghan ultimately identified eight different scroll fragments from Cave Seven that appear to be quotes from New Testament passages. The scholarly magazine *Bible Review* ran a fascinating article on Dr. O'Callaghan, these scrolls, and their possible connection with the New Testament in an article in December 1995.

The fragments appeared to O'Callaghan to be portions of the following verses from the Gospels and Paul's Epistles:

"For the earth bringeth forth fruit of herself . . ."
 (Mark 4:28).
"And he saw them toiling in rowing; . . ." (Mark 6:48).
"And Jesus answering said unto them, Render to Caesar
 . . ." (Mark 12:17).

"So when they had eaten enough, they lightened the
ship . . ." (Acts 27:38, NKJV).

"And not only so, but we also rejoice in God through
our Lord Jesus Christ . . ." (Romans 5:11-12, NKJV).

"And without controversy great is the mystery of godliness: . . ." (1 Timothy 3:16, NKJV).

"For if anyone is a hearer of the word, and not a doer . . ."
(James 1:23-24, NKJV).

As one example of Dr. O'Callaghan's study, he examined a small scroll fragment known as 7Q5 that contained
only twenty Greek letters on five lines of text. Many of the
thousands of scroll fragments that were successfully identified from the Qumran site are equally small. Another
scroll scholar, Carsten Thiede, agrees with O'Callaghan
that portions of the Mark 6:52–53 passage appear in this
scroll fragment. While other scroll scholars disagree with
the identification of this fragment as a verse from the New
Testament they do admit that almost all of the scrolls
found in Cave Seven were written in the period between 50
B.C. and A.D. 50, which is consistent with the time of the
writing of the Gospel of Mark.

Naturally, as with other matters connected with the
controversial Dead Sea Scrolls, many scholars disagreed
with the conclusions of Dr. O'Callaghan. The debate still
continues twenty years later. At this stage we cannot be certain that O'Callaghan's conclusion is correct. More work
needs to be done. However, the recent publication of the
discovery of Scroll 4Q246 and its identical reference to "the
Son of God" as found in Luke 1:32 and 35 provide strong

support for the possibility that these fragments are related to these New Testament passages. In addition, I have great hopes that the new archeological exploration of recently detected caves at Qumran by my friend Gary Collett may provide new evidence including New Testament references. Many of these mysteries will be solved when the final four hundred unpublished scrolls are finally published in the next few years. The new dig at Qumran may also uncover additional scrolls that will help us understand more clearly the Messianic beliefs of this group of religious men and women who lived at this desert site during the time when Jesus walked the earth.

When we consider the total amount of evidence that confirms the biblical record about Jesus of Nazareth, we can have confidence that we know more about the life and resurrection of Christ than we know about any other person in the ancient world. God has not left us in darkness concerning the truthfulness of the miracles, prophecies, and teaching of His Son, Jesus Christ.

Six

Scientific Proof that the Bible Is Accurate

One of the greatest proofs that the Scriptures are inspired by God is that they reveal a staggering amount of advanced scientific knowledge. The Bible is not a scientific book; however, when it does make scientific statements, they are stunning in their accuracy. These biblical statements are thousands of years in advance of the scientific knowledge present in the day when the writers penned the words of the Holy Scriptures. The psalmist David wrote, "That I may publish with the voice of thanksgiving, and tell of all thy wondrous works" (Psalm 26:7). As you consider God's "wondrous works" and the astonishing level of scientific knowledge from the Bible presented in this chapter, ask yourself a question: How could the writers of the Scriptures possibly know these facts unless they were supernaturally inspired by God?

Throughout the Word of God are statements that can now be tested as to their accuracy due to the incredible advances in scientific knowledge in the last few decades. The Book of Genesis describes the supernatural creation of man in these words, "And the LORD God formed man of the dust of the ground, and breathed into his nostrils the breath of life; and man became a living soul" (Genesis 2:7). For many years scientists laughed at the apparent simplicity of the scriptural account that God used "the dust of the ground" to construct the complex elements and molecules that make up a human being. However, after a century of scientific examination of the elements within the human body, scientists have been startled to discover that clay and earth contain every single element found in the human body. A *Reader's Digest* article in November 1982 described a fascinating discovery by the researchers at NASA's Ames Research Center that confirmed the Bible's account that every single element found in the human body exists within the soil. The scientists concluded, "We are just beginning to learn. The biblical scenario for the creation of life turns out to be not far off the mark."

It might surprise you to know that many of the greatest scientific minds of the last several centuries were Bible-believing Christians who totally accepted the scientific accuracy of the Word of God. For example, Isaac Newton, perhaps the greatest scientific mind in history, firmly accepted the Word of God and creation. Other strong believers in God who changed the face of scientific knowledge included: Lord Kelvin, the creator of the science of thermodynamics; Louis Pasteur, the discoverer of pasteurization; Johann Kepler, the brilliant astronomer who created modern astronomy; and Robert Boyle, the greatest chemist of his age. With every new scientific discovery we find additional proof of the complexity of the great design that God used to create our universe.

The Creation of the Universe

The Book of Genesis begins with the words, "God created the heaven and the earth." Until 1950, most scientists believed in some variation of the "steady state theory," which suggested that the universe had always existed as we observe it today. This theory was in total contradiction to the Word of God, which, as recorded in its opening pages, affirms that God had created the entire universe at a definite point of time in the past. New discoveries in astronomy and astrophysics then forced the scientific world to change their theory. Today, virtually all scientists accept some variation of the "Big Bang Theory," which suggests the whole universe came into existence at a particular point of time, when an incredibly dense mass of matter exploded, forming all of the stars, galaxies, and planets we witness today. Dr. P. Dirac, a Nobel Prize winner from Cambridge University, wrote: "It seems certain that there was a definite time of creation." Until quite recently, the word *creation* was never written or spoken by scientists with approval. Then, a scientific article in the 1982 issue of *Physics Letters*, an international journal of physics, contained an article by Dr. A. Vilenkin, which was entitled "Creation of the Universe from Nothing." While scientists claim the creation of the universe is "outside the scope of presently known laws of physics" (S. Hawking and G. Ellis, *The Large Scale Structure of Space-Time* [Cambridge, England: University Press, 1973], p. 364), the Word of God clearly tells us that "God created the heaven and the earth" (Genesis 1:1). However, in opposition to theoretical explosion of the Big Bang Theory, the Bible affirms that God created everything in the universe with absolute purpose and intelligence. The evidence from nature and the incredible scientific discoveries pointed out in this book reveal the meticulous design of the supernatural intelligence and power of God in that initial moment of creation when "God created the heaven and the earth."

The Lord challenged Abraham to count the stars to demonstrate the awesome number that He had created by His supernatural power. "Then He brought him outside and said, 'Look now toward heaven, and count the stars if you are able to number them.' And He said to him, 'So shall your descendants be' " (Genesis 15:5, NKJV). The unaided human eye can see and count about 1,029 stars. With a pair of binoculars or an inexpensive telescope you can see over 3,300 stars. In the last few years modern telescopes have allowed us to view over two hundred million stars in our own galaxy called the Milky Way. As late as 1915, astronomers believed that our galaxy composed the entire universe. Then in 1925, the great astronomer Edwin Hubble used his new one-hundred-inch mirror telescope on Mount Wilson, the largest in the world at that time, to view whole new galaxies of stars that were more than six million trillion miles away from earth. Professor Hubble proved that the universe contained as many galaxies outside our galaxy as there were stars inside our home galaxy, the Milky Way. During the last century very powerful telescopes of astronomers revealed that the known universe contains over ten billion galaxies like our Milky Way. However, in the last few months, scientists have used the Hubble Telescope to focus on a tiny point in space so small that it is equal to focusing your eye on an area the size of a grain of sand held at arm's length.

After intensely examining this very small area of space, the astronomers determined that it contained an additional fifteen hundred galaxies, each the size of our Milky Way. They were astonished to discover that the universe is more than five times larger than we previously believed. They now know that the known universe contains more than fifty billion galaxies with each galaxy containing more than two hundred million stars. The mind of man can scarcely conceive of such a vast universe in which stars extend out from our solar system for millions of trillions of miles in every direction. To obtain a sense of the vastness of our universe, try this exercise. Take a piece of paper and draw two circles with one small circle representing our sun at the top of the page. Using the scale of one inch to represent ten million miles, draw a much smaller circle nine inches lower at the bottom of the page to represent our earth. Now let's draw another small circle to represent our nearest neighboring star, Alpha Centauri. You would need to draw the circle representing the star Alpha Centauri over forty miles away from your piece of paper to correctly represent the vast distance between the earth and the closest star. Light travels through space at an amazing speed of 186,000 miles every second or six trillion miles every year. A ray of light leaving our closest neighbor, Alpha Centauri, would take four years to reach our planet as it crosses an astonishing twenty-four trillion miles of empty space.

The psalmist David wrote, "By the word of the LORD the heavens were made, And all the host of them by the breath of His mouth. . . . For He spoke, and it was done; He commanded, and it stood fast" (Psalm 33:6, 9, NKJV). Despite all of the billions spent on astronomy, scientists have failed to come up with a credible theory to account for the existence of either the universe or even our own earth. In 1980, the astronomer Professor Herman Bondi declared the total failure of modern science to account for the universe: "As an erstwhile cosmologist, I speak with feeling of the fact that theories of the origin of the universe have been disproved by present day empirical evidence as have various theories of the origin of the solar system" (Herman Bondi, *New Scientist*, Nov. 21, 1980, Letters Section: Reference to quote by Karl Popperp, p. 611). Another great astronomer, Sir Harold Jeffreys, wrote, "To sum up, I think that all suggested accounts of the origin of the solar system are subject to serious objections. The conclusion in the present state of the subject would be that the system cannot exist" (Harold Jeffreys, *The Earth: Its Origin, History, and Physical Constitution* [Cambridge, England: University Press, 1970], p. 359). In other words, Professor Jeffreys admitted that none of the atheistic theories can account for the universe as it exists. Perhaps they should return to the first words in Genesis as recorded by Moses, "In the beginning God created the heaven and the earth" (Genesis 1:1).

The Bible declares that God separated the waters below from the waters that were above (in the heavens): "And God said, Let there be a firmament in the midst of the waters, and let it divide the waters from the waters. And God made the firmament, and divided the waters which were under the firmament from the waters which were above the firmament: and it was so" (Genesis 1:6–7). This biblical statement declares that God created a large amount of water, which He placed in the heavens or outer space. Does any evidence exist to prove the accuracy of this statement from the Bible? The existence of water in space seemed improbable, to say the least, to scientists until quite recently. However, further astronomical discoveries have proven conclusively that massive amounts of water do exist in space, just as the Bible claimed. Naturally, because of extreme temperatures, the waters in space are frozen into permanent ice. Recently our satellites discovered large quantities of ice in the ice caps of Mars as well as in the rings of Saturn. In addition, we now know that the huge comets that travel through our solar system are composed of massive amounts of ice.

A massive block of ice from space collided with the earth at the beginning of this century at a point in northern Russia: "In the morning of 30 June 1908, a fantastic explosion occurred in central Siberia. . . . Witnesses described an enormous meteoric bolide visible in the sky for a few seconds. Other witnesses from a distance of 60 kilometers (36 miles) from the point of impact were knocked over. . . . Seismic shocks were registered over the whole world . . . this event was due to the collision with the earth of a block of ice weighing 30,000 tons which . . . released energy equivalent to that of a thermonuclear bomb of 12 megatons" (J. Audouzze, *The Cambridge Atlas of Astronomy* [Cambridge, England: University Press, 1985], p. 219). Researchers found that this Siberian explosion was caused by a small fragment of the comet Encke that broke away during its passage through our solar system. The latest scientific research has revealed that massive amounts of ice also exist at the outer edge of our solar system. The Oort Cloud at the edge of our solar system is a vast region of space that is estimated to hold as many as a trillion large comets composed of ice and rock. Each large comet is calculated to contain as much as one trillion tons of ice. The vast amount of water in our oceans is less than a fraction of the quantities of water that exist in the "firmament above" in the heavens as reported in the Book of Genesis. A passage in Job also refers to the ice and frost in the heavens: "Hath the rain a father? or who hath begotten the drops of dew? Out of whose womb came the ice? and the hoary frost of heaven, who hath gendered it? The waters are hid as with a stone, and the face of the deep is frozen. Canst thou bind the sweet influences of Pleiades, or loose the bands of Orion?" (Job 38:28–31).

The Law of Conservation of Energy

After exhaustive experiments, modern scientists have developed two fundamental laws of the science of thermodynamics that describe the nature of our known universe. The first law is the Law of Conservation of Energy, which reveals that "energy can be neither created nor destroyed." The Law of Conservation of Energy was explained by the science writer Isaac Asimov as follows: "Energy can be transferred from one place to another, or transformed from one form to another, but it can be neither created nor destroyed." In other words, this law states that the whole amount of energy that exists throughout our universe remains constant and can never change. For example, when they explode a nuclear device, the uranium 235 and plutonium within the warhead are not annihilated. The matter is simply transformed into a staggering release of heat and light energy. Every experiment has confirmed this Law of Conservation of Energy as the most basic fundamental understanding of the way the universe works. This law describes the present state of the universe after its initial creation by God.

Although this fundamental law of the universe was only discovered and proven scientifically during the last century, the Word of God recorded this principle thousands of years ago. Moses wrote in Genesis: "And on the seventh day God ended his work which he had made; and he rested on the seventh day from all his work which he had made. And God blessed the seventh day, and sanctified it: because that in it he had rested from all his work which God created and made" (Genesis 2:2–3). This inspired passage clearly declares that when God completed the creation of man on the sixth day, "he rested . . . from all his work which he had made." After He created man on the sixth day, His work was complete: this accounts for the First Law of Conservation of Energy. In addition, the Scriptures reveal why nothing can now be either totally destroyed or annihilated because Jesus Christ, who created all things, is "upholding all things by the word of his power" (Hebrews 1:3). In another passage the writer of the Book of Hebrews declared that Jesus, the Creator of the universe, had finished His acts of creation: "For he that is entered into his rest, he also hath ceased from his own works, as God did from his" (Hebrews 4:10).

The Law of Entropy

The second law of science is the Law of Entropy. This second Law of Thermodynamics describes the fact that all systems and elements of the universe tend to disintegrate to a lower order of available energy or organization. Another way of expressing this universal fact of entropy is to note that, over time, all things, whether a house or a sword, will tend to disintegrate to dust or rust, a lower order of organization than the original house or sword. Throughout history mankind has observed that everything, from a human body to a castle, begins to decay from the moment of maximum amount of order or organized information at the beginning until, years later, the object ceases to function. When you think seriously about this universal principle you can immediately see that this principle proves that it is absolutely impossible for the theory of evolution to be true. Evolution suggests that all simple systems and elements become increasingly more organized and complicated by random chance. However, common sense and scientific observation have proven that all systems and elements over time tend to disintegrate to something less organized and less useful. In fact, the second Law of Thermodynamics, the Law of Entropy, absolutely proves the theory of evolution is nonsense.

Consider the implications. The Law of Conservation of Energy proves that the universe could not have created itself. It had to be created by a supernatural force outside the universe. "In the beginning God created the heaven and the earth" (Genesis 1:1). However, the Law of Entropy shows that the whole universe is running down as it decays to a lower order of available energy. This fact reveals that the universe must have been created at some point in the past and has been running down like a clock ever since that initial moment of creation. The current evolutionary theory that postulates a universe that was created from nothing by itself is totally contradicted by all the known laws of science. In addition, the Law of Entropy reveals that the universe must have been created at some definite point in the past to account for the fact that all scientific observation confirms that everything continues to decay. As an example, the fact that the sun burns up its nuclear fuel, at the rate of 200,000 nuclear explosions every second, provides the enormous radiation that floods our solar system. However, since it is burning up its store of fuel, logic declares that there must have been a point in time somewhere in the distant past when the sun was created and began this process.

The Gospel writer Luke described the coming of Christ in the daytime as follows: "Even thus shall it be in the day when the Son of man is revealed." However, several verses later, Luke described the same event by declaring that Christ will come in the night: "I tell you, in that night there shall be two men in one bed; the one shall be taken, and the other shall be left" (Luke 17:34). To the natural mind of his day, Luke's words must have sounded like a contradiction. How could a single event, the coming of the Messiah, occur simultaneously "in the day" and "in the night"? This statement by Luke must have appeared impossible and contradictory at any time from the first century until recently. However, we can now understand that, on whatever day Christ returns, it will be a daytime event for those on one side of the globe while the event will occur during the night for those living on the other side of the planet. How could Luke have known this scientific fact two thousand years ago?

The psalmist David wrote a wonderful song of praise to God in recognition of the awesome glory of the heavens that he could witness from the roof of his palace in Jerusalem: "Their line has gone out through all the earth, And their words to the end of the world. In them He has set a tabernacle for the sun, Which is like a bridegroom coming out of his chamber, And rejoices like a strong man to run its race. Its rising is from one end of heaven, And its circuit to the other end; And there is nothing hidden from its heat" (Psalm 19:4–6, NKJV). In his song of praise King David declared that the sun traveled in "his circuit unto the ends of it [the heavens]." During the last few centuries many Bible critics denounced this statement as inaccurate because they falsely claimed the Bible's statement declared that the sun moved in an orbit around the earth. However, the Bible never made that claim. The Scriptures declare that the sun moved in "his circuit unto the ends of it [the heavens]." Recent discoveries by the Hubble Telescope confirmed the accuracy of the Scriptures when they proved that the sun actually moves through space in a circuit covering an enormous orbit that lasts over two hundred and sixty million years.

One of the most curious scientific revelations in the Bible regarding astronomy was pointed out by my friend David Harris, an astronomer from Toronto, Canada. This statement is found in the Book of Amos where we read about the seven stars in the constellation known as Pleiades. The King James Version translators set out the verse Amos 5:8 as: "Seek him that maketh the seven stars and Orion." The King James Version translators confirmed that Amos's original Hebrew statement about "the seven stars" referred to the constellation Pleiades. However, modern translators render this verse as, "He made the Pleiades and Orion" (Amos 5:8, NKJV). Early translators were puzzled by this verse because there were only six stars that could be seen by the naked eye in the constellation Pleiades. Now, however, modern telescopes have revealed the existence of a seventh star in Pleiades; it is so dim that only a telescope can detect it. How else did Amos know that there were "seven stars" in the constellation unless God told him? The Bible was correct all along in its description of "seven stars" as recorded by the prophet Amos over twenty-five centuries ago.

The Earth—Created by God for Humans

Critics of the Bible have often falsely suggested that the Bible stated the earth was flat because of the biblical expression "the four corners of the earth" (Isaiah 11:12; Revelation 7:1), as if the writers actually believed in a flat earth. However, this phrase was simply a colloquial expression. It is still used by educated individuals to indicate either the whole earth or the four extremities of the globe from a central position. God inspired the prophet Isaiah to reveal that our planet was a globe, knowledge that was far in advance of what the men in that day knew. "It is he that sitteth upon the circle of the earth, and the inhabitants thereof are as grasshoppers; that stretcheth out the heavens as a curtain, and spreadeth them out as a tent to dwell in" (Isaiah 40:22). This expression "the circle of the earth" clearly describes the earth as a sphere or globe.

The Book of Job tells us that, "He stretches out the north over empty space; He hangs the earth on nothing" (26:7, NKJV). This was an astonishingly advanced and accurate scientific statement. The ancient pagans, who were contemporary with Job, believed that the earth was balanced on the back of an elephant that rested on the back of a turtle. Other pagans believed that the mythological hero Atlas carried the earth on his shoulders. However, four thousand years ago, Job was inspired by God to declare correctly that God "hangs the earth on nothing." Only a century ago scientists believed that the earth and stars were supported by some kind of ether. Yet Job accurately stated that our planet moves in its orbit through empty outer space. An astonishing discovery by astronomers recently revealed that the area to the north of the axis of our earth toward the polar star is almost empty of stars in contrast to the other directions. There are far more distant stars in every other direction from our earth than in the area to the far north of our planet. As Job reported, "He stretches out the north over empty space" (Job 26:7). Mitchell Waldrop wrote the following statement in an article in *Science* magazine. "The recently announced 'hole in space,' a 300 million-light-year gap in the distribution of galaxies, has taken cosmologists by surprise. . . . But three very deep core samples in the Northern Hemisphere, lying in the general direction of the constellation Boötes, showed striking gaps in the red shift distribution" (Mitchell Waldrop, "Delving the Hole in Space," *Science*, Nov. 27, 1981). This relative emptiness in the direction to the north of our solar system is not visible by the naked eye. It is only as the result of very careful observation by telescopes that scientists have recently proven that Job was correct.

Jewish scholars in Israel have calculated that the Torah describes the exact duration of the time that passes between the appearance of new moons as precisely 29 days, 12 hours, 44 minutes, and 5 seconds, or 29.53059 days. With billions of dollars of research and sophisticated observation through telescopes, NASA has only recently calculated that a new moon appears every 29.530588 days! The Scriptures declare, "In the beginning God created the heaven and the earth" (Genesis 1:1). This statement revealed that God created our earth and the universe in a single moment of time. However, Genesis also reveals God's purpose: "Then God blessed them, and God said to them, 'Be fruitful and multiply; fill the earth and subdue it; have dominion over the fish of the sea, over the birds of the air, and over every living thing that moves on the earth'" (Genesis 1:28, NKJV).

After examining the complexity of the variables that govern this solar system and our planet earth, many scientists have declared that this solar system is "anthropic." This word simply means that this earth bears evidence that it was designed by a superior intelligence to allow human life to exist. The scientists use this word *anthropic* to indicate that they have discovered an astonishing number of scientific variables that fit within a very narrow range that allows human life to exist on this planet. Let me explain. If our earth were located much farther away from our sun we would freeze like the planet Mars. If it were much closer to the sun then we would be burned up like the hot surface of Mercury or the 860-degree temperature on Venus. If the magnetic forces within our planet were stronger or weaker, life could not exist. If our earth did not revolve every twenty-four hours, then one-half of the planet would be in permanent darkness without vegetation. Meanwhile, if the earth did not revolve, the other side of the planet would be an uninhabitable desert as it suffered from the overwhelming heat of permanent exposure to the sun. If our earth were not tilted at twenty-three degrees, we would not have the seasonal variation that produces the incredible abundance of crops that feed our planet's huge population. Without the twenty-three-degree tilt, less than half of the present land used for cultivation of crops would grow vegetables. The moon produces the tides that continually replenish the oceans with oxygen allowing the fish to breathe. If the earth were significantly smaller, the lessened gravity would be incapable of holding the atmosphere that is essential for breathing. A much thinner atmosphere would provide no protection from the 25,000 meteors that burn up in the atmosphere over the earth every day. In addition, a thinner atmosphere would be incapable of retaining the higher temperatures required for human and animal life to exist. If our planet earth were twice as large, the effect of increased gravity would make everything on the planet's surface weigh eight times what it weighs today. This increased weight would destroy many forms of animal and human life.

Professor Robert Jastrow has stated that "the smallest change in any of the circumstances of the natural world, such as the relative strengths of the forces of nature, or the properties of the elementary particles, would have led to a universe in which there could be no life and no man. For example, if nuclear forces were decreased by a few percent, the particles of the universe would not have come together in nuclear reactions to make the ingredients, such as carbon atoms, of which life must be constructed" (Dr. Robert Jastrow, *The Intellectuals Speak Out About God* [Regnery Gateway, 1984], p. 21). The professor noted that the same argument can be made about the strength of the electromagnetic force and the strength of the gravitational force. In other words, if the universe were changed in the slightest way, no human life could exist. The ultimate conclusion of these scientists is that our universe, our solar system, and, especially, our earth were purposely constructed by a very powerful intelligence within very narrow scientific parameters to allow human life to flourish. The prophet Nehemiah wrote the following declaration centuries before the birth of Jesus Christ: "You alone are the LORD; You have made heaven, the heaven of heavens, with all their host, the earth and everything on it, the seas and all that is in them. And You preserve them all. The host of heaven worships You" (Nehemiah 9:6, NKJV).

The Hydrological Cycle of Weather

People living in past centuries did not have a clear understanding about the weather and climatic patterns that controlled our planet's environment. However, the books of Job, Ecclesiastes, Isaiah, and Jeremiah all describe details about the complexity of the weather system far beyond the knowledge of the inhabitants living at that time. The complete hydrological cycle governing evaporation, cloud formation, thunder, lightning, and rain is explained in surprising detail in the words of the Old Testament. For example, Ecclesiastes states, "If the clouds are full of rain, they empty themselves upon the earth" (Ecclesiastes 11:3, NKJV). Throughout history most people assumed evaporation of water from lakes and rivers was responsible for the clouds. However, Ecclesiastes confirms that most clouds are formed by evaporation from the oceans: "All the rivers run into the sea, yet the sea is not full; to the place from which the rivers come, there they return again" (Ecclesiastes 1:7, NKJV). Incredibly, a recent study by the United States Department of Agriculture proved that most of the water that forms into the clouds worldwide comes from the evaporation of the waters found in the oceans that cover over 70 percent of the planet's surface.

The Book of Job asked the question, "Do you know how the clouds are balanced, those wondrous works of Him who is perfect in knowledge?" (Job 37:16, NKJV). When you consider the weight of water compared to air it is astonishing that enormous quantities of water are raised from the oceans and lakes every hour by evaporation and lifted thousands of feet in the air where they remain suspended for long periods. Air rises upward as it cools, supporting the water vapor in the clouds until the drops become large and heavy enough to fall to earth as rain. The answer is also found in Job, "For He draws up drops of water, which distill as rain from the mist, which the clouds drop down and pour abundantly on man. Indeed, can anyone understand the spreading of clouds, the thunder from His canopy?" (Job 36:27–29, NKJV). This incredible biblical passage reveals the complete hydrological cycle of evaporation, cloud formation, and precipitation.

The Complexity of Weather Patterns

King Solomon described the complex climatic circular wind patterns that determine the weather throughout the globe. "The wind goes toward the south, and turns around to the north; the wind whirls about continually, and comes again on its circuit" (Ecclesiastes 1:6, NKJV). How could Solomon have known three thousand years ago that the planetary winds followed a circular pattern from south to north and south again? Job speaks of God controlling the weather: "For He looks to the ends of the earth, and sees under the whole heavens, to establish a weight for the wind, and mete out the waters by measure. When He made a law for the rain, and a path for the thunderbolt . . ." (Job 28:24–26, NKJV). In this intriguing statement, the Bible reveals that the winds are governed by their weight, a fact that scientists have only determined in the last century. How could Job have known that the air and the wind patterns are governed by their actual weight? Meteorologists have found that the relative weights of the wind and water greatly determine the weather patterns.

This passage also reveals a profound appreciation of the fact that there is a scientific connection between lightning, thunder, and the triggering of rainfall. Apparently, a slight change in the electrical charge within a cloud is one of the key factors that cause microscopic water droplets in the clouds to join with other droplets until they are heavy enough to fall to earth. In addition, we now know that a powerful electrical charge as high as 300 million volts in a cloud sends a leader stroke down through the air to the ground. Instantaneously, only one-fiftieth of a second later, a second, more powerful return stroke travels back up to the cloud, following the path through the air opened by the leader stroke. The thunder occurs because the air within this channel or path has been vaporized by superheating it to fifty thousand degrees by the lightning. The superheated air expands outward at supersonic speed, creating the noise of thunder. Job's description, "He made a law for the rain and a path for the thunderbolt" (Job 28:26, NKJV), is startling in its accuracy. No human could have known this in ancient times without the divine revelation of God.

King David, the writer of Psalms, refers mysteriously to "the paths of the seas." He wrote, "The fowl of the air, and the fish of the sea, and whatsoever passeth through the paths of the seas" (Psalm 8:8). It wasn't until 1786 that Benjamin Franklin published the information he gleaned from conversations with ocean-going captains that huge currents, such as the Gulf Stream, ran like deep rivers far beneath the surface of the Atlantic Ocean. The massive Gulf Stream carries more than five thousand times as much water as the great Mississippi River. This awesome current, which warms the climate of the U.K. and Western Europe, carries more than twenty-five times as much water as all the rivers on the planet. Scientists have discovered that the Gulf Stream is only a small part of an enormous "gyre," a huge thirteen-thousand-mile current of water circling the Atlantic Ocean. They have recently discovered that the Pacific Ocean has its own "Black Current" gyre as well.

CNN ran a news report in May 1996 of marine scientists' discovery of a massive river of water flowing north beneath the Pacific Ocean, parallel to the coast of the western United States. However, they also found that another huge current ran under the surface of the ocean above the first current, only this higher current flowed south at a very fast flow rate. The turbulence produced by these opposing currents passing each other at different depths in the Pacific produced massive storms beneath the surface of the ocean. These massive currents not only warm the north of the planet but they are also essential to refreshing the otherwise stagnant waters of the ocean and constitute an essential part of the life system of the planet. How could King David have known thousands of years ago that there were huge currents or rivers that existed in the depths of the boundless oceans?

In another passage Job referred to deep springs of water at the bottom of the ocean. "Have you entered the springs of the sea? Or have you walked in search of the depths?" (Job 38:16). In this verse the Bible refers to the existence of springs of water flowing beneath the depths of the sea. It is only in the last thirty years that underwater exploration of the ocean depths has revealed a remarkable phenomenon of numerous huge springs of fresh water pouring out of the ocean floor. The Book of Job also contains questions that suggest a level of knowledge that would be impossible for a human writer living in the Middle East during ancient times. For example, Job refers to deep oceans whose surface waters are frozen hard like a stone: "From whose womb comes the ice? And the frost of heaven, who gives it birth? The waters harden like a stone, and the surface of the deep is frozen" (Job 38:29–30). How could someone like Job, living in the area of Saudi Arabia in ancient times, have known about Arctic ice caps?

Evolution or Creation?

Billions of people have been taught throughout their lives that science has proved that evolution is true and that the Bible is scientifically wrong about creation. As a result of this virtually universal acceptance, evolution has destroyed the faith of countless people during the past one hundred and fifty years. This false theory of evolution has caused untold numbers of people to refuse to consider seriously the claims of the Bible regarding personal salvation because they wrongly believed the Bible was full of errors. The theory of evolution holds that there is no God and that everything in the whole universe, including the complexities of biological life, has developed by random chance over billions of years.

However, the theory of evolution is falling apart today in the face of the total lack of evidence to support its hypothesis. Very few scientists still subscribe to the original theory of evolution as proposed by Charles Darwin over a century ago. Many of them accept that the mathematical odds against life forming by random chance are impossible. As one example, Dr. Harold Urey, a Nobel Prize winner for his research in chemistry, wrote about the impossibility of evolution, but still admitted he believed in the theory! "All of us who study the origin of life find that the more we look into it, the more we feel that it is too complex to have evolved anywhere." Incredibly, Dr. Urey then added these words, *"We believe as an article of faith that life evolved from dead matter on this planet. It is just that its complexity is so great, it is hard for us to imagine that it did"* (italics added). His admission proved that his acceptance of evolution was not based on logic or evidence, but on blind faith. He found the alternative to evolution, a divine Creator, totally unacceptable. At the Alpach Symposium conference, which dealt with the growing problems with the theory of evolution, one of the speakers admitted that the reason evolution was still supported by intellectuals, the education establishment, and the media had nothing to do with whether it was true or false. "I think that the fact that a theory so vague, so insufficiently verifiable and so far from the criteria otherwise applied in 'hard' science has become a dogma can be explained only on sociological grounds" (Gershon Robinson, Mordechai Steinman, *The Obvious Proof* [New York: CIS Publishers, 1993], p. 87). In other words, evolution survived despite the lack of evidence because they wanted to believe it was true.

Darwin admitted that millions of "missing links," transitional life forms, would have to be discovered in the fossil record to prove the accuracy of his theory that all species had gradually evolved by chance mutation into new species. Unfortunately for his theory, despite hundreds of millions of dollars spent on searching for fossils worldwide for more than a century, the scientists have failed to locate a single missing link out of the millions that must exist if their theory of evolution is to be vindicated. It is significant that the various educational groups supporting evolutionary teaching have encouraged their members to refuse to enter debates about evolution with creation science supporters at high schools and colleges. The evolution supporters found to their dismay that the audiences almost always believed in evolution before the debate began but that they accepted the evidence for divine creation by the end of the debate.

It is not my purpose to fully explore the errors of evolution, nor to fully present the overwhelming evidence for the creation of the universe by God. Many excellent scholars have written books that demolish the theory of evolution in defense of the Bible's account of creation. In the Selected Bibliography at the end of this book, I list several excellent books that I strongly recommend to anyone who wishes to study this subject in depth. However, I will outline in this chapter some of the astonishing evidence that proves that evolution is simply impossible and supports creation as out-lined in the Bible. As we explore this topic we will also encounter overwhelming evidence proving the inspiration of the Scriptures.

When you understand the incredible number of prob-lems with the theory of evolution you are immediately struck with the thought that there is something very strange about the continuing universal acceptance of this theory. However, the answer is clear. If the theory of evolution is rejected, then people have no other credible alternative than the Bible's account of creation by a personal God. This alter-native is unacceptable to many people in modern society because they dread the thought of facing their God. They would like to evade this issue by firmly avoiding examining the overwhelming evidence against evolution through the use of ridicule and rejection. In the final analysis the greatest obstacle to seeing the truth about God's role in creation is often our own attitudes and prejudices. If we will lay aside our former attitudes and carefully examine the evidence, the truth about creation as well as our relationship with God will become evident through the Word of God.

The odds against life's evolving by chance on earth are absolutely staggering. It is impossible to believe that the awe-some complexity involved in the simplest living cell could have occurred as a result of chance even if this process had occurred over billions of years. Scientists found that over twenty different amino acids are required to produce the proteins that exist in the smallest living cell. Despite scientif-ic experiments where they tried to create these twenty amino acids in the laboratory, they failed every time. The proteins that make up living cells are composed of long thin lines of amino acids only one-millionth the size of a human hair. The smallest living thing contains more than five hundred amino acids. All amino acids have side groups of atoms. Scientists found that 50 percent of the side groups of atoms that are attached to non-living amino acids are on the left side and another 50 percent are on the right side. When biologists examined proteins within living cells they discovered that all proteins are "left-handed." In other words, all living cells contain amino acids with their side group of atoms on the left side only. Amino acids produced in a laboratory are exactly like those found in non-living matter with 50 percent "left-handed" and 50 percent "right-handed." Yet, living cells can only exist when the atoms are solely "left-handed." To calculate the likelihood of life occurring by chance, the scientists calculated the probability that amino acids would form chains of atoms solely on the "left-hand." The odds against this happening by chance are one chance in 10^{123}. In other words, it is absolutely impossible that even a single protein could have been formed by chance alone, let alone the staggering number of awesomely complex proteins that make up the multitude of living creatures in our world. The only logical explanation for this situation is the instantaneous creation by God.

The proteins in living creatures are composed of long chains of different amino acids that must be linked together in a precise sequence to allow the protein to live. The evolutionary scientist believes that these complex amino acids simply came together by chance in the exact necessary sequence to allow life to exist. This is mathematically impossible.

Mathematicians have calculated that the odds against these five hundred amino acids lining up in the correct order to produce one single living cell are equal to one chance in 10^{200}, which is ten followed by two hundred zeros. Even if the amino acids and chemicals could combine together a trillion times faster than they do in the laboratory, and the experiment used every single atom on the planet, the odds against a single living protein forming by chance would be less than one chance in ten followed by one hundred and sixty-six zeros. This incredible number vastly exceeds the total number of atoms within the known universe. The odds against a single living protein being formed by chance alone are equal to the chance that a blindfolded man could locate a single grain of sand painted gold within a universe composed of fifty billion galaxies of two hundred million stars apiece composed of nothing but sand.

However, the formation of life requires far more complex structures than simple amino acids and proteins. DNA (deoxyribonucleic acid) creates the genetic code that commands the various elements in the cell to form the building blocks of life itself. Mathematicians have calculated that the odds against a single DNA gene forming by chance are equal to one chance in ten followed by one hundred and fifty-five zeros, a number that staggers the mind. Anyone who can believe that life on earth evolved by random chance without the presence of a supernatural intelligence designer must do so on absolute blind faith. Their decision to accept evolution reflects a deep need to evade the overwhelming evidence and logic that prove the universe was created by God.

The Genetic Code Governing Life

The incredibly intricate genetic DNA code controls every element and cell in the body of any biological creature. The genetic code contains a staggering amount of information. Professor Leslie Orgel, a scientist working in this area, wrote: "The origin of the genetic code is the most baffling aspect of the origins of life" (Leslie Orgel, "Darwinism at the Very Beginning of Life," *New Scientist* [April 1982], p. 151). Scientists who study genetics realize that the amount of genetic information encoded in the DNA of the most simple form of life contains a staggering amount of information that is far more complicated than the computer software that runs the complete accounting program controlling the inventory, costs, sales, and financial records of hundreds of General Motors plants throughout the world. Sir Fred Hoyle, one of the greatest biologists in this century, wrote: "Precious little in the way of biochemical evolution could have happened on the earth. If one counts the number of trial assemblies of amino acids that are needed to give rise to the enzymes, the probability of their discovery by random shufflings turn out to be less than one in 10^{400000}" (Fred Hoyle, "Where Microbes Boldly Went," *New Scientist*, pp. 412–415). As a result of his findings, Hoyle eventually abandoned his agnosticism and became a believer in a special creation of life. Several top scientists have concluded that life must have been brought from outer space to the earth due to the impossible mathematical odds against the spontaneous development of life on earth. Some of these scientists, such as Sir Fred Hoyle and Dr. Frances Crick, arrived at the theory that life originated in some far part of the universe and was later imported to earth by some extraterrestrial intelligence. However, this novel solution does not solve their problem at all. This solution only pushes the problem away from the earth to some unknown place in space. How could life have been created by random chance in some far part of the universe? Obviously, only God could have created life with all of its incredible complexity and order.

The Book of Proverbs declares that "a merry heart does good, like medicine, but a broken spirit dries the bones" (Proverbs 17:22, NKJV). While many Bible readers accepted this advice from Proverbs as a general statement, they would be surprised to learn that modern psychiatry has discovered that good humor and laughter truly improve our overall health. An article in the *Birmingham News* entitled "Laughter: Prescription for Health," confirms the statement found in Proverbs. "At some point during laughter, your body issues a prescription from the pharmacy in your brain." The article revealed that scientists discovered that the emotion of humor triggers the release of certain hormones and endorphins that greatly improve our overall sense of well-being.

Moses, in Leviticus 17:11, declared, "For the life of the flesh is in the blood." This statement revealed advanced scientific knowledge at a time when the level of pagan medical knowledge was abysmal. This statement by Moses was incredibly astute because doctors have discovered that our blood is essential to many of our body's life processes. The blood carries nutrients and material that produce growth, healing, store energy as fat, and support every organ in our body. When the blood supply is restricted to any part of the body, that part begins immediately to die. Blood is essential to fighting disease, clotting wounds, and growing new skin and cells. For centuries ignorant doctors used to "bleed" their patients by draining large amounts of blood from their bodies in a vain attempt to defeat disease. They did not realize that our blood is the key to our flesh. Truly, as the Bible declares, "the life of the flesh is in the blood."

The Population of the Earth

Those who reject the Bible's account of divine creation believe the evolutionary argument that mankind evolved by chance from lower life forms over billions of years. One of their conclusions is that mankind has existed on this earth for more than a million years. In contradiction to this evolutionary position, the Bible declares that mankind was created approximately six thousand years ago according to the chronological data presented in the Old Testament. The Bible clearly declares, through a detailed list of the generations from Adam to Christ, that mankind was created on the earth approximately four thousand years before the birth of Jesus Christ. Obviously, a huge discrepancy exists between the evolutionists' suggestion of man's origin approximately one million years ago compared to the Bible's declaration of man's creation by God approximately six thousand years ago.

Let us consider the growth rate of our human population to determine whether the Bible's account of man's creation only six thousand years ago, or the evolutionary scientists' account of man's evolution over one million years ago, is consistent with known scientific data. According to the Scriptures, eight people comprising four couples survived the great Flood approximately forty-three hundred years ago as described in biblical chronology. To be conservative, we will make these calculations assuming that mankind started forty-three hundred years ago with only one surviving couple and that all families produced only 2.5 children on average over the following centuries. This rate of population growth is much slower than we are experiencing in this century. If families produce only two children on average, then the population would remain static without any growth. This conservative assumption of an average of 2.5 children per family will account for the natural depletion caused by war, famine, and disease. Throughout history the average lifespan has lasted only forty-three years per generation. Using these assumptions, during the last forty-three hundred years, there would have been one hundred generations lasting forty-three years each. The calculations reveal that our population would have grown from the time of the Flood till today to reach approximately five billion people. It is fascinating to note that the earth's population today (5.5 billion world-wide) is almost identical with what we would expect if mankind began repopulating the earth after the Flood forty-three hundred years ago. I am indebted to Professor Henry M. Morris for his brilliant work on this topic in his excellent book, *The Biblical Basis for Modern Science*, which I highly recommend for any reader who wishes to explore this topic in greater depth (Henry M. Morris, *The*

Biblical Basis for Modern Science [Grand Rapids: Baker Book House, 1984], pp. 414-426). In this chapter I am simplifying the calculations but the results are the same.

Now let us consider what the earth's population would be if the evolutionary theory were correct. The evolutionary scientists who believe that man has existed for over a million years have an almost insurmountable problem. Using the same assumption of forty-three years for an average human generation, the population growth over a million years would produce 23,256 consecutive generations. We calculate the expected population by starting with one couple one million years ago and use the same assumptions of a forty-three-year generation and 2.5 children per family. The calculations reveal that we should have a total human population on earth today of 10^{2091} people. The evolutionary theory of a million years of growth would produce trillions x trillions x trillions x trillions of people that should be alive today on our planet. To put this in perspective, this number is vastly greater than the total number of atoms in our vast universe. If mankind had lived on earth for a million years, we would all be standing on enormously high mountains of bones from the trillions of skeletons of those who had died in past generations. However, despite the tremendous archeological and scientific investigation in the last two centuries, the scientists have not found a fraction of the trillions of skeletons predicted by the theory of the evolutionary scientists. The conclusion is obvious. The Bible's account of Noah's family repopulating the earth following the Flood approximately forty-three hundred years ago is in agreement with the current population of the earth.

The Wonders of Creation

The Bible claims that God created all of the living creatures on earth. When we examine these creatures we discover an awesome degree of complexity that simply defies the evolutionary theory that claims these animals and their behavior have occurred by chance alone. One of the most amazing examples of God's design is found in the fact that birds have hollow bones. This makes them much lighter than they would be with normal solid bones and facilitates flight. As an example of God's providential design, consider the woodpecker that is so familiar to North Americans. As I write this chapter, a beautiful woodpecker is standing on a branch of the tree only five feet beyond my library window, pecking away in diligent search for an insect beneath the bark of the tree. The woodpecker has two toes in front and two toes in the rear, allowing it to grip the trunk of a tree firmly while pecking for insects. While all other birds have their bills connected directly to their skulls, only the woodpecker has an unusual spongy tissue between its bill and skull that acts as a shock absorber while it pecks forcefully at the trunk of a tree for hours at a time seeking to locate insects. Some woodpeckers have actually pecked through solid concrete in their quest for insects or to bury seeds for future food. The woodpecker's short tail feathers act as support to brace its body against the trunk of the tree while it pecks, searching for food. When it locates a tunnel bored through the tree by an insect, the woodpecker inserts its extremely long tongue into the narrow tunnel until it reaches its prey. Unlike those of other birds, the tongue of a woodpecker is not attached to the rear of its mouth. Incredibly, the woodpecker's tongue is five inches long and coiled within its skull, allowing the bird to locate its insect prey deep within the tree trunk.

Those who reject divine creation believe that the awesome complexities of biological life have occurred by simple chance through evolution without intelligent design. This argument appears ridiculous to people who examine the awesome complexity of animal and human life. Those who honestly and carefully consider the evidence must conclude that God has created this incredible design. As an example of this design we should consider the migratory pattern of birds. The Manx shearwater birds that live in Wales migrate from America to their home every year, flying approximately 250 miles every day. A Manx shearwater captured in Wales was transferred by plane in a crate to America. Then scientists released the bird in Boston. Incredibly, the bird flew home across the trackless expanse of the Atlantic Ocean to Wales, more than 3,100 miles away, in only twelve days, despite the fact that the bird had never flown over the ocean before. How could this occur unless God planted within the bird the knowledge of where its home was located thousands of miles away? Another example of God's creative design is found in the ability of the rattlesnake to detect its prey. This ability depends on a small sense organ, found between the nostril and the eyes of the snake, which is so sensitive it can detect a difference of temperature of only one thirty-third of a degree. This ability to detect the precise temperature of an object in front of the snake enables it to measure precisely the distance and direction to its prey. This ability to detect such a small temperature variation is so difficult that only a computerized thermometer device can detect so small a difference. How could such a sensitive awareness of temperatures have evolved in the rattlesnake by chance?

Evolutionists believe that the complex systems found in living creatures have been formed as a result of random chance. However, King David declared: "You [God] formed my inward parts; You covered me in my mother's womb. I will praise You, for I am fearfully and wonderfully made" (Psalm 139:13–14, NKJV). Consider the case of the human eye and ask yourself whether or not such an astonishingly complex system could have occurred by chance alone. When a baby is conceived in its mother's womb, the genetic code governing the eye programs the baby's body to begin growing optic nerves from both the brain and the eye. Each eye will have a million nerve endings that begin growing through the flesh toward the baby's brain. Simultaneously, a million optic nerves will begin growing through the flesh toward the baby's eye. Each of the million optic nerves must find and match up to its mate to enable sight to exist. We are impressed when highway engineers are able to correctly align two thirty-foot-wide tunnels dug from opposite sides of the mountain to meet somewhere precisely in the middle of the mountain. However, every day hundreds of thousands of children are born with the ability to see; their bodies have precisely aligned a million separate optic nerves from each eye to meet matching optic nerve endings growing out from the baby's brain. If you think this miracle of design has happened by random chance, you probably still believe in the Tooth Fairy.

The human eye has the ability to transmit to the brain over one and a half million messages simultaneously. The retina at the back of the eye contains a dense area of rods and cones that gather and interpret information presented to the eye. The retina contains over one hundred and thirty-seven million nerve connections that the brain uses to evaluate data in its attempt to interpret the scene in front of your eyes. One hundred and thirty million of these special cells are rods that enable us to have black and white vision. However, about seven million eye cells are cone-shaped cells that allow us to see color. Each of these one hundred and thirty-seven million cells communicates directly with the brain, allowing us to interpret the visual image in front of us. Amazingly, scientists have discovered that while the image we receive in our eye is "upside-down," the cellular structure in our eye actually reverses the image to "right-side up" within the eye before sending it to the mind. The eye then transmits the corrected image at three hundred miles an hour to the brain where we "see" the image that is before us.

The human brain is the most complex organ in the known universe. While it weighs less than three pounds, it contains an amazingly intricate connection of nerves with more than thirty billion special cells known as neurons. In addition, there are another two hundred and fifty billion glial cells that facilitate communication between neurons. Incredibly, every one of the thirty billion neurons is connected to other neurons in a staggering degree of complicated connections. Every neuron is connected directly with more than fifty thousand other neurons allowing instantaneous transfers of messages across your brain. In less than a second, your brain can calculate the trajectory of a football thrown at thirty miles an hour toward you without warning. In a moment, your brain calculates your position and the ball's ultimate trajectory, and sends detailed electronic messages to the muscles in your arms and legs at more than three hundred miles a second to move you into position to catch the ball. Despite hundreds of billions of dollars and fifty years of advanced research by computer scientists, there are no computer systems on the planet that can equal this marvelous instantaneous computing that is required to allow a ten-year-old boy to catch a football! When we carefully consider the evidence, I believe that any fair-minded observer will conclude that our universe and all of life were designed by God exactly as revealed in the Bible.

The Bible reveals that a supernatural God designed and created our extremely complicated universe. Any person with an unbiased mind who examines the evidence must conclude that only a designer with miraculous powers could possibly account for the marvelously designed universe. The many scientific statements found throughout the Bible are perhaps the greatest proof of God's inspiration. There are no scientific errors or mistakes found in its thousands of passages. These conclusive evidences provide overwhelming proof that God exists, and that He inspired the writers of Scripture to record His message to all of mankind. The incredible scientific insights and revelations found throughout the Bible, from Genesis to Revelation, act as God's genuine signature on the pages of the Scriptures authenticating the Word of God.

Seven

Advanced Medical Knowledge in the Bible

Keep in mind as you read this chapter that man's medical knowledge was virtually abysmal until the beginning of the twentieth century. Even the existence of germs was unknown until around A.D. 1890. Yet, the first five books of the Bible, known as the Torah, or the Law, recorded by Moses approximately 1491–1451 B.C., reveal surprising advanced scientific principles. In addition, the Bible contains advanced medical and scientific knowledge about hygiene and sanitation. As you will discover, the Scriptures contain God's medical instructions for Israel that far exceeded the level of knowledge possessed by the Egyptians and other ancient societies of that day. This advanced information in the Bible, written over three and a half millennia ago, is strong proof that a divine Creator inspired it. What other rational explanation is there for this precise medical knowledge in the five books of the Law recorded while Moses led the Israelites through the wilderness of Sinai? God inspired Moses to record these medical commandments to protect the health of His chosen people. The Book of Exodus reveals one of the most astonishing promises God ever made to mankind.

God's Promise: "The Lord will take away from you all sickness"

God promised that, if they obeyed all of His commandments and statutes that He gave to Moses, the Lord would protect them from the plagues and sicknesses that afflicted the ancient Egyptians. This incredible promise is found in Exodus 15:26, "If you diligently heed the voice of the LORD your God and do what is right in His sight, give ear to His commandments and keep all His statutes, I will put none of the diseases on you which I have brought on the Egyptians. For I am the LORD who heals you"(NKJV). Throughout the Bible, especially the first five books of Moses from Genesis to Deuteronomy, we discover incredibly advanced medical laws and principles that are designed to protect us from the devastating diseases that have afflicted mankind throughout history.

For centuries, the Jews had lived as slaves among the pagan Egyptians. Obviously, they learned and adopted the traditional folk medicine and remedies of their Egyptian masters. As a result, the Israelites would have been afflicted during their long captivity by the same terrible diseases and plagues that repeatedly devastated the people of ancient Egypt. Deuteronomy 28:27–28 records a number of these terrible diseases of the Egyptians. "The LORD will strike you with the boils of Egypt, with tumors, with the scab, and with the itch, from which you cannot be healed. The LORD will strike you with madness and blindness and confusion of heart" (NKJV). However, if the Israelites would turn from their sins and follow the commandments of God, the Lord promised that "none of the terrible diseases of Egypt which you have known" would afflict the Jews from that moment on. "And the LORD will take away from you all sickness, and will afflict you with none of the terrible diseases of Egypt which you have known, but will lay them on all those who hate you" (Deuteronomy 7:15, NKJV).

When the children of Israel left Egypt through the miraculous intervention of God, the Lord demanded that they obey His commandments against sinning. God's specific medical laws and sanitation commandments that were given to Moses would protect the Jews from the most terrible diseases of the Egyptians and their attendant high mortality rates. An examination of the medical remedies of the ancient Egyptians and other pagan cultures of the Middle East reveals an appalling ignorance of even the most rudimentary medical knowledge as we know it today. However, the laws of Moses contained specific laws and sanitation procedures that, if faithfully followed, would eliminate the dreadful diseases that afflicted the Egyptians of that day and still afflict most of mankind in the Third World today.

The Medical Knowledge of Ancient Egypt

It is fascinating to study the several hundred prescriptions in the *Papyrus Ebers* to gain an understanding of the level of medical and sanitary knowledge possessed by the Egyptians, the most advanced society on earth in the days of Moses. Despite their advanced astronomical and engineering knowledge, as evidenced by their great temples at Karnak and the three great pyramids at Giza, the Egyptians' level of medical knowledge was extremely primitive and dangerous. Yet, they prided themselves on their great medical knowledge as revealed in various medical manuscripts that have survived the ravages of time, including the *Papyrus Ebers,* written about the time of Moses.

As an example of the medical ignorance and primitive state of their medical knowledge, consider the Egyptian doctor's suggestion for healing an infected splinter wound. The prescription involves the application of an ointment mixture composed of the blood of worms mixed with the dung of a donkey. The various germs, including tetanus, contained in donkey's dung must have assured that the patient would rapidly forget the pain of his splinter as he died from an assortment of other diseases produced by his doctor's contaminated medicine. The medical solution for a patient's hair loss involved the application to his scalp of a solution composed of various fats from a horse, a crocodile, a cat, a snake, and a donkey's tooth crushed in honey. The Egyptian doctors had an equally wondrous cure for a poisonous snake bite. They poured "magical water" over a pagan idol and then gave it to the victim for what probably turned out to be his last drink on earth.

According to these ancient documents, the pharmacies of ancient Egypt provided popular prescriptions including "lizards' blood, swines' teeth, putrid meat, stinking fat, moisture from pigs' ears, milk, goose grease, asses' hoofs, animal fats from various sources, excreta from animals, including human beings, donkeys, antelopes, dogs, cats, and even flies." Believe it or not, this list is quoted from pages of the *Papyrus Ebers* manuscript as translated in S. E. Massengill's *A Sketch of Medicine and Pharmacy.* During my last research trip to the Middle East, I located a fascinating book about ancient Egyptian medical knowledge. This book, *An Ancient Egyptian Herbal* by Lise Manniche (London: British Museum Press, 1989), describes a number of Egyptian cures that use ingredients such as "cat's dung," "hippopotamus dung," "donkey's hoof," "gazelle dung," "snakeskins," and, of

The Tomb of Cyrus

Grant and Kaye Jeffrey in Front of the Western Wall

A Clay Brick from Babylon Inscribed
with the Name of King Nebuchadnezzar

Wadi Mukatteb.
The Valley of the Inscriptions in the Sinai

ΕΝΑΡΧΗΗΝΟΛΟΓοϲ
ΚΑΙΟΛΟΓΟϲΗΝ
ΠΡΟϲΤΟΝΘΝΚΑΙ
ΘϹΗΝΟΛΟΓΟϹΟΥ
ΤΟϹΗΝΕΝΑΡΧΗ
ΠΡΟϹΤΟΝΘΝΠΑ
ΤΑΔΙΑΥΤΟΥΕΓΕΝε
ΤΟΚΑΙΧΩΡΙϹΑΥΤΟΥ
ΕΓΕΝΕΤΟΟΥΔΕΝ
ΟΓΕΓΟΝΕΝΕΝΑΥ
ΤΩΖΩΗΕϹΤΙΝ
ΚΑΙΗΖΩΗΗΝΤο
ΦΩϹΤΩΝΑΝΘΡω
ΠΩΝΚΑΙΤΟΦωϲ
ΕΝΤΗϹΚΟΤΙΑΦΑΙ
ΝΕΙΚΑΙΗϹΚΟΤΙ
ΛΑΥΤΟΟΥΚΑΤΕ
ΛΑΒΕΝ·
ΕΓΕΝΕΤΟΑΝΘΡω
ΠΟϹΑΠΕϹΤΑΛΜε

A New Testament Greek Manuscript

(Top.)

The Trilingual Inscription in a Mountain Cave on Djebel Maghara. Two Columns Are Hieroglyphics; One Column Is in the Sinaitic Alphabet.

The Mountains and Valleys of Sinai

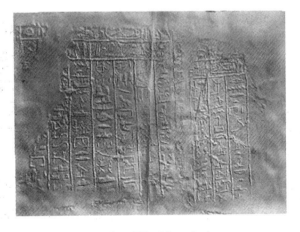

Example of Sinai Inscription

Sinai Inscription
No. XL.

Causes to descend into the deep valley[1] Moses the tribes.
Leader of the way he causes to descend into the deep the young
   ostrich[2] the sea foaming.
Divides it asunder power given him by GOD.

   [1] "That led them through the deep, as an horse in the wilderness, that they should not stumble: *As a beast goeth down into the
valley,* the Spirit of the Lord caused him to rest: so didst thou lead
thy people, to make thyself a glorious name."—*Isaiah* lxiii. 13,14.
   [2] "The daughter of my people is become cruel, like
ostriches in the *wilderness.*"—*Lam.* iv. 3.

Reproduced from
Sinai Photographed by Rev. Charles Forster
A.D. 1862

Sinai Inscription
No. XLI.

The People like a she-ostrich fleet-winged crying aloud causeth to
    haste Moses, the Cloud bright shining.[3]
A mighty army propelled into the Red Sea[4] gathered into one by
    GOD, they go jumping and skipping[5] journeying through the
    fissure taking flight from the face of the enemy.
The flux of the sea divided.[6]

[3]Exod. xiv. 20.
[4]Hab. iii. 15.
[5]Wisdom xix. 9.
[6]Exod. xiv. 21.

Reproduced from
Sinai Photographed by Rev. Charles Forster
A.D. 1862

Example of Sinai Inscription with Hieroglyphs

Sinai Inscription with Girl Praying.
Found in Tomb at Turbet es Yahoud
—"The Graves of the Jews."

Close-up of Girl
Praying

course, the ever popular "fly dung" that appears in numerous prescriptions. The Egyptian's remedy for "constipation: zizyphus bread, gurma, cat's dung, sweet beer, wine." In another passage we read, "A painful tumour was treated with fly dung mixed with sycamore juice applied to the tumour so that it goes down by itself." Among these amazingly dangerous medicines we find an incredible suggestion for curing a baby of excessive crying: "A remedy for too much crying in a child: spn-seeds; fly dung from the wall; is made to a paste, strained and drunk for four days. The crying will cease instantly." No doubt the crying would cease with the death of the poor child receiving this deadly potion. As the author noted, "In general, Coptic medicine is not held in very high esteem." A majority of the medicines described in documents from ancient Egypt included dung from either humans or animals. The mortality rate from infection must have been dreadful with such unhelpful and deadly advice from doctors. Due to the total lack of knowledge of germs and infection, almost any serious illness or injury treated by the medical system of pagan Egypt would result in a painful and virtually certain death.

The Bible records that Moses was adopted by and grew up as the son of "Pharaoh's daughter." Moses would have had access to the knowledge of the royal and priestly colleges of Egypt. The Jewish historian Flavius Josephus tells us in his *Antiquities of the Jews* that Moses, as a prince of Egypt, became a great general in his successful war against the Ethiopian Empire. As a royal prince, he was taught all that Egypt, as the most advanced culture of the day, could transmit to his genius. The Book of Acts (7:22) tells us: "And

Moses was learned in all the wisdom of the Egyptians, and was mighty in words and in deeds." Therefore, as a royal heir, he would have been educated in all of these amazing medical cures. Both the writer of the Torah and the millions of ancient Israelite slaves would have absorbed the medical knowledge and traditional treatments of the Egyptians during the centuries of Israel's captivity. However, a close examination of the first five books of the Bible written by Moses does not reveal a single reference to these "deadly" medical cures of the pagan Egyptian society in which Moses and the Israelites were raised. Rather, we discover in the pages of ancient Scriptures the most advanced sanitation instructions and the most sophisticated medical knowledge that the world has ever known, until the explosion of medical research in this century following World War I. Despite the natural human tendency to add our own natural education and knowledge to what God tells us, Moses resisted such temptations by writing exactly what God inspired him to write as he composed the Torah. There are no references to the disgusting and dangerous ancient Egyptian medical practices in the five books of Moses.

Any intelligent reader must ask this question: Where did Moses obtain his incredibly advanced medical knowledge? Obviously he did not receive this accurate medical knowledge from the Egyptians or any other pagan culture of that time. This advanced and accurate knowledge reveals a profound understanding of germs, infectious transmission routes, human sanitation needs, and many other medical advances unknown outside the Bible during the last thirty-five centuries. Moses abandoned the medical ignorance of the Egyptians when he left the palace in Egypt and spent the next eighty years of his life in the wilderness. The first five books of the Bible contain detailed medical laws regarding the careful kosher inspection of meat and exacting sanitation regulations regarding the burial of bodies. How could Moses have acquired such a profound and medically advanced knowledge without help from some outside force? The only answer that makes sense is that found in the first five books of the Bible as written by Moses. Moses declared that he received this knowledge from God by direct and supernatural inspiration. A careful examination of the medical treatises from the Egyptians and the comprehensive Babylonian Code of Hammurabi reveals absolutely nothing about preventive medicine to enable people to avoid these deadly diseases that devastated ancient societies. However, the presence of incredibly advanced and accurate knowledge of diseases, sanitation, and preventive medicine in the ancient Scriptures is one more incontrovertible proof that the Bible is truly the inspired Word of God. It is fascinating to note that a total of two hundred and thirteen out of the six hundred and thirteen biblical commandments found in the Torah were detailed medical regulations that ensured the good health of the Children of Israel if they would obediently follow the laws of God.

God's Ancient Laws of Hygiene and Sanitation

Medical science did not know of the existence of germs and their methods of transmission of infection until the end of the last century. Doctors until this century believed that the presence and transmission of disease were entirely haphazard and governed by simple chance or bad luck. Those who were sick with deadly diseases were cared for in the home without any awareness of the contagious transmission of disease from one sick individual to others around them. People had no idea that invisible and deadly microscopic germs could exist on eating and cooking utensils. However, Leviticus 6:28, written over thirty-five hundred years ago, reveals a clear commandment to discard broken pottery (because the cracks could contain harmful germs): "But the earthen vessel in which it is boiled shall be broken. And if it is boiled in a bronze pot, it shall be both scoured and rinsed in water (NKJV)." In other words, a cracked vessel should not be used for cooking or eating but should be discarded. The Bible tells us further that "if it be sodden in a brasen pot, it shall be both scoured, and rinsed in water," indicating that a metal pot should be disinfected by scouring and rinsing in water. These instructions certainly saved hundreds of thousands of Jews from infections over the centuries at a time when the rest of the world didn't even know that germs existed. How could Moses have known of the dangers of infectious germs in cooking and eating utensils thousands of years ago unless God actually inspired him to write these words?

Moses' writing also reveals an astonishing knowledge of deadly germs associated with dead animal bodies and anything they touch. Throughout history people stored and cooked their meat with ample spices to delay the rotting and to disguise the smell of decay. Without refrigeration, the eating of meat was often hazardous because of the great danger of infection. In Leviticus 11:35, Moses revealed his knowledge of the danger of germs from animal carcasses when he wrote, "And everything on which a part of any such carcass falls shall be unclean; whether it is an oven or cooking stove, it shall be broken down; for they are unclean, and shall be unclean to you." God inspired Moses to record these medical and sanitation instructions in the Bible to protect the Israelites from invisible, infectious germs found in dead animal bodies that would kill them. It is important to remember that, until this century, even medical researchers and doctors denied that disease could be transmitted by invisible germs or viruses.

The Book of Leviticus 7:24 forbids the people to eat of the flesh of any animal that has died naturally of disease or by wild animals: "And the fat of an animal that dies naturally, and the fat of what is torn by wild beasts, may be used in any other way; but you shall by no means eat it" (NKJV). Any animal carcass found after natural death would be dangerous to eat because it would likely contain the germs that caused its premature death or the infectious germs that would develop within hours of an animal's violent death following an attack by another animal. The children of Israel were saved from countless invisible germs and diseases by following these religious laws and prohibitions given by their God through the prophet Moses.

Laws Designed to Prevent Infectious Disease

God provided the Israelites with wise and beneficial laws to protect their health, including advanced sanitation laws to prevent the spread of infections. "This is the law when a man dies in a tent: All who come into the tent and all who are in the tent shall be unclean seven days; and every open vessel, which has no cover fastened on it, is unclean. Whoever in the open field touches one who is slain by a sword or who has died, or a bone of a man, or a grave, shall be unclean seven days. And for an unclean person they shall take some of the ashes of the heifer burnt for purification from sin, and running water shall be put on them in a vessel" (Numbers 19:14–17, NKJV).

Throughout history mankind has suffered billions of untold deaths due to infections from microscopic germs. Germs from a dead human body are more dangerous to another human than germs from an animal's body because of the greater likelihood of transmission of infection. These deadly germs are everywhere, but especially within the bodies of those who are already sick or those who have died due to some disease. Mankind's ignorance of these deadly microscopic germs has exposed countless humans to premature death. However, thirty-five centuries ago the Bible clearly gave instructions that would protect us from many of these infectious diseases.

A brilliant Hungarian doctor of the last century, Ignaz Semmelweis, created a tremendous improvement in practical medical treatment and the control of deadly infectious diseases. I am indebted to the fascinating book, *None of These Diseases* by S. I. McMillen, M.D., for making me aware of the importance of the medical contributions of Dr. Semmelweis. An article in the *Encyclopædia Britannica* documents that, as a young doctor in Vienna in 1845, Semmelweis was appalled by the staggering rate of death by infection of women who gave birth in hospitals. While most children were born at home at that time, a number of women, usually the homeless or sick, gave birth to their children in the local hospitals. The level of infectious puerperal (child-bed) fever was horrendous with between 15 and 30 percent of such mothers dying in hospital. This tragic situation was considered normal at that time. Dr. Semmelweis noted that every morning the young interns examined the bodies of the mothers who had died and then immediately, without washing their hands, went to the next ward where they would examine the expectant mothers. This astonishing behavior was considered normal medical practice in the last century because the existence of microscopic infectious germs was unknown and unsuspected.

However, the young doctor insisted that the doctors under his supervision follow his new orders to wash their hands vigorously in water and chlorinated lime prior to examining living patients. Immediately, the mortality rate caused by infection among the expectant mothers fell to less than 2 percent. Despite these fantastic improvements the senior hospital staff despised Dr. Semmelweis's medical innovations and eventually fired him. Most of his medical colleagues rejected his new techniques and ridiculed his demands that they wash their hands because they could not believe infections could be caused by something invisible to the naked eye. Later he took a position with another hospital in Pest, Hungary [Budapest], the St. Rochus Hospital, which was experiencing an epidemic of puerperal fever in the ward where mothers were giving birth. Immediately, his new san-itary procedures had a positive effect, with the mortality rate dropping to less than 1 percent instead of the 15 percent that was normal in other hospitals in the area. During the following six years, he received the approval of the Hungarian government, which sent medical advisory letters to all district authorities demanding that all medical staff follow Dr. Semmelweis's instructions for washing hands and general hospital sanitation. Although the beneficial results of washing hands were obvious, the medical establishments of Europe and North America continued to ignore his techniques. Patients continued to die needlessly of infectious diseases while they were in the hospital. Decades of rejection by his colleagues finally drove Dr. Semmelweis to a nervous breakdown that placed him in a mental institution. Tragically, due to an infection he received through a cut on his hand during an operation in 1865, Dr. Semmelweis succumbed to the same disease he spent his life trying to alleviate. Dr. Joseph Lister, the father of modern antisepsis (the science of fighting infection), said of him, "I think with the greatest admiration of him and his achievement."

Thousands of years ago, God commanded the Israelites to wash their hands in "running water" when dealing with those afflicted with infectious diseases. "And when he who has a discharge is cleansed of his discharge, then he shall count for himself seven days for his cleansing, wash his clothes, and bathe his body in running water; then he shall be clean" (Leviticus 15:13, NKJV). Until this century most doctors who did choose to wash their hands did so in a bowl of water, which obviously would allow the germs to remain on their hands. However, Moses instructed the Israelites to wash in "running water," which is the only way to effectively remove these infectious germs.

Laws to Prevent Plague and Leprosy

Throughout history, the scourge of leprosy has killed untold millions of people and afflicted many more with misery. There is some debate among medical scholars about whether the Hebrew word translated "leprosy" in the Bible is exactly the same disease as the modern variant. It may have been another deadly infectious disease that differs from modern forms of leprosy. Amazingly, an examination of the detailed laws of Numbers and Leviticus reveals an advanced system for the control of infectious diseases at a time when ancient pagan nations did not understand the dangers of infections. For example, the Bible commands that the priests act as medical control officers, examining all sick individuals and taking action to protect them and the community. "Then the priest shall examine it; and indeed if the swelling of the sore is reddish-white on his bald head or on his bald forehead, as the appearance of leprosy on the skin of the body, he is a leprous man. He is unclean. The priest shall surely pronounce him unclean; his sore is on his head" (Leviticus 13:43–44, NKJV). In addition to identifying the diseased individual, the priest was responsible for the isolation of those afflicted with leprosy. "He shall be unclean. All the days he has the sore he shall be unclean. He is unclean, and he shall dwell alone; his habitation shall be outside the camp" (Leviticus 13:46, NKJV).

The Lord's concern to protect His children from infectious disease was manifested in His command to forbid those who were still infected with disease from participating in the three great annual festivals of the Jews, lest they infect others. "But the man who is unclean and does not purify himself, that person shall be cut off from among the congregation, because he has defiled the sanctuary of the LORD. The water of purification has not been sprinkled on him; he is unclean" (Numbers 19:20, NKJV). Even after a man recovered from his disease and returned from medical isolation, the individual was subject to strict medical supervision for seven days under the medical orders of the priest to ascertain that he was truly healed. "He who is to be cleansed shall wash his clothes, shave off all his hair, and wash himself in water, that he may be clean. After that he shall come into the camp, and shall stay outside his tent seven days" (Leviticus 14:8, NKJV). After this period of quarantine, the individual must submit to a careful medical examination by the priests to ascertain that he was truly free of disease and able to resume his position in society. "But on the seventh day he shall shave all the hair off his head and his beard and his eyebrows—all his hair he shall shave off. He shall wash his clothes and wash his body in water, and he shall be clean" (Leviticus 14:9, NKJV). When you consider these ancient medical instructions, you can see that they are amazingly similar to the medical quarantine orders a modern public health official would issue to determine absolutely that someone was cured of his disease and able to reenter society safely.

The continents of Europe and Asia have been periodically engulfed by epidemics of leprosy and plague, such as those in the medieval period, especially A.D. 1200 to A.D. 1400. These dreaded diseases terrified the populations of Europe and appeared unbeatable. More than sixty million people, almost one-third of the population of Europe in the fourteenth century, are estimated to have died by the Black Death (bubonic plague). Entire counties and towns were devastated with no known survivors. Those who survived portrayed scenes that sounded like the haunting visions of Dante's descriptions of hell. Renowned doctors of the time were unable to respond adequately because of their lack of knowledge. They were reduced to offering medical advice to prevent the plague such as, "Stop eating pepper or garlic." Some suggested the plague was caused by the positions of the planets and stars. Mostly, the doctors helplessly comforted their dying patients and finally succumbed to the disease themselves.

How was this dreaded plague finally stopped before it killed everyone in Europe? As ministers prayed and held their Bibles in their hands, little did they realize that God had already provided the divine solution in the pages of Holy Scripture. While doctors failed the people totally, some church leaders wisely looked to God and the Bible for a divine medical solution to the apparently hopeless situation. During my last trip to Vienna, I examined a strange-looking statue in the center of the city dedicated to the Black Death's countless victims and the actions of the church fathers, in accordance with Scripture, to abolish the curse of that disease. The history of that time reveals that the doctors could do nothing. It was only after the people began to follow the ancient biblical laws of sanitation and disease control that the epidemic was broken. In the midst of fear and panic, several church leaders in Vienna began to search the Bible to discover whether or not there was a practical biblical solution to this plague. They discovered in

Leviticus 13:46 that Moses laid down strict regulations from God regarding the medical treatment of those afflicted with leprosy or plague: "He shall be unclean. All the days he has the sore he shall be unclean. He is unclean, and he shall dwell alone; his habitation shall be outside the camp (NKJV)." God answered their prayers for deliverance when they finally began to obey His declared commands. Both the scourge of leprosy and the Black Death were eliminated by following God's inspired commands given to Moses in the ancient past.

The Divine Laws of Quarantine

This divine medical rule demanded that a person who contracted leprosy or the plague must be isolated and segregated from the general population during his infectious period, until he was healed or died. God's commands included detailed instructions regarding protection from infection for those who treated the segregated patient. After feeding and caring for the plague sufferer, the care givers must change their clothes, wash in running water, and expose both themselves and their clothing to sunlight. Doctors today know that sunlight and vigorous washing in running water are among the most effective preventive steps to minimize infectious transmission between patients. Moses' instruction to segregate infected patients from their families and other people was one of the most important medical advances in human history. The biblical instructions reveal a profoundly advanced scientific understanding that invisible germs can be transmitted to others unless preventive sanitary steps are taken. Until this century, all previous societies, except for the Israelites who followed God's medical laws regarding quarantine, kept infected patients in their homes—even after death, exposing family members and others to deadly disease. During the devastating Black Death of the fourteenth century, patients who were sick or dead were kept in the same rooms as the rest of the family. People often wondered why the disease was affecting so many people at one time. They attributed these epidemics to "bad air" or "evil spirits." However, careful attention to the medical commands of God as revealed in Leviticus would have saved untold millions of lives. Arturo Castiglione wrote about the overwhelming importance of this biblical medical law: "The laws against leprosy in Leviticus 13 may be regarded as the first model of a sanitary legislation" (Arturo Castiglione, *A History of Medicine* [New York: Alfred A. Knopf, Inc., 1941], p. 71).

Fortunately, the church fathers of Vienna finally took the biblical injunctions to heart and commanded that those infected with the plague must be placed outside the city in special medical quarantine compounds. Care givers fed them there until they either died or survived the passage of the disease. Those who died in homes or streets were instantly removed and buried outside the city limits. These biblical sanitary measures quickly brought the dreaded epidemic under control for the first time. Other cities and countries rapidly followed the medical practices of Vienna until the Black Death was finally halted.

Laws of Cleanliness—Next to Godliness

While people repeat the phrase "Cleanliness is next to godliness," they often forget that God has actually provided stringent laws of cleanliness that, if followed, would immeasurably prevent disease and premature death. Throughout the Scriptures we find God commanding His people to follow laws of hygiene and cleanliness. To put these laws and instructions in perspective, we need to understand that cleanliness and bathing were almost unknown through much of human history. Most people lived from the cradle to grave in past centuries without ever having a bath. In fact, most Europeans until the 1840s believed that taking a bath was the most dangerous thing you could do to your health. Most Europeans, until the end of the last century, experienced a bath less than once a year. King James I of England, who ordered the translation of the Bible known as the King James Version, never bathed once. He kept a bowl of talc beside him that he applied to his fingers and hands to keep them soft. When Kaye and I visited the thousand-room Hampton Court several years ago, the guide pointed out that King James's numerous guests did not have access to a single bathtub in the whole castle. One of the reasons they loved snuff and perfume so much in those days was to mask dreadful body odors.

However, thousands of years ago God commanded the Israelites to deal with their uncleanliness by following His specific instructions to avoid infection and death. For example, even before God gave Moses the Ten Commandments at Mount Sinai, He told the Israelites to sanctify themselves by washing their clothes: "Then the LORD said to Moses, Go to the people, and sanctify them today and tomorrow, and let them wash their clothes" (Exodus 19:10, NKJV). Preparations for ministering in the Tabernacle required that Aaron and his sons wash their bodies before putting on their priestly garments: "And Aaron and his sons thou shalt bring unto the door of the tabernacle of the congregation, and shalt wash them with water" (Exodus 29:4) prior to giving them their priestly garments. "Moses, Aaron, and his sons would wash their hands and their feet with water . . . whenever they went into the tabernacle of meeting, and when they came near the altar, they washed, as the LORD had commanded Moses" (Exodus 40:31, 32, NKJV). This rule still applied years later when the priests ministered in the Temple.

When you consider that the priests were responsible for preparing and sacrificing animals on the altar, the need for strict rules of washing is obvious in light of our present knowledge of the dangers from infectious germs. The Bible also contains detailed sanitation instructions concerning the purification following the birth of a child, and very detailed instructions were laid out regarding hygiene for women.

Incineration of Animal Waste to Prevent Disease

One of the most astonishing of the sanitation commandments found in the Bible is the demand that the internal organs and waste of the animals to be sacrificed were to be carefully burned "without the camp" to prevent the possibility of transmitting infection to the Israelites from the germ-filled waste of the sacrificed animals. Incredibly, the Israelites were commanded to create, in effect, an incinerator "outside the camp" to safely dispose of the dangerous infectious materials produced by their sacrifices. "But the bull's hide and all its flesh, with its head and legs, its entrails and offal—the whole bull he shall carry outside the camp to a clean place, where the ashes are poured out, and burn it on wood with fire; where the ashes are poured out it shall be burned" (Leviticus 4:11–12). At a time when no one knew that animal waste and decaying organs would be dangerous because of the microscopic germs, the Bible commands the Israelites to destroy these infectious agents in the most sanitary method available to an ancient culture—burning outside the camp.

The Medical Importance of the Red Heifer Sacrifice

In Numbers 19, Moses wrote these inspired instructions regarding the mysterious Sacrifice of the Red Heifer: "Then the heifer shall be burned in his sight: its hide, its flesh, its blood, and its offal shall be burned. And the priest shall take cedar wood and hyssop and scarlet, and cast them into the midst of the fire burning the heifer. Then the priest shall wash his clothes, he shall bathe in water, and afterward he shall come into the camp; the priest shall be unclean until evening. And the one who burns it shall wash his clothes in water, bathe in water, and shall be unclean until evening. Then a man who is clean shall gather up the ashes of the heifer, and store them outside the camp in a clean place; and they shall be kept for the congregation of the children of Israel for the water of purification; it is for purifying from sin. And the one who gathers the ashes of the heifer shall wash his clothes, and be unclean until evening. It shall be a statute forever to the children of Israel and to the stranger who sojourns among them. He who touches the dead body of anyone shall be unclean seven days. He shall purify himself with the water on the third day and on the seventh day; then he will be clean. But if he does not purify himself on the third day and on the seventh day, he will not be clean. Whoever touches the body of anyone who has died, and does not purify himself, defiles the tabernacle of the LORD. That person shall be cut off from Israel. He shall be unclean, because the water of purification was not sprinkled on him; his uncleanness is still on him" (Numbers 19:5–13, NKJV).

The primary spiritual significance of the Sacrifice of the Red Heifer is the fact that it symbolically points to the ultimate sacrifice of Jesus Christ as our only hope of being cleansed from the uncleanliness of our sins. The Talmud claims that the Red Heifer sacrifice was the only one of God's commands that King Solomon, the wisest man who ever lived, claimed he did not understand. Although the priest obediently offered the sacrifice as demanded by God, Solomon apparently did not understand why Numbers 19 declared that the priest would be "unclean until evening." This unusual sacrifice symbolically pointed to Jesus Christ and His sacrifice because our Lord, who was perfectly sinless, judicially took upon Himself the sins of the world so that we who are sinful could become righteous before God. Christ paid the price for our sins. Just as the Red Heifer was sacrificed "outside the camp" in contrast to all other sacrifices that took place in the Tabernacle or Temple, Jesus was sacrificed outside the city of Jerusalem. In contrast to the normal male animals sacrificed, the Red Heifer was one of the few female animals the Law commanded to be sacrificed. Significantly, our Lord was betrayed for thirty pieces of silver, the price of a female slave.

In addition to the obvious spiritual significance of the law of the Sacrifice of the Red Heifer, we now understand that the water of purification described in Numbers 19 actually had the ability to destroy germs and infection. The resulting water of purification solution contained ashes from the Red Heifer sacrifice combined with cedar, hyssop, and scarlet thread. This water of purification contained "cedar" oil that came from a kind of juniper tree that grew in both Israel and in the Sinai. This cedar oil would irritate the skin, encouraging the person to vigorously rub the solution into his hands. Most important, the hyssop tree—associated with mint, possibly marjoram—would produce hyssop oil. This hyssop oil is actually a very effective antiseptic and antibacterial agent. Hyssop oil contains 50 percent carvacrol, which is an antifungal and antibacterial agent still used in medicine, according to the book *None of These Diseases*. When we note that the waters of purification from the Red Heifer sacrifice were to be used to cleanse someone who had become defiled and unclean due to touching a dead body, we begin to understand that this law was an incredibly effective medical law as well as a spiritual law. The Book of Hebrews reveals that Paul, an educated rabbi, understood that the Red Heifer sacrifice had a practical medical effect as well as its more obvious spiritual element. Paul declared that "the blood of bulls and goats and the ashes of a heifer, sprinkling the unclean, sanctifies for the purifying of the flesh" (Hebrews 9:13, NKJV). The Jews stood apart from the pagan nations in their attention to sanitation and personal cleanliness as a result of the commands of God revealed in the Old Testament.

Another of the medical commands that is simply astonishing in its understanding of the need for disinfecting items is found in the command of God regarding all captured material from an enemy's camp. This command of the Lord stated that "whoever has killed any person, and whoever has touched any slain, purify yourselves and your captives on the third day and on the seventh day. Purify every garment, everything made of leather, everything woven of goats' hair, and everything made of wood" (Numbers 31:19–20, NKJV). The clear instructions for disinfecting these items was as follows: "Everything that can endure fire, you shall put through the fire, and it shall be clean; and it shall be purified with the water of purification. But all that cannot endure fire you shall put through water. And you shall wash your clothes on the seventh day and be clean, and afterward you may come into the camp" (Numbers 31:23–24, NKJV). These instructions would purify any materials captured from pagans that might carry dangerous germs.

Life Is in the Blood

Moses makes a fascinating statement in the Book of Leviticus about the importance of blood: "For the life of the flesh is in the blood" (Leviticus 17:11). Incredibly, Moses reveals that our blood is the essence of life. Our blood is one of the most amazing features in our wonderful bodies. We have over seventy-five thousand miles of blood vessels in our bodies, enough to circle the world three times! These incredibly tiny veins, arteries, and capillary vessels carry blood cells with nutrients to feed every one of the sixty trillion cells in our bodies. The sixty trillion amazingly complex cells that make up a human body are produced from a single microscopic cell formed when a father's sperm is joined to a mother's egg. This complex system of interconnected blood vessels must bring the needed nutrients to the particular cells that require these chemicals. This is the equivalent of a courier company delivering trillions of packages daily to sixty trillion business customers over a route covering seventy-five thousand miles of territory. Each of our cells requires a number of different nutrients and chemicals. Special chemical sensors detect the nutrient needed as the blood passes through the bloodstream and allow that cell to connect with the necessary substance. In addition, we have over a million special types of white cells, antibodies specially designed to fight one particular disease. As soon as the body detects that it has been invaded by a particular germ or virus, the whole blood system goes on special alert to produce an explosive increase in whatever antibody is required to fight the disease.

The Hebrew word for the heart is *lev*. This word and variations of it appear at least eight hundred and twenty-five times in the Old Testament and another one hundred and sixty times in the New Testament. Our enormously complex blood system that allows life to exist is pumped by our heart, the most powerful muscle in our body. Though it is only the size of a clenched fist, it is far stronger than our legs or arms. However, while the heart works non-stop for eighty years or more, the muscles of our legs or arms are exhausted after only a short time of exertion. Weighing less than a pound, this fantastically reliable organ pumps over one and a half million gallons of blood every year of our life. In the course of a normal lifespan, the average human heart will pump forty million times, pushing almost one million pounds of blood through the seventy-five thousand miles of blood vessels that make up our body. How could Moses have understood thirty-five centuries ago that "the life of the flesh is in the blood" unless God revealed it to him by inspiration?

God's Command Concerning Circumcision

One of the most interesting of the medical details in the Bible is found in the specific instructions regarding the process of circumcising every Hebrew male child at the age of eight days as a sign of their obedience to the Covenant of God. Abraham was commanded specifically that "he who is eight days old among you shall be circumcised, every male child in your generations" (Genesis 17:12, NKJV). For thousands of years righteous Jews have faithfully obeyed this commandment. Why would God demand that Moses command the Israelites to circumcise their male children on the eighth day of life rather than any other day? The Arabs, for example, circumcise their male children on their thirteenth birthday. Medical scientists have been examining the biological processes that lead to blood clotting. The rapid healing of a wound begins with clotting of the blood. Any wound that continues to bleed, especially in a primitive environment, will provide a tremendous likelihood of infection. Recently they discovered that two specific factors in our blood are closely related to the ability of our blood to clot quickly and safely to facilitate healing and resistance to infection. These medical researchers found that two different blood clotting factors, Vitamin K and prothrombin, are at the highest levels of your life (110 percent of normal) on the eighth day of life. In addition, they discovered that the blood clotting factor, Vitamin K, is formed in the blood of a baby between day five and day seven of the baby's life. Therefore, of all the days of the baby's life, the eighth day of life is the optimum day for an operation because of the high levels of Vitamin K and prothrombin, which will clot the blood and facilitate wound healing. How would Moses have known that the eighth day of life was the ideal time to circumcise the Israelite male children unless God inspired him to write this command?

The Bible's Laws on Sanitation

Since the beginning of human civilization, mankind has suffered from the many diseases that are carried in human waste. When men lived primarily in widely distributed rural areas, there was little danger of infection. However, as men began to move into villages, towns, and cities, the danger of contamination grew geometrically. Throughout the medieval and Renaissance periods, and in many societies of the Third World today, waste is thrown into the gutter in the street and allowed to be flushed through the drains by occasional rains or floods. The stench from such a primitive system is beyond imagination. During the days of Shakespeare, the River Thames in London was an open sewer containing untreated human waste. Even then, four hundred years ago, salmon could not survive in the river because of toxic poisons. People could not bear to walk near the River Thames because of the stench from the open cesspool. It is interesting to note that modern pollution treatment has now succeeded in reclaiming the Thames to the point where fishermen are actually catching edible salmon from the bridges of London. According to an article in the *Encyclopædia Britannica*, the foul smells arising from the River Thames in London in past centuries were so terrible that they hung burlap sacks saturated in chloride of lime in the windows of Parliament in an ineffective attempt to kill the odors.

The smells in cities and towns were as indescribable and deadly as the comparable odors in Calcutta today. The result of this deplorable condition is that humans died in huge numbers every year as they succumbed to a variety of germ-related diseases including typhoid, dysentery, and cholera. As difficult as it might be to believe, even the educated people of the day ignored the appalling threat to their health represented by the lack of any sanitation whatsoever. It is not an exaggeration to claim that hundreds of millions of people have died throughout history due to infectious disease produced by the absence of even the most elementary sanitation regarding human waste. Yet obedience to God's law of sanitation, proclaimed thousands of years ago in the pages of Scripture, would have saved countless millions of lives from needless death caused by germs spread through untreated and unburied sewage.

My reason for dwelling on this unpleasant subject is an attempt to emphasize the extraordinary nature of the advanced sanitation commands issued by God over three and a half thousand years ago. At a time when no one humanly understood anything about the true deadly nature of microscopic germs and infections, God instructed Moses about how he could ensure adequate sanitation for his huge Jewish refugee population. As the history of refugee situations reveals, they almost inevitably lead to terrible infections, such as cholera and typhoid, due to the lack of adequate sanitation facilities. The germs from untreated human waste produced in such unorganized refugee groups contaminate the ground water and lead to horrendous epidemics.

God's basic sanitation order regarding human waste for the children of Israel was recorded in the Book of Deuteronomy: "Also you shall have a place outside the camp, where you may go out; and you shall have an implement among your equipment, and when you sit down outside, you shall dig with it and turn and cover your refuse" (Deuteronomy 23:12–13, NKJV). While such a basic sanitation law concerning latrines may seem very normal and obvious to us today, it is an extraordinary instruction when you consider that it was made thirty-five centuries before the existence of invisible germs was discovered.

As a student of biblical and military history, I have long noted the historical truth that the vast majority of soldiers who have been killed during the countless wars have succumbed to infectious disease rather than bullets or other weapons of war. The history of war until A.D. 1900 reveals that five times as many soldiers usually died due to disease as from wounds inflicted by enemy weapons. Sickness and plague often determined the outcome of a battle. Often the army that suffered the greatest diseases lost the war. A huge percentage of the diseases of mankind, especially in war or refugee situations, developed due to the lack of sanitation regarding waste disposal. Even as late as the Boer War in South Africa (1899–1902), an analysis of military casualties indicates that five times as many soldiers died or were incapacitated due to infections, often caused by exposure to germs generated from waste, as were killed in combat. When armies marched across a country and besieged a city, tens of thousands of soldiers were forced to camp in the open for months. Without obedience to the strict sanitation rules found in the Bible, the unburied waste from these soldiers inevitably ended up in the ground water system and ultimately infected the rest of the army.

It is certain that the strict obedience to the Law of God by the soldiers of Israel allowed them to escape many of the terrible diseases that would have afflicted their pagan enemies. It is likely that Israel was assisted in winning many of its ancient battles against the pagan troops of Syria and Moab because Jewish soldiers were not exposed to the tremendous infections that would afflict their enemies who did not know God's rules of sanitation. Consider the logistic problems of trying to meet the human needs of hundreds of thousands of Jews during the forty years in the wilderness. Most Israelites would have died due to infectious diseases during those years if God had not instructed Moses to teach His chosen people these advanced laws of sanitation. In his book *A History of Medicine*, the medical historian Arturo Castiglione declared that Moses' sanitation commands to his army were "certainly a primitive measure, but an effective one, which indicates advanced ideas of sanitation" (p. 70).

These simple but profoundly important instructions from God told the Israelites that each soldier must carry a shovel and bury his waste. Such instructions would assure that there would be no risk of infection to himself and his fellow soldiers from the waste. This command on latrines is so obvious to us today that it is easy to overlook its importance as a proof of the divine inspiration of the Scriptures.

Before the medical advances of the last one hundred and thirty years, medical doctors did not know that microscopic infections from human and animal waste were among the deadliest dangers to mankind. Yet, here we find this advanced sanitation and medical knowledge clearly expressed in the Bible written thousands of years ago. Where could Moses have learned this incredibly important and lifesaving medical knowledge about the dangers of human waste unless he received a divine revelation as he recorded? Moses could not possibly have learned this knowledge from his schooling in the medicine of Egypt. Remember that one of the favorite ingredients found in the traditional medicines of ancient Egypt, as described in the Egyptian *Papyrus Ebers,* was manure from insects, animals, and humans. How could Moses have written these incredibly accurate and advanced medical instructions unless God inspired him?

Eight

Precise Fulfillment of Bible Prophecy—The Signature of God

> *"From all the angelic ranks goes forth a groan,*
> *'How long, O Lord, how long?'*
> *The still small voice makes answer 'Wait and see,*
> *O sons of glory, what the end shall be.'"*
>
> Thomas Macaulay—*Marriage of Tirzah and Ahirad*

This study of the fulfillment of biblical prophecy provides overwhelming proof that God is controlling human history. Despite the apparent anarchy of daily events, the hand of God is still moving behind the scenes of current history to bring about His divine will. The details in the history of God's chosen people were precisely prophesied throughout the Bible. Each of the three long captivities of Israel was prophesied: their first exile in Egypt, which lasted four hundred and thirty years; the seventy years of captivity in Babylon; the final worldwide dispersion of the Jewish people for the last two thousand years. Every time Israel was out of the Promised Land, the duration of the captivity was foretold regarding how long God would keep the Jews in exile. Incredibly, the actual time of the miraculous rebirth of Israel, on May 15, 1948, was foretold by the prophet Ezekiel over twenty-five centuries before it occurred. It is obvious to any who will examine this evidence that history is following a purposeful pattern, a design laid down centuries ago in the Word of God. The question we must ask is this, "Who is the designer?" And, "What is His purpose in history and in our own lives?"

The Bible itself declares that the evidence of fulfilled prophecy is the unmistakable proof of God's inspiration of Scripture. It is clear from the words of the prophet Isaiah that God Himself declared that the phenomenon of correctly and precisely prophesying future events is the absolute proof that the Lord inspired biblical writers to write the Scriptures. The prophet Isaiah recorded God's declaration: "Behold, the former things are come to pass, and new things do I declare; before they spring forth I tell you of them" (Isaiah 42:9).

No one except God can accurately predict future events in detail. Neither Satan nor his demons can predict the future. Twenty-five centuries ago the prophet Isaiah recorded these powerful words directly from God Almighty: "Remember the former things of old: for I am God, and there is no other; I am God, and there is none like Me, declaring the end from the beginning, and from ancient times things that are not yet done, saying, My counsel shall stand, and I will do all My pleasure" (Isaiah 46:9–10, NKJV). The Bible contains 1,817 individual predictions concerning 737 separate subjects found in 8,352 verses. These numerous predictions comprise 27 percent of the 31,124 verses in the whole of the Scriptures. Multitudes of biblical scholars over the last two thousand years have explored many of these prophecies and their detailed fulfillments as proven by ample historical evidence.

Only God Can Correctly Prophesy the Future

Despite the fact that the world is full of spiritual texts by multitudes of religious writers, a close examination of this literature reveals that not one of these texts contains detailed prophecies that have been fulfilled. The reason is quite simple: Since no one but God can know the future accurately, religious philosophers who wrote other texts were wise enough to refrain from attempting detailed prophecies that would quickly prove their authors to be in error. "Thus says the LORD, the King of Israel, and his Redeemer, the LORD of hosts: 'I am the First and I am the Last; besides Me there is no God. And who can proclaim as I do? Then let him declare it and set it in order for Me, since I appointed the ancient people. And the things that are coming and shall come, let them show these to them'" (Isaiah 44:6–7, NKJV). The classical and religious literature of the Greeks, Romans, and other Middle Eastern cultures contains no specific, detailed prophecies regarding future events, people, or trends. There were no prophecies concerning the coming of Buddha, Mohammed, or any other religious leader. Only Old Testament prophecies predicted numerous, precise details about the life, death, and resurrection of Jesus of Nazareth.

Despite the impossible odds against correctly guessing future events, multitudes of false prophets have attempted to make predictions in the past and continue to do so in our generation. However, these human predictions are almost always wrong with the exception of very few lucky guesses. As I noted in my first book, *Armageddon—Appointment with Destiny* (pp. 14, 15), a fascinating study of the predictive claims of New Age psychics called *The Shattered Crystal Ball* proved that these modern psychics are hopelessly wrong in their predictions. "The study analyzed the accuracy of the ten top psychics whose prophecies were published over a three-year period, 1976 to 1979. The study compared all of the published predictions with their subsequent success or failure rate. The results are certainly intriguing: 98 percent of their predictions were totally incorrect! Only 2 percent of their predictions were fulfilled . . . six out of the ten psychics were wrong 100 percent of the time."

Some New Age writers have claimed that several non-biblical prophets such as Nostradamus (A.D. 1555) were able to predict the future correctly. Many modern New Age writers have claimed that Nostradamus actually predicted that Adolf Hitler would be the future leader of Germany in his hundreds of predictions called "centuries." This claim is totally false! In fact, Nostradamus never mentioned Adolf Hitler by name in any of his predictions. The closest he came to "Hitler" was his mention of the word *Ister* in several predictions that the majority of interpreters admit refers clearly to a European river called the Ister River, a tributary of the River Danube. However, some writers who wrote their analysis after World War II have falsely claimed that Nostradamus actually predicted the history of Hitler, the German dictator. Incredibly, they claim that the name "Hitler" is quite close to the word *Histler* which is not all that different from the actual word *Ister* that appeared in Nostradamus's prediction! The New Age writer Erika Cheetham, who wrote *The Final Prophecies of Nostradamus* in 1989, admitted in her book that "until 1936, approximately, all commentators on the Centuries thought that the word referred to the River Danube, the Ister." Even strong supporters of Nostradamus, such as Henry C. Roberts, the editor of *The Complete Prophecies of Nostradamus* (Jericho, N.Y.: Nostradamus, Inc., 1976), admitted in his Introduction that these prophetic writings of Nostradamus are "unintelligible." He wrote that these predictions are "unintelligible and garbled to the uninitiate. The strange, broken, and often incoherent nature of the quatrains, both in French and English, is the hallmark of prophetic media."

Other New Age writers have made great claims for the accuracy of the predictions of Edgar Cayce, the so-called American "sleeping prophet" who lived in the early part of this century. I had the experience of interviewing both Hugh Lynn Cayce, the son of Edgar Cayce, and his grandson in the early 1970s at their research center in Virginia Beach, Virginia. It was fascinating to hear them describe the research they had completed on a manuscript revealing numerous mistaken predictions Edgar Cayce made during his career. Some of these false predictions were prophecies Cayce made about where they could locate oil wells or mineral deposits. Not surprisingly, they indicated that they did not intend to publish the manuscript.

No One but God Knows the Future

The ability of humans to predict future events or trends correctly is virtually non-existent outside of lucky guesses. Despite the great knowledge and genius of mankind, we are unable to predict future events and trends correctly. As examples of this blindness as to the future, consider the following statements. The director of the U.S. Patent Office resigned his high position in 1875. He complained in his letter to the government that there was no point in continuing the Patent Office because "there's nothing left to invent." Since his resignation, we have witnessed an astonishing number of brilliant inventions and developments every year in all areas of knowledge and science. Only a few years later, in 1887, the brilliant French chemist Marcellin Berthelot wrote, "From now on there is no mystery about the universe." In the years that followed, we have seen the mysteries of the atomic structure of matter unfold and the creation of a hundred new sciences including biophysics, astrophysics, and molecular biology. Another great scientist at that time, Professor Simon Newcomb, wrote a highly acclaimed manuscript that proved that it was mathematically impossible for any machine that was heavier than a balloon to fly in the air. Every day thousands of large airplanes take off from thousands of airports carrying a staggering number of passengers throughout the world. An equally brilliant French philosopher by the name of Poincaré ridiculed a scientist's speculations about unleashing the power of the atom through chain reactions in uranium. "Common sense alone is enough to tell us that the destruction of a town by a pound of metal is an evident impossibility." Tragically, the discoveries of awesome nuclear energies locked within the metal uranium allowed scientists to create atomic weapons of staggering power that annihilated two Japanese cities, Hiroshima and Nagasaki, in only seconds with only a few pounds of metal (*Morning of the Magicians,* Louis

Pauwels and Jacques Bergier [New York: Stein and Day, 1964], pp. 9, 10, 14).

More recently, in 1943, Thomas Watson, the chairman of IBM, declared, "I think there is a world market for maybe five computers." Today, the world contains over a billion computer devices. In the 1940s, the first-generation computers were so large that they filled whole rooms and weighed several tons. The magazine *Popular Mechanics* examined the state of scientific knowledge in 1949 and made this forecast about the future of computer development: "Computers in the future may weigh no more than 1.5 tons." Today we have sophisticated computers capable of billions of calculations per second that weigh less than five pounds and are much smaller than a TV set. In 1981, Bill Gates, the brilliant creator of Microsoft, the largest computer software company in history, declared, "640K (640,000 bytes of memory) should be enough for anybody." Little did he realize that in less than fifteen years the average personal desktop computer, such as the Macintosh system Power Tower 180MHz I use, would contain as much as 48MB (48 million bytes) of RAM (Random Access Memory) and 2 billion bytes of fast computer memory on its hard drive. These inaccurate predictions reveal the profound limitations of man's intelligence and his inability to forecast future events correctly.

However, when we turn to the pages of the Holy Scriptures, we discover a staggering number of precise predictions that were made thousands of years ago concerning the future of nations and individuals. A careful analysis of these predictions reveals that every one has been fulfilled with an awesome precision that can only be explained by divine knowledge predicting the event, and the hand of God bringing the event to pass. Let's examine one of the most incredible of the thousands of Old Testament prophecies that actually predicted that rebirth of Israel in the spring of 1948.

Ezekiel Prophesied Israel's 1948 Rebirth

Several years ago, I discovered that God had hidden in the pages of Scripture a precise prophecy about the exact time when He would miraculously restore His chosen people to their ancient Holy Land. While everyone knew that the Scriptures contained numerous prophecies that the Jews would return to Israel in the last days, God's prediction about the exact time of Israel's return to the Promised Land was not revealed until after the fulfillment of the prophecy. In God's divine purpose, many details about the prophecies concerning the last days were sealed in biblical visions in such a way that they could not be clearly discerned prior to their accomplishment. Then, when the prophecy was fulfilled, this confirmed the inspiration of the Scriptures and glorified God. An examination of the prophecies reveals that God often specified in great detail the exact duration of time involved in various predictions concerning Israel. However, times were never given in prophecies that deal with the Church. There are no prophecies that reveal the time of the Rapture. The Lord has specifically hidden the time of the future resurrection of the saints from all but Himself. The Lord Himself told us, "But of that day and hour knoweth no man, no, not the angels of heaven, but my

Father only" (Matthew 24:36). The failure to appreciate this fact has led to many errors in prophetic interpretation. The interpretation of Ezekiel's prediction about the time of Israel's rebirth appeared in my book *Armageddon— Appointment with Destiny* in 1988. Despite the fact that over five hundred thousand people have read this material in various editions and languages of *Armageddon,* no one has been able to refute the accuracy of this incredible biblical prophecy that was given to the prophet Ezekiel when he was taken captive to Babylon twenty-five centuries ago.

Israel's Return to the Land

Israel's relationship to the Holy Land is a major focus of biblical prophecy, both fulfilled and unfulfilled. God prophesied precisely when Israel would return to the Promised Land after her citizens went into exile in the first two captivities, the Egyptian and Babylonian. The Egyptian captivity was prophesied to last exactly 430 years and it is significant that it ended precisely to the day when the 430-year captivity ended. "And it came to pass at the end of the four hundred and thirty years, even the selfsame day it came to pass, that all the hosts of the LORD went out from the land of Egypt" (Exodus 12:41). The prophet Jeremiah predicted the exact duration of the captivity of the Jewish exiles in Babylon would last 70 years. "And this whole land shall be a desolation, and an astonishment; and these nations shall serve the king of Babylon seventy years" (Jeremiah 25:11). The Babylonian army conquered Israel in the spring of 606 B.C. Both secular history and the Bible reveal that, as predicted, the Babylonian Captivity ended exactly 70 years later in the spring of 536 B.C., in the Jewish month Nisan, when the Persian king Cyrus freed the Jews to return to their land (Ezra 1:3).

The three major Jewish prophets, Daniel, Jeremiah, and Ezekiel, were all alive at this time. Naturally, the prophet Ezekiel was aware of the prophet Jeremiah's prophecy that the Jews could return from Babylon after 70 years in 536 B.C. However, God gave him a new revelation that looked much farther into the future revealing how long it would be until the Jewish people would finally re-establish their nation in the last days. The prediction began with God's declaration that "this shall be a sign to the house of Israel" (Ezekiel 4:3). The full prediction is found in Ezekiel 4:3–6: "This will be a sign to the house of Israel. Lie also on your left side, and lay the iniquity of the house of Israel upon it. According to the number of the days that you lie on it, you shall bear their iniquity. For I have laid on you the years of their iniquity, according to the number of the days, three hundred and ninety days; so you shall bear the iniquity of the house of Israel. And when you have completed them, lie again on your right side; then you shall bear the iniquity of the house of Judah forty days. I have laid on you a day for each year" (NKJV).

In this passage the prophet Ezekiel clearly declares that this prophecy would be "a sign to the house of Israel" and that each day represents one biblical year. The prediction revealed that Israel would be punished for a combined period of 430 years (390 years plus another 40 years). The beginning point for this worldwide captivity occurred in the spring of 536 B.C., at the end of the seventy years of predicted captivity in

Babylon (Jeremiah 25:11). However, in the month of Nisan, 536 B.C., only a small remnant of the Jews from the nation of Judah chose to leave their homes in Babylon and return to Jerusalem. The Jewish exiles who remembered their former homes in Israel were now over 70 years old. Their children who had been born in Babylon naturally had little connection or attachment to the former home of their parents. The vast majority were quite happy to remain in the pagan Persian Empire as colonists rather than immigrate six hundred miles to rebuild the devastated colony of Israel. God decreed to Ezekiel a period of punishment of 430 years for Israel's and Judah's sin (390 years + 40 years = 430 years). However, when we deduct the 70 years of punishment the Jews had endured during the 70-year Babylonian captivity, which ended in 536 B.C., there still remained a total of 360 years of further punishment beyond the year 536 B.C. When we examine the history of that period we note that the Jews did not return to establish an independent country at the end of either 360 or 430 years of additional punishment. In light of the precision of Ezekiel's prophecy, it was difficult to understand why nothing occurred at that time to fulfill the detailed prediction.

Both the Bible and history reveal that Israel did not repent of its sins at the end of the seventy-year captivity in Babylon. In fact, the Scriptures record in the books of Ezra and Nehemiah that the minority of fifty thousand who chose to return with Ezra to the Promised Land did so with little faith. The vast majority of the Jews remained in pagan Babylon. They failed to repent of their disobedience, which was the reason God sent them into captivity in the first place.

This majority who refused to immigrate home to Israel, composing more than 95 percent of the Jewish captives, simply settled down as colonists in what is now Iraq-Iran. Over the centuries that followed, travelers such as Benjamin of Tuldela reported that thousands of Jews still lived in several of the cities of present-day Iraq, Iran, and Afghanistan.

I discovered the solution to the mystery of the duration of Israel's worldwide dispersion and return in a divine principle that God revealed to Moses in Leviticus 26. In this chapter, the Lord established promises and punishments for Israel based on her obedience and her disobedience to His commands. God declared to Israel four times in this passage that if, after being punished for her sins, she still did not repent, the punishments previously specified would be multiplied by seven (the number of completion). "And after all this, if you do not obey Me, then I will punish you seven times more for your sins" (Leviticus 26:18, NKJV; see also Leviticus 26:21, 23–24, 27–28). In other words, if Israel failed to repent of her disobedience, the punishments already decreed by God would be multiplied or extended seven times. Since the majority of Israel refused to repent of her sin after the Babylonian Captivity ended, the period of 360 years of further punishment declared by Ezekiel 4:3–6 was multiplied seven times. This meant that the Jews would remain without an independent nation for another 2,520 biblical years from 536 B.C., the beginning point of the prediction (360 years x 7 = 2,520 biblical years).

The Biblical Year of 360 Days

The period of punishment was to last 2,520 biblical years rather than 2,520 calendar years. The reason is that the Bible always used the ancient Jewish calendar composed of 360 days, making up a biblical year, in both the historical and prophetic passages. The true length of the Jewish, biblical prophetic year was only 360 days because it was a lunar-solar year composed of twelve months of thirty days each. The modern solar year of 365.25 days was unknown to the ancient nations in the Old Testament. According to articles on Chronology in the *Encyclopædia Britannica* and *Smith's Bible Dictionary,* Abraham used a 360-day year. The Genesis record of Noah's flood confirms that the ancient year consisted of twelve months of thirty days each. Moses declared in Genesis that the period of 150 days when the flood waters were at their height lasted precisely five months from the seventeenth day of the second month to the seventeenth day of the seventh month, proving that each month consisted of thirty days. Sir Isaac Newton relates that "all nations, before the just length of the solar year was known, reckoned months by the course of the moon, and years by the return of winter and summer, spring and autumn; and in making calendars for their festivals, they reckoned thirty days to a lunar month, and twelve lunar months to a year, taking the nearest round numbers, whence came the division of the ecliptic into 360 degrees."

Therefore, if we wish to understand the precise times involved in the fulfillment of prophecy, we need to calculate using the same biblical lunar-solar year of 360 days that the prophets used. Both the prophet Daniel and John, in the Book of Revelation, clearly used a year of 360 days. The failure to understand the true length of the biblical year as 360 days has prevented some prophecy students from clearly understanding many prophecies that contain a precise time element. This 360-day prophetic year is also borne out in the Book of Revelation where John's vision refers to the future Great Tribulation period. He describes the Great Tribulation of three and one-half years as lasting precisely 1,260 days (Revelation 12:6), "a time and times and half a time" where a "time" in Hebrew stands for a year of 360 days (14), and "forty-two months" of thirty days each (13:5). All of these biblical references confirm that the 360-day biblical year is the one we must use to correctly understand biblical prophecy and chronology.

Therefore, Ezekiel's prophecy of the 430 years declared that the end of Israel's punishment and her final restoration to the land would be accomplished in 2,520 biblical years of 360 days each, which totals precisely 907,200 days. To convert this period into our calendar year of 365.25 days we simply divide the period of 907,200 days by 365.25 days to reach a total of 2,483.8 of our modern calendar years. Therefore, Ezekiel prophesied that the end of Israel's worldwide captivity would occur precisely 2,483.8 years after the end of the Babylonian Captivity, which occurred in the spring of 536 B.C. In these calculations we must keep in mind that there was only one year between 1 B.C. and A.D. 1. There was no year Zero. As an illustration, there were only twelve months between the Feast of Passover on the 14th of Nisan in the spring of 1 B.C. and the next annual Feast of Passover in the spring of A.D. 1.

To Calculate when Ezekiel Prophesied the Jews Would Become a Nation Again

The Babylonian Captivity ended in the spring of 536 B.C.	536.4 B.C. *MINUS*
The duration of Israel's captivity (from Ezekiel 4:3–6)	<u>2,483.8</u> calendar years 1,947.4
To adjust for the fact there was no year Zero between 1 B.C. and A.D. 1, we adjust one year, Therefore the end of Israel's captivity would occur:	1
The Rebirth of Israel	1948–May 15

On the afternoon of May 14, 1948, the Jews proclaimed the independence of the reborn state of Israel. As an old rabbi blew on the traditional shofar, a ram's horn, the Jewish people celebrated the end of their tragic worldwide dispersion and captivity in precise fulfillment of the prophecy made thousands of years earlier by the prophet Ezekiel. At midnight, as May 15, 1948, began, the British Mandate officially ended and Israel became an independent nation. This great day marked the first time since the days of Solomon that a united Israel took its place as a sovereign, independent state among the nations of the world.

In Ezekiel's amazing prophecy we are witnessing a fulfillment of prophecy in our generation of such incredible
precision that one is forced to marvel at the power of God
to foresee and control all of man's plans and their outcomes.
Despite the apparent anarchy of the events of our time, God
is still on the throne of this universe and remains in full
control of events. The universe is unfolding precisely as our
Lord ordained and foresaw millennia ago. In addition, this
amazingly accurate fulfillment of prophecy in our lifetime
should focus our attention on the prophecy of Jesus Christ
about the budding of the fig tree. The Bible used the symbol
of the fig tree or figs in six different passages as an exclusive
symbol of the nation Israel (Judges 9:8-15; Hosea 9:10;
Jeremiah 24:1–10; Matthew 21:18–20, etc.). "Now learn this
parable from the fig tree: When its branch has already
become tender and puts forth leaves, you know that summer
is near. So you also, when you see all these things, know that
it is near—at the doors! Assuredly, I say to you, this generation will by no means pass away till all these things take
place" (Matthew 24:32–34, NKJV). In light of the startling precision of the fulfillment of Ezekiel's prophecy about Israel's
rebirth and the prophecy of Jesus that the generation who
witnessed this rebirth "will by no means pass away till all
these things take place," every one of us should realize that
we are living in the generation when Christ indicated He
will return to judge mankind.

Predictions About Jesus Christ the Messiah

The Old Testament contains over three hundred passages
that refer to the first coming of the Messiah. Within these

hundreds of prophecies, Bible scholars have found forty-eight specific details about the life, death, and resurrection of Jesus. These scriptural prophecies were published over five centuries before Christ was born in Bethlehem. In this chapter we will discuss seventeen of these prophecies, examine the evidence for their fulfillment, and prove that Jesus of Nazareth fulfilled them, showing that He is the promised Messiah, the Son of God.

The Laws of Probability

The study of statistics includes the theory and Laws of Mathematical Probability. The Laws of Probability are not abstract. They are so dependable that huge insurance companies write policies promising to pay a million dollars to the family of a thirty-year-old male in return for a small premium of only $30 per month. How can they take on such a huge risk in return for only $30 in monthly premiums? The answer is found in the Laws of Probability. After careful analysis of the mortality tables, insurance companies know that only a tiny fraction of the thirty-year-old clients they insure will actually die within the next year. Every day, insurance companies risk billions of dollars on similar well-established calculations of mathematical probability.

The Laws of Probability reveal that if the probability of a single event occurring randomly is one chance in five, and the probability of another event occurring is one chance in ten, then the combined probability that both events will occur together in sequence is five multiplied by ten. Thus, the combined chance of both events occurring in sequence is one chance in fifty. To put this in a perspective we can appreciate, consider the odds when we toss a coin in the air. Since a coin has two sides, the odds are 50 percent or one chance in two that you will get "heads" when you toss a dime. However, suppose that you toss two dimes in a row. What are the odds against getting "heads" twice in a row? The answer is four. The combined odds are 2 x 2 = 4. The odds of tossing ten coins in a row and getting ten "heads" one after another are quite staggering. According to the laws of probability, the odds against getting ten "heads" are one chance in 1,024. Don't bet your salary that you can beat such odds. However, when you consider the odds against these seventeen prophecies about the life and death of Jesus Christ happening by chance, you will realize that the evidence proves that Jesus was the promised Messiah and the Savior of all who will believe in Him.

To further prove the inspiration and authority of the Bible, let us examine only one area of specific prophecy, out of literally hundreds, that has to do with the life and death of the coming Messiah who will save humanity from their sins. In this chapter we will examine a series of specific predictions that were made by different Jewish prophets who lived in widely separated communities over a period of a thousand years. These predictions were fulfilled over five hundred years after they were recorded. We will also examine the possibility that these individual predictions could have occurred by random chance alone. After considering the evidence presented in this chapter, you will understand that the precise fulfillment of these different predictions in the life of one man was so improbable that any unbiased observer must accept that the Bible was truly inspired by God and that Jesus Christ is the promised Messiah.

Seventeen Incredible Prophecies About the Messiah

In this chapter we will examine seventeen specific prophecies in this analysis of Old Testament predictions that were fulfilled in the life of Jesus of Nazareth. As you consider the likelihood that any one of these particular prophecies could have occurred by chance, ask yourself if it was possible that all seventeen of these predictions could have been fulfilled by random chance in the life of one man, Jesus Christ.

The Old Testament Predictions About the Coming Messiah

The odds against these events occurring by chance

The First Prediction:
His birth in Bethlehem from the tribe of Judah.

Probability: 1 chance in 2,400

The Old Testament Prediction:

"But you, Bethlehem Ephrathah, though you are little among the thousands of Judah, yet out of you shall come forth to Me the One to be Ruler in Israel, whose goings forth are from of old, from everlasting" (Micah 5:2, NKJV).

"The scepter shall not depart from Judah, nor a lawgiver from between his feet, until Shiloh comes; and to Him shall be the obedience of the people" (Genesis 49:10, NKJV).

The New Testament Fulfillment:
"Now after Jesus was born in Bethlehem of Judea in the days of Herod the king, behold, wise men from the East came to Jerusalem" (Matthew 2:1, NKJV).

There were twelve tribes in ancient Israel from which the Messiah could have been born. Yet He was born from the tribe of Judah as Moses predicted fifteen hundred years earlier. Since there were twelve tribes, the odds were 12 to 1 against Moses guessing correctly the tribe of Christ's birth. In addition, there were over two thousand villages and towns in the densely populated area allotted to the tribe of Judah during the first century of this era. However, to be conservative I used the figure of 1 chance in 2,400 to estimate the odds against anyone guessing that He would be born in Bethlehem and that He would descend from the tribe of Judah centuries before Jesus was born.

The Second Prediction:
He would be preceded by a messenger.

Probability: 1 chance in 20

The Old Testament Prediction:
"The voice of one crying in the wilderness: 'Prepare the way of the LORD; make straight in the desert a highway for our God'" (Isaiah 40:3, NKJV).

The New Testament Fulfillment:
"In those days John the Baptist came preaching in the wilderness of Judea, and saying, 'Repent, for the kingdom of heaven is at hand!'" (Matthew 3:1–2, NKJV).

I estimated the odds as 1 in 20, but historical records do not reveal any other king to my knowledge who was preceded by a messenger such as John the Baptist. To calculate the combined probability of these two predictions we must multiply 2,400 times 20, which equals only one chance in 48,000 that Jesus would fulfill both predictions by chance.

The Third Prediction:
He would enter Jerusalem on a colt.

Probability: 1 chance in 50

The Old Testament Prediction:
"Rejoice greatly, O daughter of Zion! Shout, O daughter of Jerusalem! Behold, your King is coming to you; He is just and having salvation, lowly and riding on a donkey, a colt, the foal of a donkey" (Zechariah 9:9, NKJV).

The New Testament Fulfillment:
"Then they brought him to Jesus. And they threw their own clothes on the colt, and they set Jesus on him. And as He went, many spread their clothes on the road. Then, as He was now drawing near the descent of the Mount of Olives, the whole multitude of the disciples began to rejoice and praise God with a loud voice for all the mighty works they had seen" (Luke 19:35–37, NKJV).

Of all the kings of history I do not know of a single king who ever entered his capital on a colt, as Jesus did on Palm Sunday, A.D. 32, in fulfillment of this prophecy. The combined odds of the three predictions occurring by chance are 50 x 48,000, which equals one chance in

2,400,000. With the addition of every subsequent prediction, the laws of probability reveal that the combined odds against anyone fulfilling these multiple prophecies are simply astronomical.

The Fourth Prediction:
He would be betrayed by a friend.

Probability: 1 chance in 10

The Old Testament Prediction:
"Even my own familiar friend in whom I trusted, who ate my bread, has lifted up his heel against me" (Psalm 41:9, NKJV).

The New Testament Fulfillment:
"And while He was still speaking, behold, Judas, one of the twelve, with a great multitude with swords and clubs, came from the chief priests and elders of the people. Now His betrayer had given them a sign, saying, 'Whomever I kiss, He is the One; seize Him'" (Matthew 26:47–48, NKJV).

Although it is not that unusual for a secular king to be betrayed by a close associate, the betrayal of a religious leader is quite unusual historically. However, to be conservative, I have assigned the odds of this occurring by chance as only one chance in ten. The combined probability for these four predictions (10 x 2,400,000) is now only one chance in 24 million.

The Fifth Prediction:
His hands and feet would be pierced.

Probability: 1 chance in 100

The Old Testament Prediction:
"For dogs have surrounded Me; the congregation of the wicked has enclosed Me. They pierced My hands and My feet" (Psalm 22:16, NKJV).

The New Testament Fulfillment:
"And when they had come to the place called Calvary, there they crucified Him, and the criminals, one on the right hand and the other on the left" (Luke 23:33, NKJV).

The combined probability of these five predictions (10 x 24 million) has now reached an astonishing one chance in 2.4 billion.

The Sixth Prediction:
He would be wounded by His enemies.

Probability: 1 chance in 10

The Old Testament Prediction:
"But he was wounded for our transgressions, he was bruised for our iniquities: the chastisement of our peace was upon him; and with his stripes we are healed" (Isaiah 53:5).

The New Testament Fulfillment:
"Then released he Barabbas unto them; and when he had scourged Jesus, he delivered him to be crucified" (Matthew 27:26).

Throughout history most kings who were killed were murdered suddenly. Very few were ever subjected to torture as was inflicted on our Lord Jesus Christ. The odds against this occurring by chance were less than one chance in ten.

The combined odds for the six predictions (10 x 2.4 billion) now rise to one chance in 24 billion.

The Seventh Prediction:
His betrayal for 30 pieces of silver

Probability: 1 chance in 50

The Old Testament Prediction:
"Then I said to them, 'If it is agreeable to you, give me my wages; and if not, refrain.' So they weighed out for my wages thirty pieces of silver" (Zechariah 11:12, NKJV).

The New Testament Fulfillment:
"'What are you willing to give me if I deliver Him to you?' And they counted out to him thirty pieces of silver" (Matthew 26:15, NKJV).

Consider how impossible it would be to correctly predict five hundred years in advance the exact price of betrayal that would be paid for the death of a future king. The odds (50 x 24 billion) now rise to one chance in one trillion, two hundred billion.

The Eighth Prediction:
He will be spit upon and beaten.

Probability: 1 chance in 10

The Old Testament Prediction:
"I gave My back to those who struck Me, and My cheeks to those who plucked out the beard; I did not hide My face from shame and spitting" (Isaiah 50:6, NKJV).

The New Testament Fulfillment:

"Then they spat in His face and beat Him; and others struck Him with the palms of their hands" (Matthew 26:67, NKJV).

Although many kings throughout history were killed, very few were tormented, beaten, and ridiculed. However, Jesus Christ bore those stripes for our healing and salvation. The odds of these eight predictions (10 x one trillion, two hundred billion) occurring by chance are now one chance in 12 trillion.

The Ninth Prediction:
His betrayal money would be thrown into
the Temple and then given to buy a potter's field.

Probability: 1 chance in 200

The Old Testament Prediction:

"And the LORD said to me, 'Throw it to the potter'—that princely price they set on me. So I took the thirty pieces of silver and threw them into the house of the LORD for the potter" (Zechariah 11:13, NKJV).

The New Testament Fulfillment:

"Then he threw down the pieces of silver in the temple and departed, and went and hanged himself. But the chief priests took the silver pieces and said, 'It is not lawful to put them into the treasury, because they are the price of blood.' And they consulted together and bought with them the potter's field, to bury strangers in" (Matthew 27:5-7, NKJV).

This complicated prophecy actually seems contradictory on its surface. However, despite its apparent impossibility every detail of this prophecy was fulfilled in precise detail. Judas threw the thirty pieces of betrayal money into the Temple. Later the priests used this money to purchase a potter's field to bury strangers, including Judas, who, overcome with guilt, hanged himself. I calculated the odds extremely conservatively as one chance in 200. However, the combined odds (200 x 12 trillion) against these nine predictions occurring have risen to one chance in 2,400 trillion.

The Tenth Prediction:
He would be silent before His accusers.

Probability: 1 chance in 100

The Old Testament Prediction:
"He was oppressed and He was afflicted, yet He opened not His mouth; He was led as a lamb to the slaughter, and as a sheep before its shearers is silent, so He opened not His mouth" (Isaiah 53:7, NKJV).

The New Testament Fulfillment:
"And while He was being accused by the chief priests and elders, He answered nothing. Then Pilate said to Him, 'Do You not hear how many things they testify against You?' But He answered him not one word, so that the governor marveled greatly" (Matthew 27:12–14, NKJV).

When we are accused of a crime we naturally defend ourselves, even when we are guilty. Consider how unlikely this prediction was that a totally innocent man would stand before His accusers in absolute silence without speaking to defend Himself. While I assigned the odds as one chance in one hundred, the realistic chances against this event occurring are much higher. The odds against these ten predictions occurring (100 x 2,400 trillion) is now one chance in 24,000 trillion.

The Eleventh Prediction:
He would be crucified with thieves.

Probability: 1 chance in 100

The Old Testament Prediction:
"Therefore I will divide Him a portion with the great, and He shall divide the spoil with the strong, because He poured out His soul unto death, and He was numbered with the transgressors, and He bore the sin of many, and made intercession for the transgressors" (Isaiah 53:12, NKJV).

The New Testament Fulfillment:
"Then two robbers were crucified with Him, one on the right and another on the left" (Matthew 27:38).

The continued multiplication of these odds reaches a truly staggering number when we examine the chances that all seventeen prophecies occurred by chance. At the end of this analysis I will give the final calculation of these incredible odds.

The Twelfth Prediction:
People would gamble for His garments.

Probability: 1 chance in 100

The Old Testament Prediction:
"They divide My garments among them, and for My clothing they cast lots" (Psalm 22:18, NKJV).

The New Testament Fulfillment:

"Then the soldiers, when they had crucified Jesus, took His garments and made four parts, to each soldier a part, and also the tunic. Now the tunic was without seam, woven from the top in one piece. They said therefore among themselves, 'Let us not tear it, but cast lots for it, whose it shall be,' that the Scripture might be fulfilled which says: 'They divided My garments among them, and for My clothing they cast lots'" (John 19:23–24, NKJV).

Think of how unlikely it was that Roman soldiers would bother to gamble to see who would win the right to claim the garments of a crucified prisoner. Yet the prophecy was fulfilled precisely.

The Thirteenth Prediction:
His side would be pierced.

Probability: 1 chance in 100

The Old Testament Prediction:

"And I will pour on the house of David and on the inhabitants of Jerusalem the Spirit of grace and supplication; then they will look on Me whom they pierced. Yes they will mourn for Him as one mourns for his only son, and grieve for Him as one grieves for a firstborn" (Zechariah 12:10, NKJV).

The New Testament Fulfillment:

"But one of the soldiers pierced His side with a spear, and immediately blood and water came out" (John 19:34, NKJV).

The cruelty of the Romans was expressed in the unspeakable pain inflicted on prisoners in their lengthy death on the cross. However, despite their orders to produce a drawn-out death, the Roman centurion was motivated by God to pierce Christ's side with his spear. The blood and water flowing out of Christ's side proved that He had already died before the spear entered His side. The odds against anyone plunging a spear into the side of a man being crucified on a cross is estimated conservatively as one chance in 100.

The Fourteenth Prediction:
None of His bones would be broken.

Probability: 1 chance in 20

The Old Testament Prediction:
"He keepeth all his bones; Not one of them is broken" (Psalm 34:20).

The New Testament Fulfillment:
"But when they came to Jesus and saw that He was already dead, they did not break His legs" (John 19:33, NKJV).

When a prisoner of Rome was crucified, his body was placed on the cross in such a manner that the only way he could breathe was by painfully lifting his upper body, using the strength of his legs to expand his diaphragm. When the Roman soldiers wished to speed up the death of the condemned prisoner, they would break his legs with a club and thus prevent him from lifting himself up to breathe. Within minutes the prisoner would die due to oxygen deprivation and fluid accumulating in his lungs. To avoid desecrating the Sabbath, which was about to begin, the soldiers broke the legs of the prisoners on both sides of Jesus to assure their quick death. However, in fulfillment of the ancient prophecy, Jesus had already "given up the ghost" and died by His own will. Therefore, they did not break Christ's legs and thus fulfilled the prophecy.

The Fifteenth Prediction:
His body would not decay.

Probability: 1 chance in 10,000

The Old Testament Prediction:
"For You will not leave my soul in Sheol, nor will You allow Your Holy One to see corruption" (Psalm 16:10, NKJV).

The New Testament Fulfillment:
"He, foreseeing this, spoke concerning the resurrection of the Christ, that His soul was not left in Hades, nor did His flesh see corruption" (Acts 2:31, NKJV).

Obviously, the odds against anyone dying and their body not decaying, but later rising from the dead, are astronomical. However, I have estimated the odds as only one chance in 10,000 because several individuals were resurrected in the Old Testament, such as the Shunammite widow's son who was raised from the dead by Elisha (2 Kings 4:28–37).

The Sixteenth Prediction:
His burial in a rich man's tomb

Probability: 1 chance in 100

The Old Testament Prediction:

"And they made His grave with the wicked—but with the rich at His death, because He had done no violence, nor was any deceit in His mouth" (Isaiah 53:9, NKJV).

The New Testament Fulfillment:

"Now when evening had come, there came a rich man from Arimathaea, named Joseph, who himself had also become a disciple of Jesus. This man went to Pilate and asked for the body of Jesus. Then Pilate commanded the body to be given to him. When Joseph had taken the body, he wrapped it in a clean linen cloth, and laid it in his new tomb which he had hewn out of the rock; and he rolled a large stone against the door of the tomb, and departed" (Matthew 27:57–60, NKJV).

The probable site of the tomb of Christ is located just north of the Damascus Gate of the old walled city of Jerusalem, only a few hundred yards from the probable site of Golgotha. When the tomb was discovered in the last century, archeologists found that only one body depression was ever used. The owner did not complete the stone carving work to bury a second body. In addition, they found a huge cistern capable of holding 200,000 gallons of water beneath the garden, indicating that it was a rich man's garden tomb. Furthermore, they found the remains of an ancient wine press in the garden.

The Seventeenth Prediction:
The darkness covering the earth

Probability: 1 chance in 1,000

The Old Testament Prediction:

"'And it shall come to pass in that day,' says the Lord GOD, 'that I will make the sun go down at noon, and I will darken the earth in broad daylight'" (Amos 8:9, NKJV).

The New Testament Fulfillment:

"Now from the sixth hour until the ninth hour there was darkness over all the land" (Matthew 27:45, NKJV).

Although this prophecy is one of the most incredible of the seventeen, the *Third History of Thallus,* by a pagan historian of the third century, reported that there was an unusual darkness that blotted out the sun for a number of hours at the time of Passover in the year A.D. 32, the year of Christ's crucifixion. Although Thallus speculated that this darkness was the result of an eclipse, any astronomer can tell you that it is absolutely impossible that an eclipse could have occurred at that time, because Passover was carefully calculated to occur at the time of the full moon. The positions of the sun, moon, and earth at the time of the full moon make it impossible that this darkness recorded by the historian Thallus could have been the result of a natural eclipse. However, his report does confirm that the Bible's prophecy and the New Testament record of its fulfillment are accurate.

This analysis has shown that seventeen detailed prophecies, made five centuries before the birth of Jesus of Nazareth, were fulfilled with absolute precision in the life, death, and resurrection of Jesus Christ. The question to consider is this: What are the chances that all seventeen of these predictions occurred by chance rather than by the divine plan of God? Either these seventeen predictions are simply the result of chance or this evidence provides overwhelming proof that God inspired the Bible and is in control of history.

The combined probability **against** these 17 predictions occurring is equal to

1 chance in 480,000,000,000,000,000,000,000,000,000,000
   or
1 chance in 480 billion x 1 billion x 1 trillion

In other words, there is only one chance in 480 billion x 1 billion x 1 trillion that these Old Testament prophets could have accurately predicted these seventeen specific prophecies about the life, death, and resurrection of Jesus Christ by chance alone. The odds are equally impossible that any man could have fulfilled these detailed prophecies by chance alone. Let any reader assign any other estimates they might choose for these probabilities that these predictions occurred. Regardless of the size of the estimates for probability you assign to these individual predictions, you will still be confronted with a combined probability so staggering in its magnitude that it will be impossible to convince yourself honestly that these things occurred by chance. In the unlikely event that you still are not convinced, consider the fact that we have examined only seventeen of the forty-eight major prophecies given in the Old Testament about the promised Messiah. If we were to calculate the odds against all forty-eight predictions occurring by chance, we would arrive at a number so large that it would exceed our capacity to comprehend it.

Some Bible critics have suggested that Jesus of Nazareth, as a rabbi, knew about these predictions and simply arranged the events of His life to fulfill them. However, consider the impossibility of any normal human arranging the fulfillment of these specific predictions. How would you arrange to be born in Bethlehem and manage to be descended from the tribe of Judah? How would you arrange the price of your betrayal to be precisely thirty pieces of silver? How would you arrange to be crucified with thieves and then to be buried in a rich man's grave? Obviously, only God could either foresee these events in advance or fulfill these precise predictions in the life of Jesus Christ.

These Prophecies Prove the Bible Is Inspired by God

When we consider these seventeen specific Messianic prophecies, the odds against any one person fulfilling these predictions by chance alone are absolutely astronomical. To fully grasp the reality that these fulfilled prophecies prove that Jesus Christ is the promised Messiah and Son of God, consider the following illustration:

First, the odds against the prophets correctly guessing all seventeen prophecies are:

1 chance in 480 billion x 1 billion x 1 trillion!

Next, to fully grasp these incredible odds we must try to get a picture of these odds in our minds. Imagine that every one of these chances was represented by a small grain of sand. Furthermore, imagine that a single grain of sand is painted gold and represents the one chance out of this astronomical number that Christ fulfilled these predictions by chance. We are going to blindfold you and ask you to search for the single gold-painted grain of sand. Imagine that the entire galaxy known as the Milky Way, encompassing two hundred million stars like our sun plus millions of planets, moons, and asteroids, is composed only of these 480 billion x 1 billion x 1 trillion grains of sand. In a galaxy filled with this incredible number of grains of sand, your target is the only grain of sand that is painted gold. Remember the galaxy is so vast that if you could travel in the starship Enterprise at the speed of light, 186,000 miles per second, it would still take you a hundred thousand years to cross the galaxy. If we were to blindfold you and send you blindly searching through our entire galaxy to find a single gold-painted grain of sand, you would face the same impossible odds in finding the gold grain of sand as the odds against these seventeen prophecies occurring by chance alone.

With such odds against you, would you bet a thousand dollars that you would find a single grain in a whole galaxy filled with sand? I doubt that you would risk your money on such impossible odds. Yet, tragically, every year millions will die who have bet their lives and their eternal souls on the "chance" that these fulfilled prophecies about Jesus Christ are not reliable. They believe they can safely ignore the claims of Christ upon their lives. However, in light of the overwhelming evidence for the authority of the Bible and the reality of Jesus Christ as God's Messiah, each of us needs to personally consider the decision we must make about our response to Christ's life, death, and resurrection.

In light of the Bible's own declaration that fulfilled prophecy is the absolute proof that it was written under the direct inspiration of God, I believe the evidence in this chapter provides a staggering level of proof for the authority of the Scriptures.

Nine

Evidence from Prophecies Fulfilled in Our Generation

> *"Now as He sat on the Mount of Olives, the disciples came to Him privately, saying, 'Tell us, when will these things be? And what will be the sign of Your coming, and of the end of the age?'"*

> (Matthew 24:3, NKJV)

One of the greatest proofs that the Bible is inspired is the evidence of thousands of detailed prophecies that were fulfilled to the smallest particular throughout history. Centuries before the events occurred the ancient prophets foretold the rise and fall of empires and cities including Babylon, Tyre, and Nineveh. However, in the balance of this chapter, I would like to examine several astonishing prophecies that were fulfilled in our lifetime that prove the Bible's inspiration and also point to the nearness of Christ's return.

For thousands of years, men have studied the Bible's ancient prophecies and wondered if they would live to witness the return of Christ to redeem the earth. Many today are longing for the return of Jesus Christ. Naturally, skeptics remind us that past generations also looked for the Second Coming but never saw the promise fulfilled. Why should we believe our generation will witness the return of Christ when other generations were disappointed? Thirty years of study of Bible prophecies have convinced me of the overwhelming evidence that Christ will likely return in our lifetime. Jesus and the other prophets described numerous prophecies that would occur in the lifetime of those who would see Him return with their own eyes. Is ours the generation that will see Christ coming for His Church? The answer to this question will have profound implications for our life, our witnessing, and our priorities.

In this chapter we will examine numerous prophecies relating to the last days and the biblical passages where the original prophecies were announced over two thousand years ago. Each of these prophecies is a unique event that was never fulfilled in any other generation. By their very nature, many of these predictions could not be fulfilled again in another generation. Our Lord Jesus Christ warned, "Now when these things begin to happen, look up and lift up your heads, because your redemption draws near" (Luke 21:28, NKJV). Let's examine in detail several of these fascinating predictions to illustrate the tremendous precision of biblical prophecies as proof that God inspired the writers of the Bible.

The Rebirth of Israel

The rebirth of Israel is one of the most extraordinary and unlikely of all the prophecies in the Bible. In an earlier portion of this book, we examined the marvelous precision of the prophecy in which Ezekiel predicted that Israel would be reborn in the spring of 1948.

Jesus Christ foretold the rebirth of Israel in His famous prophecy of the "fig tree" budding that was recorded in Matthew's Gospel. Our Lord declared in Matthew 24:32–35: "Now learn a parable of the fig tree; when his branch is yet tender, and putteth forth leaves, ye know that summer is nigh: So likewise ye, when ye shall see all these things, know that it is near, even at the doors. Verily I say unto you, This generation shall not pass, till all these things be fulfilled. Heaven and earth shall pass away, but my words shall not pass away." No other ancient nation ever ceased to exist for a period of centuries and then returned to take its place on the stage of world history. "Who hath heard such a thing? who hath seen such things? Shall the earth be made to bring forth in one day? or shall a nation be born at once? for as soon as Zion travailed, she brought forth her children" (Isaiah 66:8).

Most nations evolved gradually over the centuries, such as Egypt or France. In the time of the ancient prophecies, no one had ever witnessed a nation being created "in one day." Yet, in his prediction, Isaiah prophesied that Israel would come into existence in "one day." The prophecies of Isaiah and Ezekiel were fulfilled precisely as predicted on May 15, 1948.

Predictions About the Present Arab-Israeli Conflict

However, the prophecies surrounding the rebirth of Israel did not stop with the declaration of Israel's independence in 1948. Three thousand years ago, God inspired King David to predict that the reborn nation of Israel would be immediately surrounded by enemies, including the Arab nations of Jordan, Egypt, Saudi Arabia, and Syria. "For, lo, thine enemies make a tumult: and they that hate thee have lifted up the head. They have taken crafty counsel against thy people, and consulted against thy hidden ones. They have said, Come, and let us cut them off from being a nation; that the name of Israel may be no more in remembrance. For they have consulted together with one consent: they are confederate against thee: The tabernacles of Edom, and the Ishmaelites; of Moab, and the Hagarenes; Gebal, and Ammon, and Amalek; the Philistines with the inhabitants of Tyre; Assur also is joined with them: they have holpen the children of Lot. Selah" (Psalm 83:2–8). In this incredible prophecy, David described the modern states of the Middle East by naming the ancient nations that have now joined with the Palestinians in their attempt to destroy the Jewish state in the last days.

The Miraculous Restoration of the Hebrew Language

The prophet Zephaniah had predicted something as equally impossible as the rebirth of Israel. God predicted through His prophet Zephaniah that He would restore the ancient dead language of Hebrew as the living, spoken language of Israel. Hebrew ceased to be the common language of the Jews long before the life of Christ. "For then will I turn to the people a pure language, that they may all call upon the name of the LORD, to serve him with one consent" (Zephaniah 3:9). No other nation has ever lost its language and later recovered it. No one is speaking ancient Egyptian or Chaldee today. A Jewish scholar by the name of Eliazar ben Yehuda began working earlier in this century in Israel, in his attempt to revive the dead language of Hebrew with its original seven thousand words related to Temple worship as used by the priests. He invented thousands of new words for fountain pen, airplane, etc. Ultimately, Eliazar created modern Hebrew as the living language of five million

Israelis. As the Jews began to return from seventy different nations to their Promised Land in 1948 after two thousand years of exile, the government and army began to unify these widely divergent peoples into a united people through teaching them the revived Hebrew language. The Jews of Israel will someday fulfill the prophecy of Zephaniah by calling "upon the name of the Lord, to serve him with one consent."

The Return of the Ethiopian Jews to Israel

The prophet Zephaniah predicted another seemingly impossible prophecy when he declared that God would return the Ethiopian Jews to the land of Israel after they were separated from their Jewish brethren for almost three thousand years. In the days of King Solomon, a group of Jews from each of the twelve tribes immigrated to Ethiopia with Prince Menelik, the son of King Solomon, and the Queen of Sheba, as detailed in my book *Armageddon*. The prophet foretold their return to their homeland in the last days in these words, "From beyond the rivers of Ethiopia my suppliants, even the daughter of my dispersed, shall bring mine offering" (Zephaniah 3:10). Another prophet, Isaiah, also confirmed this prediction. "I will say to the north, Give up; and to the south, Keep not back: bring my sons from far, and my daughters from the ends of the earth" (Isaiah 43:6). Isaiah predicted the miraculous return of the Jews from both Russia (the north) and from Ethiopia (the south). In the later part of the 1980s, and especially in 1991, over eighty-five thousand black Jews returned home to Israel from Ethiopia in fulfillment of Zephaniah's ancient prophecy.

Ezekiel 37:21 and numerous other prophecies foretold of the return of the exiles to the Holy Land.

The Astonishing Fertility of Israel

In addition to recovering their homeland, their lost language, and their exiles, the prophet Isaiah predicted that Israel would become fertile again. "He shall cause them that come of Jacob to take root: Israel shall blossom and bud, and fill the face of the world with fruit" (Isaiah 27:6). The returning Jews have transformed the previously deserted and desolate land into the most agriculturally efficient land on earth according to the United Nations. Israel now supplies over 90 percent of the citrus fruit consumed by hundreds of millions of Europeans. Another prophecy connected with Israel's return was made by the prophet Joel who declared that the desert nation of Israel would experience tremendous increases of rain in the last days. "Be glad then, ye children of Zion, and rejoice in the LORD your God: for he hath given you the former rain moderately, and he will cause to come down for you the rain, the former rain, and the latter rain in the first month" (Joel 2:23). As the rainfall increased dramatically by over 10 percent every decade for the last century, the returning Jewish exiles planted over two hundred million trees and transformed the complete environment of the Promised Land. "And the parched ground shall become a pool, and the thirsty land springs of water: in the habitation of dragons, where each lay, shall be grass with reeds and rushes" (Isaiah 35:7).

Another curious prediction was found in Ezekiel 38 which claimed that Israel would dwell "without walls or gates" in the last days. In the ancient past even small villages, as well as cities, depended on walls for defense against invading armies. Yet God inspired Ezekiel to record the following verse in his prophecy about the coming Russian-Arab invasion of Israel. "And thou shalt say, I will go up to the land of unwalled villages; I will go to them that are at rest that dwell safely, all of them dwelling without walls, and having neither bars nor gates" (Ezekiel 38:11). How could Ezekiel have known twenty-five centuries ago that the development of modern weapons such as bombs, airplanes, and missiles would have made walls and gates irrelevant for defensive purposes in the last days? Even army bases and Israel's settlements in the West Bank and Gaza have no walls today.

Israel's Plans to Rebuild the Temple

The Bible contains numerous prophecies that tell us that Israel will rebuild the Temple in the last days. The prophet Isaiah wrote, "And it shall come to pass in the last days, that the mountain of the LORD's house shall be established in the top of the mountains, and shall be exalted above the hills; and all nations shall flow unto it" (Isaiah 2:2). In the Book of Revelation (11:1–2) John tells us that the angel took him into the future to measure the Temple that will exist during the seven-year tribulation period. The apostle Paul confirms this in his prophecy about the Antichrist occupying the future Temple. "Let no man deceive you by any means: for that day shall not come, except there come a falling away first, and that man of sin be revealed, the son of perdition; who opposeth and exalteth himself above all that is called God, or that is worshipped; so that he as God sitteth in the temple of God, shewing himself that he is God" (2 Thessalonians 2:3–4). The prophet Ezekiel described his vision of the future Temple with Levites and priests worshiping God: "And thou shalt give to the priests the Levites that be of the seed of Zadok, which approach unto me, to minister unto me, saith the Lord GOD, a young bullock for a sin offering" (Ezekiel 43:19).

The Oil of Anointing

One of the most unusual aspects of the ancient Tabernacle and Temple was the oil of anointing that was specially prepared with five specific ingredients to anoint the Temple and the High Priests. Moses described God's command to Israel: "And thou shalt make it an oil of holy ointment, an ointment compound after the art of the apothecary: it shall be an holy anointing oil. And thou shalt anoint the tabernacle of the congregation therewith, and the ark of the testimony" (Exodus 30:25–26). One of the five ingredients needed to make the oil was afars'mon. However, the oil and its ingredients were lost, seemingly forever, when the Romans destroyed the Temple in A.D. 70 and burned the only two groves where afars'mon trees grew. Without this special ingredient, they could never obey God's command to anoint the rebuilt Temple.

In addition, the prophet Daniel foretold that, when the Messiah returns, He will be anointed with this oil of anointing. "Seventy weeks are determined upon thy people and upon thy holy city, to finish the transgression, and to make an end of sins, and to make reconciliation for iniquity, and to bring in everlasting righteousness, and to seal up the vision and prophecy, and to *anoint the most Holy*" (Daniel 9:24, italics added). How could these prophecies be fulfilled when some of the key ingredients were lost forever? Incredibly, Dr. Joseph Patrich of Hebrew University found a clay flask buried near the Dead Sea caves filled with the ancient oil of anointing. Scientists confirmed that the oil is two thousand years old and is composed of the precise ingredients described in Exodus 30:25–26. (Associated Press, February 16, 1989).

Vessels for the Future Temple Worship

Ezekiel foretold that the sacred vessels and linen robes will be prepared for use in the Temple in the Millennium. "They shall enter into my sanctuary, and they shall come near to my table, to minister unto me, and they shall keep my charge. And it shall come to pass, that when they enter in at the gates of the inner court, they shall be clothed with linen garments; and no wool shall come upon them, whiles they minister in the gates of the inner court, and within" (Ezekiel 44:16–17). It is significant that the Temple Institute in the Old City of Jerusalem has prepared over seventy-five of the objects, vessels, and linen priestly garments required for future Temple services. The yeshivas, or Jewish Bible colleges in Jerusalem, have trained over five hundred young men from the tribe of Levi to correctly fulfill their future duties of Temple worship and sacrifice. The prophecies describe the resumption of the sacrifice of the Ashes of the Red Heifer to produce the waters of purification (Numbers 19) needed to cleanse the defiled Temple objects, the priests, and the stones on the Temple Mount. The prophet Ezekiel confirmed that the waters of purification will be used to cleanse the future Temple and the Jewish people. "Then will I sprinkle clean water upon you, and ye shall be clean: from all your filthiness, and from all your idols, will I cleanse you" (Ezekiel 36:25).

The Revival of the Roman Empire

The Bible foretold the revival of the Roman Empire in the final generation when the Messiah will return to establish His eternal kingdom: "And the fourth kingdom shall be strong as iron: forasmuch as iron breaketh in pieces and subdueth all things: and as iron that breaketh all these, shall it break in pieces and bruise. And whereas thou sawest the feet and toes, part of potters' clay, and part of iron, the kingdom shall be divided; but there shall be in it of the strength of the iron, forasmuch as thou sawest the iron mixed with miry clay. And as the toes of the feet were part of iron, and part of clay, so the kingdom shall be partly strong, and partly broken. And whereas thou sawest iron mixed with miry clay, they shall mingle themselves with the seed of men: but they shall not cleave one to another, even as iron is not mixed with clay. And in the days of these kings shall the God of heaven set up a kingdom, which shall never be destroyed: and the kingdom shall not be left to other people, but it shall break in pieces and consume all these kingdoms, and it shall stand for ever" (Daniel 2:40–44). Other prophecies in Daniel 7 and Revelation 13 and 17 confirm the revival of the Roman Empire in the last days in the unique form of a ten-nation superstate. Following the devastation of two world wars, the leadership of Europe came together after World War II to plan the creation of a confederate form of superstate bringing the major nations of Europe together for the first time since the days of Rome. In 1957, six countries signed the Treaty of Rome, laying the foundation for the future United States of Europe. Henri Spaak, the former secretary-general of NATO, admitted in a BBC documentary on the European Union that "we felt like Romans on that day. . . . We were consciously re-creating the Roman Empire once more." Since then, the Maastricht Treaty consolidated the fifteen nations of the European Union into the world's first superstate. It is now an economic, political, and potentially, military colossus that will dominate world events in the near future.

The Rebuilding of Babylon

One of the most unusual of the Bible's prophecies reveals that the city of Babylon will be rebuilt and later destroyed by God at Armageddon by supernatural fire from heaven like Sodom and Gomorrah. The prophet Isaiah foretold this destruction as follows: "Howl ye; for the day of the LORD is at hand; it shall come as a destruction from the Almighty. . . . And Babylon, the glory of kingdoms, the beauty of the Chaldees' excellency, shall be as when God overthrew Sodom and Gomorrah" (Isaiah 13:6, 19). In this remarkable prediction, the prophet declared that Babylon will not only exist again but it will be destroyed on the Great Day of the Lord. As unlikely as it seems, the Iraqi government of Saddam Hussein has spent over one billion dollars rebuilding the ancient city of Babylon and intends that it will become the center of their future renewed Babylonian Empire. Interestingly, the whole city of Babylon was built over an underground lake of asphalt and oil. God has already provided the fuel for its final destruction. In another prophecy, God foretold that the wicked city will burn forever. "For it is the day of the LORD's vengeance, and the year of recompences for the controversy of Zion. And the streams thereof shall be turned into pitch, and the dust thereof into brimstone, and the land thereof shall become burning pitch. It shall not be quenched night nor day; the smoke thereof shall go up for ever: from generation to generation it shall lie waste; none shall pass through it for ever and ever" (Isaiah 34:8-10). Several years ago during the Gulf War, we had a foretaste of this burning of Babylon when Saddam Hussein set hundreds of Kuwaiti oil wells on fire and covered the desert with smoke and fire.

One World Government

Over two thousand years ago, the prophets Daniel and John described that there would be a global world government led by the coming dictator, the Antichrist, in the last days (Daniel 7:14). "And it was given unto him to make war with the saints, and to overcome them: and power was given him over all kindreds, and tongues, and nations. And all that dwell upon the earth shall worship him" (Revelation 13:7–8). There has never been a world government during thousands of years of human history. However, as I outlined in my last book, *Final Warning*, the elite are moving behind the scenes to produce a world government as quickly as possible. The rising powers of the United Nations, the World Trade Organization, and World Court are moving us quickly beyond the days of national sovereignty and individual nations.

Deadly Pestilence

The Bible describes terrible plagues and horrible sores occurring throughout the world's population in the Great Tribulation. The plagues that will destroy hundreds of millions in the last days may include the effects of biological and chemical weapons. Zechariah also described the terrible plagues at the Battle of Armageddon: "And this shall be the plague wherewith the LORD will smite all the people that have fought against Jerusalem; their flesh shall consume away while they stand upon their feet, and their eyes shall consume away in their holes, and their tongue shall consume away in their mouth" (Zechariah 14:12).

"So I looked, and behold, an ashy pale horse, . . . and its rider's name was Death, and Hades . . . followed him closely. And they were given authority and power over a fourth part of the earth to kill with the sword and with famine and with plague (pestilence, disease) and with wild beasts of the earth" (Revelation 6:8, Amplified Bible). The prophecy of the Four Horsemen of the Apocalypse warned that a fourth of humanity will be killed by plague and pestilence symbolized by the fourth horseman during the Tribulation. How could this prophecy be fulfilled literally? Tragically, the AIDS epidemic throughout Africa, South America, and Asia is demonstrating how this prophecy may be fulfilled in our generation. The AIDS plague is now poised to destroy a large portion of mankind in the worst epidemic in history. Thus far, it appears that almost no one has survived AIDS for more than twelve years. Jesus warned His disciples about plagues in the last days, "For nation shall rise against nation, and kingdom against kingdom: and there shall be famines, and pestilences, and earthquakes, in divers places" (Matthew 24:7).

In North America and Europe, the AIDS virus is still primarily infecting people within the homosexual community and those who share illegal drugs through needles. However, in the Third World huge numbers of heterosexuals in Africa, South America, and Asia are now infected with AIDS. Scientists have determined that unprotected promiscuous sexual activity between males and females facilitates the rapid transmission of the AIDS virus throughout the sexually active population in the Third World. The combination of high levels of promiscuity, an absence of sanitation, minimal AIDS education, and a lack of antibiotics or protection has produced an epidemic of sexually transmitted diseases, including AIDS. The only real solution to the AIDS crisis is to return to God's laws regarding a monogamous marriage relationship between a faithful husband and wife. This is the only true "safe sex" that exists in a world of promiscuous behavior and sexually transmitted disease. In the fall of 1991, the Central Intelligence Agency produced a report on the AIDS epidemic in Africa that was staggering in its conclusions. The evidence pointed to the greatest epidemic and loss of life in human history. The CIA report concluded that up to 75 percent of the population of Africa living in the area south of the Sahara Desert may become infected with AIDS over the next twelve years. This will mean the death by AIDS of over three hundred million people in Africa alone. We are now witnessing the greatest tragedy in history in the death of a whole continent. The mind can scarcely imagine death on this massive scale. The *South African Medical Journal* in July 1991 reported that a staggering 47 percent of black male and female blood donors tested positive for AIDS during 1989. The prognosis for Asia and parts of South America is tragically similar. One study showed that almost every soldier in the armies of several East African nations that could be tested was found to have been infected by the AIDS virus.

Worldwide Famine

The apostle John described his vision of the horrible famine in the last days. "So I looked, and behold, a black horse, and he who sat on it had a pair of scales in his hand" (Revelation 6:5, NKJV). The scales represent famine, and the prophet explains that a day's wages at that time will only buy enough wheat or barley to feed the workman, not his family. The United Nations claims that over thirty million people in Africa are now at risk of dying from the most devastating famine in this century. Despite the great advances in food production and food storage techniques, more people are starving today than at any other time in history. The UN estimates that one billion people are in danger of starvation while another billion people lack proper nutrition. North American food reserves (grain and corn) are at the lowest level in sixty years. Wheat reserves worldwide are at the lowest level in this century as our government sends its surplus food to Russia, Bosnia, and Africa. In light of the massive changes in world weather patterns, we may witness devastating famine in the future in countries that felt themselves immune to hunger.

The Rise in Major "Killer" Earthquakes

Jesus prophesied that the last generation of this age would witness the greatest earthquakes in history. Other prophets, including Ezekiel, Zechariah, Haggai, and John predicted awesome earthquakes that would precede Christ's return. Jesus said these earthquakes will occur in "divers places" (strange places). Massive earthquakes are now occurring worldwide in "divers places." Enormous forces are accumulating far beneath the massive tectonic plates supporting the continents. Scientists warn that the major earthquakes felt recently in California, Japan, and other parts of the Pacific Rim are only a foretaste of the coming "Big One," the most massive earthquake in human history. Major "killer" quakes (7.2 or greater on the Richter Scale) occurred only once per decade throughout history until our century. However, since A.D. 1900, the growth in the number of major earthquakes has been relentless. From 1900 to 1949, it averaged three major quakes per decade. From 1949, the increase became awesome with 9 killer quakes in the 1950s; 13 in the 1960s; 56 in the 1970s; and an amazing 74 major quakes in the 1980s. Finally, in the 1990s, at the present rate, we will experience 125 major killer quakes in this decade (Source: *U.S. Geological Survey Earthquake Report*, Boulder, Colorado). The prophets warned that the planet will be shaken in the last days as never before. The judgment of God will finally unleash the greatest earthquake in history as part of a series of enormous earthquakes. "There were noises and thunderings and lightnings; and there was a great earthquake, such a mighty and great earthquake as had not occurred since men were on the earth" (Revelation 16:18, NKJV).

Preparations for the Mark of the Beast

The Book of Revelation describes the end of cash and the creation of a cashless society in the last days where the possession of a certain number, "666," will be essential to enable you to "buy or sell." This was an astonishing prophecy when John proclaimed it in the first century: "And he causeth all, both small and great, rich and poor, free and bond, to receive a mark in their right hand, or in their foreheads: And that no man might buy or sell, save he that had the mark, or the name of the beast, or the number of his name. Here is wisdom. Let him that hath understanding count the number of the beast: for it is the number of a man; and his number is Six hundred threescore and six" (Revelation 13:16–18). However, we are already 95 percent cashless in America today. Studies reveal that less than 5 percent of the total money in our society exists as paper currency or coins. Revelation describes a time when the number 666 will be placed beneath the skin on the right hand or forehead to control people in the Antichrist's empire. For the first time in history, we are developing technology that would allow tiny computer chips holding your complete medical and financial records to be placed beneath the skin of the right hand or forehead. Recently, scientists developed a miniature computer chip so powerful that it will hold up to five gigabytes of information in a chip the size of a dime. This tiny chip will hold as much information as contained in thirty complete sets of the *Encyclopædia Britannica*. This chip could also be configured in a shape the size of two grains of rice that could be injected beneath the skin. Your complete financial life records could be held by such a chip, which could be read from a distance by electronic scanners.

Business Week magazine reported on June 3, 1996, p. 123, that MasterCard International is testing a "smart card" computer chip that includes information about your fingerprint and identity that can be embedded in a credit/debit card. Card scanners in stores and banks will scan your fingerprint and compare it to the information on the card to verify your identity. How could the apostle John have known that the future would hold such incredible technology unless God inspired him to write the words recorded in Revelation 13:16–18?

Worldwide Television Communications

Another incredible prophecy relating to our era is found in the Book of Revelation that describes worldwide television communications. The prophet John prophesied that in the future Tribulation the Antichrist will kill two of God's witnesses who will stop the rain for three and a half years. The prophet declared that the people living around the world will see their deaths and observe their bodies lying unburied for three and a half days in Jerusalem. The whole world will hold a party, exchanging gifts in their relief that their tormentors are dead. Then these people will watch astonished as God resurrects His two witnesses to heaven (Revelation 11:9–10). How could the news that these men were killed travel instantaneously around the world in only three and a half days in any generation other than today? Only seventy years ago, it would have taken a week for the news to travel from Israel to Japan or New York. However, today CNN instantly transmits pictures and sound about any important event worldwide. Over a billion people around the world can simultaneously watch the Olympic events every four years. For the first time in history, this prophecy about the whole world watching an event in Jerusalem can be literally fulfilled in this last decade.

Gospel of the Kingdom Shall Be
Preached in All the World

One of the most wonderful of the prophecies concerns the prediction of Jesus Christ that "this gospel of the kingdom will be preached in all the world as a witness to all the nations, and then the end will come" (Matthew 24:14, NKJV). The Bible has now been translated into more than 3,850 languages in every nation, tribe, and dialect on this planet. Electronic communication transmits the message of hope in Jesus Christ through the air waves worldwide. According to researchers on evangelism, over eighty-five thousand people accept Jesus as their personal Savior every day. We have never witnessed such an explosion of the Gospel from the first days following the Feast of Pentecost in Jerusalem until today. There were only one million Christians in China in 1949 after a century of faithful missionary work. However, the Church in China has grown astronomically despite tremendous persecution and the killing of untold millions of believers in concentration camps. Today, the lowest estimates calculate that there are more than one hundred million true followers of Christ in communist China.

Knowledge and Travel Shall
Increase in the Last Days

Twenty-five centuries ago, the Book of Daniel predicted that there would be an explosion of knowledge and a huge increase in travel in the last days. Daniel wrote these words: "But thou, O Daniel, shut up the words, and seal the book, even to the time of the end: many shall run to and fro, and knowledge shall be increased" (Daniel 12:4). Throughout thousands of years of history the level of knowledge only increased incrementally. In some generations the level of general knowledge actually decreased. Yet, in the last century and a half, there has been an explosion of knowledge beyond anything ever experienced in human history. There are more scientists alive today than have lived in all of the rest of history. Recently, it was calculated that the total level of human knowledge is growing so quickly that it literally doubles every twenty-four months. This is staggering in light of Daniel's inspired prediction from the ancient past. In addition, Daniel stated that a characteristic of the last days would be an awesome increase in mobility as "many shall run to and fro." The speed of transportation has also exploded in the last century. Throughout history, most people have never traveled faster than a galloping horse. Today, men travel at over eighteen thousand miles an hour in the U.S. space shuttle *Discovery*. In addition, while most people in past centuries never traveled more than twenty miles from the place they were born, millions of people now travel the globe as part of their normal course of daily business or annual vacation.

Preparations for the Battle of Armageddon

Numerous prophecies deal with the climactic battle at the end of this age that will bring about the defeat of the Antichrist's armies and the ultimate victory of Jesus Christ to establish His kingdom on earth for a thousand years. The prophet John named the place of the final battle in this war between the Antichrist and the armies of the Kings of the East. "And he gathered them together into a place called in the Hebrew tongue Armageddon" (Revelation 16:16). John also stated that the army of the eastern nations from the "kings of the east" would consist of an astonishing two hundred million soldiers. This statement was almost impossible in light of the fact that the population of the entire Roman Empire in the days of John was only two hundred million people. "And the four angels were loosed, which were prepared for an hour, and a day, and a month, and a year, for to slay the third part of men. And the number of the army of the horsemen were two hundred thousand thousand: and I heard the number of them" (Revelation 9:15–16).

However, the populations of the nations of Asia are growing so quickly that they could field an army in the next few years containing almost two hundred million soldiers. As a result of the cruel and evil One Child Policy, Chinese couples routinely abort any unborn baby that tests indicate will be female. They keep aborting fetuses until the tests reveal that the woman has a male fetus. Then they allow the male child to be born. Numerous reports by human rights organizations reveal that China, India, and North Korea are involved in the selective abortion of female unborn infants. In addition, many in these nations kill young girls who are not wanted by their parents. As a result, the *Toronto Star* newspaper reported in 1995 that Chinese officials admitted that they have a staggering imbalance between boys and girls. This sexual imbalance will result in an excess of more than seventy million young men in China by the year 2000 with no women for them to marry. This growing imbalance of sexes throughout Asia will produce up to two hundred million excess young men of military age in the next decade. This situation could fulfill the prophecy of John about the two-hundred-million-man army from the East that will fight in the Battle of Armageddon.

A Military Highway Across Asia and the Drying Up of the Euphrates River

Another prophecy in Revelation declares that the Euphrates River will be dried up to allow this enormous army of two hundred million soldiers to cross from Asia to invade Israel: "And the sixth angel poured out his vial upon the great river Euphrates; and the water thereof was dried up, that the way of the kings of the east might be prepared" (Revelation 16:12). Throughout history the Euphrates River has been an impenetrable military barrier between East and West. However, the government of Turkey recently constructed the huge Ataturk Dam, which can now dam up the waters of the Euphrates for the first time in history. The prophet John foretold a future military highway across Asia that would allow this astonishing army to march toward the final battle in Israel. John describes the building of this highway in these words: "The way of the kings of the east might be prepared" (Revelation 16:12). The Chinese government has spent enormous sums and expended the lives of hundreds of thousands of construction workers building a military super-highway across Asia heading directly toward Israel. This highway has no economic purpose and no foreigners are allowed anywhere near this road. The highway has been completed through the south of China, Tibet, Afghanistan, and Pakistan. This curious prophecy about "the way of the kings of the east" is being fulfilled in the 1990s, setting the stage for the final battle of this age.

The Staggering Odds Against These Prophecies Being Fulfilled in Our Lifetime

In this chapter we have examined a number of significant prophecies fulfilled in our lifetime that point to the Lord's return in this generation. Almost two thousand years have passed from the time of Christ until our generation. At its simplest level we can ask: What are the odds that even ten of these specific prophecies would be fulfilled by chance during our lifetime? If these prophecies could not have occurred by random chance, then their fulfillment is proof that God inspired the writers of the Bible to predict these future events correctly! In the Bible there are several types of generations. One generation is defined as the length of life of the average person—seventy or eighty years. However, a generation of governing is usually defined as forty years, as indicated in the forty-year reigns of Gideon, King David, King Solomon, etc. During the last two thousand years since the days of Christ, there were fifty such forty-year generations. Therefore, the odds are one chance in fifty that any one of these specific prophecies happened by chance in our generation rather than some other generation. Examine the prediction about the rebirth of Israel, as prophesied by Matthew 24:32, as an example. There was only one chance in fifty that Israel would become a nation in our lifetime, rather than in some other generation such as A.D. 350 or A.D. 1600.

According to the laws of combined probability, the chance that two or more events will occur in a given time period is equal to the chance that one event will occur multiplied by the chance that the second event will occur. If the odds are fifty to one against Israel being reborn in our lifetime by chance and the odds are also fifty to one against the revival of the Roman Empire in our generation; then the combined probability is fifty times fifty, which equals one chance in twenty-five hundred. To calculate the probability of these prophecies occurring by chance:

What Are the Odds that These Prophecies Were Fulfilled by Chance?

There are 40 years to a generation.
There are 50 generations from Christ till today.
Therefore:
The odds are 1 in 50 of any of these prophecies occurring in our lifetime
The odds are:

1 event	= 1 x 50	1 in 50
2 events	= 50 x 50	1 in 2,500
3 events	= 50 x 50 (3 times)	1 in 125,000
4 events	= 50 x 50 (4 times)	1 in 6.25 million
5 events	= 50 x 50 (5 times)	1 in 312.5 million
6 events	= 50 x 50 (6 times)	1 in 15.6 billion
7 events	= 50 x 50 (7 times)	1 in 780 billion
8 events	= 50 x 50 (8 times)	1 in 39 trillion
9 events	= 50 x 50 (9 times)	1 in 1,950 trillion
10 events	= 50 x 50 (10 times)	1 in 97,500 trillion

Obviously, the odds against even ten prophecies occurring by random chance alone in one generation are simply staggering. The above calculation suggests that there is only one chance in 97,500 trillion that these particular predictions from the Bible could be fulfilled by chance in our lifetime. Another way of looking at this is that the chance that the prophets of the Bible correctly guessed these prophecies is also one chance in 97,500 trillion. If we calculated the odds against all twenty of these prophecies occurring by chance, the numbers would be beyond our ability to comprehend. In other words, it is simply impossible that men alone could have written the Bible without the supernatural assistance and inspiration of God.

This analysis demonstrates the truly incredible odds against even ten specific prophecies being fulfilled by chance in our generation. The odds against only ten prophecies occurring by random chance were 50 x 50 x 50 x 50 x 50 x 50 x 50 x 50 x 50 x 50 = one chance in 97,500 trillion!! This number is so large that it is hard to conceive of it. However, to illustrate these incredible odds, consider this. The odds of 97,500 trillion to one are equal to the estimated number of grains of sand that would fill our entire planet. Imagine that we were to take a single grain of sand out of this staggering number of grains of sand and paint it blue. Then we blindfold you and let you search the planet for this buried grain of sand as long as you wish. Remember the entire globe consists of grains of sand and you would need to consider the possibility that the blue-painted grain of sand was buried ten miles or, possibly, a thousand miles deep beneath the planet's surface. When you think you have found the right place, stop and pick up a random grain of sand. If you were lucky enough to pick up the only grain of sand painted blue by pure chance, you would have equalled the odds of one chance in 97,500 trillion against even these ten prophecies being fulfilled by chance in our generation. Frankly, I don't think you would find that grain of sand. Likewise, it is simply impossible that these ten prophecies were fulfilled by random chance.

The Scriptures teach that the final generation of this age will witness the fulfillment of a staggering number of prophecies pointing to the soon return of the promised Messiah. The evidence presented in this chapter also provides astonishing evidence that proves that only God could have inspired the writers of the Scriptures to accurately predict the startling number of predictions already fulfilled in our lifetime. The words of Jesus speak especially to our generation, "Now when these things begin to happen, look up and lift up your heads, because your redemption draws near" (Luke 21:28, NKJV).

Ten

The Mysterious Hebrew Codes

"It is the glory of God to conceal a thing,
But the honour of kings is to search out a matter."

Proverbs 25:2

Recently, researchers in Israel discovered a staggering phenomenon of hidden codes beneath the Hebrew text of the Old Testament that reveal an astonishing knowledge of future events and personalities that cannot be explained unless God inspired the writers to record His precise words. The material in this chapter is possibly the most important evidence I will present in this book that will prove to any unprejudiced observer that the Scriptures are truly inspired by God.

Rabbi Michael Dov Weissmandl, a brilliant Czechoslovakian Jewish scholar in astronomy, mathematics, and Judaic studies, found an obscure reference in a book by a fourteenth-century rabbi known as Rabbeynu Bachayah that described a pattern of letters encoded within the Torah. This discovery during the years before World War I inspired Rabbi Weissmandl to begin exploring for other examples of codes hidden within the Torah. During the war years, he found that he could locate certain meaningful words or phrases, such as "hammer" and "anvil," if he examined the letters at sequences that were equally spaced in the Hebrew text. In other words, if he found the first letter of a significant word such as *Torah,* and then, by skipping forward seven letters he found the second letter of the word *Torah*, he continued to skip forward the same number of letters to see whether or not the complete word *Torah* was spelled out in the text at equally spaced intervals. Rabbi Weissmandl described this phenomenon as "equidistant letter sequences" (ELS). The rabbi was astonished to find that an incredible number of significant words were hidden in code within the text of the Torah at equally spaced intervals. These spaced intervals between significant letters varied from every five letters, every seven letters, and numerous other intervals. However, once they found a particular word spelled out at, say every 22nd letter, the balance of the letters from the words in this group were also spaced at an interval of every 22nd letter.

Initially, Rabbi Weissmandl could not be certain if this phenomenon was truly significant or whether it was simply due to the great number of possible combinations of words and phrases that could occur by chance arrangement by skipping forward various intervals of letters in the Hebrew text. The proof that this phenomenon was evidence of a supernatural intelligence and design was confirmed almost forty years later in Israel. The invention of sophisticated computers and statistical analysis was finally able to analyze the text of the Bible to prove that these codes could not have been produced by random chance. Although Rabbi Weissmandl found many coded names by simply manually counting the letters in the text, he did not record his discoveries in writing. Fortunately, some of his students did record several examples of his code discoveries. Over the following decades, students in Israel who had heard about his research began searching the Torah for themselves to ascertain whether or not such codes actually existed. Their discoveries ultimately resulted in the research studies at Hebrew University that have proven the validity of this research. The introduction of sophisticated high-speed computers allowed Jewish scholars at Hebrew University to explore the text of the Torah in ways that previous generations could only dream about.

Equidistant Letter Sequences

A group of dedicated Jewish scholars in Israel, following up on Rabbi Weissmandl's research, found many additional hidden codes embedded within the text of the Torah. A paper called "Equidistant Letter Sequences in the Book of Genesis," was published in August 1994 in the scholarly journal entitled *Statistical Science*. This academic magazine is one of the most prominent mathematical and scientific journals in the world. The study was completed by Doron Witztum, Yoav Rosenberg, and Eliyahu Rips at Hebrew University and the Jerusalem College of Technology. This study has been republished in several other respected scholarly journals recently, including *Bible Review,* October 1995, and on the Internet. Their discoveries of complex Hebrew codes that reveal supernatural and prophetic knowledge about the future are causing tremendous consternation in the academic community because they challenge the long-held beliefs of liberal scholars who generally reject verbal inspiration of the Bible.

This scientific discovery is earth-shaking in its consequences because it reveals a staggering level of mathematical design and intelligence that could only have been produced by a supernatural mind, providing unshakable mathematical proof that the Bible was truly inspired by God. The incredible data demolishes forever the false claim by liberal scholars and skeptics that the Bible was written and edited by uninspired men and that it is full of errors and contradictions. Despite the fact that numerous scholars and scientists have attempted to challenge the validity of this Torah research, the evidence has not been refuted.

Every Jot and Tittle

Jesus Christ, Himself, affirmed that the actual letters composing the Scriptures were directly inspired by God and were preserved in their precise order throughout eternity. "For verily I say unto you, till heaven and earth pass, one jot or one tittle shall in no wise pass from the law, till all be fulfilled" (Matthew 5:18). The English word *jot* is our translation of the Greek word *iota*, the Greek letter *i*. This *iota* is the Greek equivalent of the Hebrew letter *yod*, which is the smallest letter in the Hebrew alphabet. The word *tittle* is the Greek word *keraia*, derived from the smallest Hebrew grammatical symbol. Jesus Christ stated that even the smallest of the letters and grammatical marks in the original text of the Bible were directly inspired by God.

This intriguing statement by Jesus about the Scriptures has been confirmed two thousand years later by means of an intricate analysis of the Hebrew text of the Bible by mathematicians and computer scientists in Israel. To their total surprise, these researchers discovered that every single letter of the Torah fits into a complicated tapestry of staggering mathematical precision. In this regard we should remember the provocative words found in Proverbs 25:2, "It is the glory of God to conceal a matter, but the glory of kings is to search out a matter."

This phenomenon of Hebrew codes was placed beneath the text of the Bible thousands of years ago. However, it has been hidden successfully by God until our generation. Many of these codes could not have been discovered by manual examination of the text. The invention of high-speed computers, developed in the last twenty years, enabled the researchers to examine every possible combination occurring in any of hundreds of possible intervals (from every second letter to every 500th letter, for example) throughout the millions of Hebrew letters in the Old Testament. However, once detected by the computer program, anyone can personally verify the existence of the code by manually counting out the letters to see that a particular name is spelled out by skipping the appropriate number of letters.

The Process of Analyzing the Torah

Using the ancient Hebrew received text (the Masoretic text) of the Torah, the scientists began by eliminating the spaces between the Hebrew letters, words, and sentences throughout the first five books of the Bible. The traditional Orthodox text was written in this manner—without punctuation marks or spaces between letters, words, grammatical marks, or sentences. To demonstrate what this would look like, let us take a sentence in English and write it out as it would appear in an ancient Hebrew manuscript.

THEBIBLEWASWRITTENINHEBREWWITHOUT
PUNCTUATIONMARKS

To understand this sentence, we break it up with appropriate spaces:

THE BIBLE WAS WRITTEN IN HEBREW WITHOUT
PUNCTUATION MARKS

There is a curious tradition in the writings of the ancient
Jewish sages who claim that Moses first saw the Hebrew letters of the Torah revealed in his vision on Mount Sinai as a
continuous sequence, without spaces between letters, composed of letters of black fire appearing upon a background of
white fire. The sages wrote that Moses wrote these divinely
revealed letters one-by-one in the five books of the Law, the
Torah, as he recorded God's commands to Israel.

In their initial experiment, reported in their 1988 paper,
the scientists arbitrarily chose three hundred Hebrew word-
pairs that were logically related in meaning, such as "hammer"
and "anvil," or tree and leaf, or man and woman. They asked
the computer program to locate any such word-pairs in the
Genesis text. Once the computer found the first letter in
Hebrew of "hammer," it would look for the second letter at
various intervals or spaces between letters. If the program
couldn't locate the second letter of the target word *hammer*
following the first letter at a two-space interval, it would then
search at a three-space interval, then a four-space interval, etc.
Once it located the second letter at, say, the twelve-space
interval, it would then look for the third letter at the same
twelve-space interval, and so on through the entire 78,064

Hebrew letters in Genesis. The computer also looked for coded words by checking in reverse order. Since the computer can compute millions of calculations every second, the scientists could quickly examine every 4th, 5th, 6th, 7th letter, for example. The sophisticated computers could examine every one of millions of possible combinations to discover encoded words that no human could ever have found manually, including such words as *Hitler, Berlin,* and *Sadat.*

After the program had examined the text for each of the three hundred word-pairs, the researchers were astonished to realize that every single word-pair had been located in Genesis in close proximity to each other. As mathematical statisticians, they were naturally astounded because they knew it was humanly impossible to construct such an intricate and complicated pattern beneath a surface text, such as Genesis, which told the history of the Jewish people. After calculating the probabilities of this phenomenon occurring randomly by chance alone, they published their calculations in their scientific journal. The odds against the three hundred word-pairs occurring by chance in the text of Genesis are less than one chance in fifty quadrillion. To express this number another way, it would look like this: one chance in 50,000,000,000,000,000! Another way to express this probability is that the odds against this phenomenon occurring by chance are equal to one chance in fifty thousand trillion. Most scientific journals consider an experimental result significant if it exceeds the probability of one chance in one hundred. The bottom line is that only a supernatural intelligence, far beyond our human capacity, could have produced the pattern of secretly coded words found in the Bible.

More Surprises

As they studied this pattern, the scientists discovered that many of the coded words described future events and personalities in human history, from ancient times until today. When they looked at the string of Hebrew letters in Genesis 1:1, they counted forward forty-nine letters from the letter ת, the first letter (*tav*) of the Hebrew word *Torah* and found the second letter in the word. Skipping forward another forty-nine letters they found the third letter of the word *Torah*. Incredibly, the Hebrew word *Torah* was spelled out using every fiftieth letter of the text.

To their surprise they found that the opening verse of Exodus, the second book in the Bible, contained the same word *Torah*, once again spelled out at the same fifty-letter intervals beginning with the first appearance of the letter ת. However, when they examined the opening verses of the third book of the Bible, Leviticus, they did not find *Torah* encoded. However, they did discover the word God was spelled out when they skipped forward every eighth letter from the first letter י *yod* that appeared in the book.

Upon examining the initial verses of Numbers and Deuteronomy, the fourth and fifth books of the Bible, the scientists again found that the word *Torah* was encoded. In the Book of Numbers, the word *Torah* is spelled out in reverse at a fifty-letter interval. However, to their surprise, while the word *Torah* was also found to be spelled out in reverse order in the Book of Deuteronomy, it appeared at a forty-nine-letter interval beginning with the fifth verse of the book.

Mathematicians calculated that the odds were more than

three million to one against the word *Torah* being encoded by chance alone within the opening verses in the first five books of the Bible. Bible students know that the number fifty is very significant in Scripture. For example, God commanded Israel to free their slaves and return family lands that had been pledged to a lender on the fiftieth Year of Jubilee. In addition, the Bible reveals that Law itself, the *Torah,* was presented to the Jewish people at Mount Sinai by God precisely fifty days after their miraculous Exodus from Egypt.

These coded words are interlaced in intricate patterns at evenly spaced intervals in the text reading both forward and backward. The scientists realized that these coded letters formed words and associations of such complexity and design that it is absolutely impossible that the patterns could have occurred by chance.

It is fascinating to observe that the key word *Eden* is encoded repeatedly sixteen times within the relatively short Genesis 2:4-10 passage of only 379 Hebrew letters dealing with the Garden of Eden. The odds against sixteen "Edens" occurring by chance in such a short passage are one chance in ten thousand. Another fascinating feature of this phenomenon was found in Genesis 2, which deals with the Garden of Eden. Scientists found twenty-five different Hebrew names of trees encoded within the text of this one chapter. The laws of probability indicate that the odds against this occurring are one hundred thousand to one (Professor Daniel Michelson, *Codes in the Torah*).

Thousands of detailed and precise patterns and codes such as these were discovered hidden in the Hebrew text of the ancient Scriptures. Mathematical and computer statisticians, after exhaustive statistical analysis, concluded that this pattern of coded words could not have occurred by chance nor could a human writer have purposely produced this phenomenon. Their conclusion is that only a divine intelligence could have directed Moses to record this precise text containing such complex codes thousands of years ago.

Other Mysterious Codes Reveal God's Prophetic Foreknowledge

The scientists discovered that some of the words coded in the text of the Torah concerned events and personalities that occurred thousands of years after Moses wrote the text. Naturally, many academics rejected out of hand the possibility that this phenomenon could be real. However, despite many attempts, no one could refute the data. They recently discovered a pair of words—"Zedekiah," the last king of Judah in 587 B.C., when Jeremiah was a prophet, and "Matanya," which was King Zedekiah's original name before he ascended the throne (2 Kings 24:17). Incredibly, they also found the word *Hanukkah,* which refers to the festival of lighting the Menorah that commemorates the rededication of the Temple after it was recaptured from Antiochus IV Epiphanes in 165 B.C. The word *Hanukkah* appears near the word *Hasmoneans* which is the famous name of the family of warriors led by Judas Maccabee, the Jewish general who defeated the Syrian armies of King Antiochus IV Epiphanes. How could the writer of Genesis have known about King Zedekiah and the Festival of Hanukkah when the Book of Genesis was written centuries before they occurred?

Egyptian President Anwar Sadat

Possibly the most astonishing of the phenomena recently discovered involves codes that reveal events that occurred in our generation. As one example, the name of the late Egyptian president Anwar Sadat occurred together with the name of the leader of the Moslem Brotherhood assassination team that killed him. The same code sequence also contained the year of his assassination, 1981, and the words *president, gunfire, shot,* and *murder.* Incredibly, even the Hebrew word for "parade" appears in this coded sequence. President Sadat was assassinated during the president's review of a military parade in 1981.

Adolf Hitler, the Nazis, and the Death Camps Were Prophesied in the Bible

Truly one of the most incredible of the hidden codes is their discovery of the words *Hitler* and *Nazis* and names of several of the actual death camps embedded within this text of the Book of Deuteronomy: "For the LORD your God is God of gods, and Lord of lords, a great God, a mighty, and a terrible, which regardeth not persons, nor taketh reward: He doth execute the judgment of the fatherless and widow, and loveth the stranger, in giving him food and raiment. Love ye therefore the stranger: for ye were strangers in the land of Egypt. Thou shalt fear the LORD thy God; him shalt thou serve, and to him shalt thou cleave, and swear by his name. He is thy praise, and he is thy God, that hath done for thee these great and terrible things, which thine eyes have seen.

Thy fathers went down into Egypt with threescore and ten persons; and now the LORD thy God hath made thee as the stars of heaven for multitude" (Deuteronomy 10:17–22).

```
17כי י_וה א_היכם הוא א_הי הא_הים וא_ני הא_נים
הא_ הגדל הגבר והנורא אשר לא-ישא פנים ולא יקח
שחד: 18ועשה משפט יתום ואלמנה ואהב גר לתת לו
לחם ושמלה: 19ואהבתם את-הגר כי-גרים הייתם בארץ
מצרים: 20את-י_וה א_היך תירא אתו תעבד ובו תדבק
ובשמו תשבע: 21הוא תהלתך והוא א_היך אשר-עשה
אתך את-הגדלת ואת-הנוראת האלה אשר ראו עיניך:
22בשבעים נפש ירדו אבתיך מצרימה ועתה שמך י_וה
א_היך ככוכבי השמים לרב:
```

Hebrew Text of Deuteronomy 10:17-22 Passage

The Hebrew text of this Deuteronomy 10:17-22 passage reads as follows. The word *Hitler* in Hebrew (היטלר) is spelled out at a twenty-two-letter interval.

היטלר – Hitler

Beginning with the second to the last appearance of the Hebrew letter *bet* ב in this passage, researchers counted every thirteenth letter from left to right. To their amazement they discovered that the coded letters spelled out the phrase "b'yam marah Auschwitz," which means, "in the bitter sea of Auschwitz." As they carried the counting forward another thirteen letters they came to the letter *resh* ר. From this resh, they counted every twenty-second letter from left to right. To their amazement they found the word היטלר, "Hitler," the name of the greatest enemy of the Jews in history, the one who almost conquered the Western world in World War II. It was Hitler's satanic obsession against the chosen people that motivated him to create the Final Solution, which ultimately slaughtered over six million Jews and another six million Poles and Russians in the murderous death camps in Eastern Europe, such as Auschwitz. Amazingly, the actual names of the Nazi concentration camps "Auschwitz" and "Belsen" were also encoded close to the words *Hitler* and *Berlin* in a cluster of letters hidden within the text of this passage in Deuteronomy.

Scientists found that Deuteronomy 33:16 also contained a hidden message about the Nazi Holocaust. Beginning with the first Hebrew letter *mem* מ, they counted every two-hundred-and-forty-sixth letter from left to right and found that the coded letters spelled out the phrase "Melek Natzim," which translates as the "King of the Nazis." Another group of nearby letters spelled out the phrase "laiv m'Laivi," which means, "the heart from Levi," referring to the Levites, one of the twelve tribes of the Jews. Incredibly, this same passage yielded another hidden code about the rise of Nazi Germany; the phrase "kemi bait rah," "an evil house rose up."

One of the most fascinating of these Nazi codes appeared in Deuteronomy 32:52. Beginning with the appearance of the first letter *aleph* א, the researchers counted from left to right every six hundred and seventy letters throughout the passage, and discovered the name "Aik'man," which is a Hebrew form of the name "Eichmann." Adolf Eichmann was a Nazi official who designed the Final Solution, the evil system of concentration camps used in the Holocaust. Eichmann and Hitler were among the greatest killers in history.

This whole series of hidden codes dealing with Nazi Germany ended in Deuteronomy 33:21 with a final astonishing code. Beginning with the letter *resh* ר that appeared in the word *Yisrael,* researchers counted every twenty-second letter from left to right and found the tragic phrase "re'tzach alm" describing the terrible sufferings of the Jews during the Holocaust, which translated as "a people cry murder, slaughter." I have often been asked by Jews about why the Bible's prophecies do not say anything about the Holocaust, the worst event in the history of God's chosen people. Now we can see that God included these coded words beneath the text of the Bible describing this terrible time of persecution.

The French Revolution in the Torah

Another passage in the Book of Genesis revealed a cluster of encoded words that deal with the French Revolution. The following words are clustered together: *Mapecha HaSarfatit* (which spells "the French Revolution" in Hebrew), *Louis,* the name of the French king, and the word *Beit* [house of] *Bourbon,* his royal dynasty. In the same cluster were the following words: *Hamarseilles* (the name of the French national anthem) and the word *Bastillia* (the infamous French prison for political prisoners that was stormed by revolutionaries). Interestingly, this cluster dealing with the French Revolution appears embedded in Genesis chapters 39 to 41, which describe Joseph's imprisonment in Egypt. The Hebrew word "Bastillia" is found encoded within the sentence in Genesis 39:20 that describes "the prison in which the king keeps his prisoners."

It is fascinating that these messages and data have been

hidden secretly within the text of the Torah for thirty-five centuries until today. However, a skeptical and scientifically minded generation in our lifetime has generally rejected the authority and inspiration of the Bible. There is a greater need for our generation to see evidence and proof that the Bible is the true Word of God. In the sovereign plan of God, it is only in this generation of sophisticated high-speed computers and new techniques of statistical analysis that men could both discover and fully appreciate this divine message from the past that introduces our skeptical generation to the God of their future.

Dr. David Kazhdan, chairman of the mathematics department at Harvard University, warned those who would casually reject this evidence of Torah codes: "The phenomenon is real. What conclusion you reach from this is up to the individual."

The Scientists Prove Their Findings

The Israeli scientists wrote a follow-up paper for submission to *Statistical Science,* a scientific journal that insisted that a group of opposing scholars review and challenge their data and examine their computer program before publication. Despite the fact that all of the reviewers held previous beliefs against the inspiration of the Scriptures, the overwhelming evidence and the integrity of the data forced the editors to approve the study's scientific accuracy and reluctantly publish the article. Robert Kass, the editor of *Statistical Science,* wrote this comment about the study: "Our referees were baffled: their prior beliefs made them think the Book of Genesis could not possibly contain meaningful references to modern day individuals, yet when the authors carried out additional analyses and checks the effect persisted. The paper is thus offered to *Statistical Science* readers as a challenging puzzle" ("Equidistant Letter Sequences in the Book of Genesis," *Statistical Science,* August 1994). The study concluded that the peculiar sequences of Hebrew letters at equal spaces from each other that formed significant words could not possibly have occurred by simple coincidence.

The Response from Recognized Experts

I realize that this information will sound almost unbelievable to many readers. However, the well-respected mathematician Professor Kazhdan of Harvard University, and his fellow scientists from other universities including Yale and Hebrew University in Jerusalem, have confirmed that this is "serious research carried out by serious investigators." These recognized experts in mathematics wrote a letter confirming the value of this research in the introduction to a recent Israeli book about this phenomenon called *Maymad HaNosaf* (*The Added Dimension*), written by Professor Doron Witztum of the Jerusalem College of Technology. Professor Witztum is the leading researcher on these Torah codes. Realizing that this discovery is extremely controversial in today's academic world, these scientists encouraged additional research on the phenomenon and declared that "the results are sufficiently striking to deserve a wide audience." In light of their known attitude of rejection of the Bible's inspiration and the supernatural, their statement is a powerful endorsement that the phenomenon is legitimate.

One of the most interesting of the experiments examined the text of Genesis 38, which describes the history of Judah and his daughter-in-law Tamar, who gave birth to two sons, Pharez and Zerah. The Book of Ruth tells us that King David, the greatest king of Israel, was descended from Pharez in this manner: Pharez was the ancestor of Boaz, who married Ruth and gave birth to Obed, the father of Jesse, who was the father of King David. Every one of the five Hebrew names of these ancestors of King David were found encoded at forty-nine-letter intervals, hidden within the text of Genesis 38. Incredibly, these five names also appeared in the correct chronological order as recorded in the Bible. The statisticians calculated that the odds against these five names occurring in this passage in the exact, chronological order they lived are more than eight hundred thousand to one.

They also examined the text of Genesis 28 dealing with Jacob's vision of the ladder to heaven, which he received at Mount Moriah, the "place of God." The scientists found the key words *Temple* and *Torah* encoded at twenty-six-letter intervals in a continuous sequence of nine Hebrew letters. The occurrence of these two significant words occurring together in sequence in a biblical passage declaring that "this is none other but the house of God, and this is the gate of heaven" is extraordinary. The researchers calculated the probability of these key words occurring by chance in this passage dealing with the "place of God" was less than one chance in seventeen billion.

In another analysis, they examined the first chapter of Leviticus, which records God's laws concerning the priesthood of Aaron, the High Priest of Israel. They found the Hebrew name "Aaron" encoded twenty-five times in this one chapter, not counting the four times the word *Aaron* appears in the normal surface text. The odds against this occurring by chance are more than four hundred thousand to one.

Scientists who have studied these results state no human could create such a Hebrew document containing hundreds of encoded, significant words hidden within this text. They concluded that it would be impossible to reproduce this phenomenon in a Hebrew text even if they had the help of a group of brilliant language geniuses, or the assistance of the world's most sophisticated super-computers. In addition, it is impossible to account for the prophetic knowledge of future personalities and events found in these codes. The inescapable, logical conclusion is that God inspired Moses to record the precise Hebrew words in the words of the Torah. In addition to demonstrating that the text of the Torah was dictated by God, this evidence of this marvelous design destroys the false theory of the skeptics that the Book of Genesis was created by different "editors" who interwove several different texts centuries after the life of Moses. Only one supernatural mind could have imposed this marvelously complex design upon these five books of the Law. Only God could have designed the text of the Torah. Recently, the researchers discovered similar codes throughout the Old Testament. As I will reveal in a later chapter, God has provided equally compelling evidence in the text of the New Testament proving that He also inspired the writers to record His precise words to His Church.

More Astonishing Discoveries

In a 1994 follow-up paper, the team of researchers recorded the results of their search for pairs of encoded words that relate to events that occurred during the period long after the time when Moses wrote the Torah. They selected the names of thirty-four of the most prominent rabbis and Jewish sages during the thousand years leading up to A.D. 1900. Interestingly, the researchers simply selected the thirty-four sages with the longest biographies in the *Encyclopædia of Great Men in Israel,* a well-respected Hebrew reference book. They asked the computer program to search the text of the Torah for close word-pairs coded at equally spaced intervals that contained the name of the famous rabbis paired with their date of birth or death (using the Hebrew month and day). The Jewish people celebrate the memory of their famous sages by commemorating their date of death. Incredibly, the computer program found every single one of the thirty-four names of these famous rabbis embedded in the text of Genesis paired at significantly close proximity with their actual date of birth or their date of death. The odds against these particular names and dates occurring by random chance were calculated by the mathematicians as only one chance in 775 million.

Scholars at the *Statistical Science* journal who reviewed this experimental data were naturally astonished. They demanded that the scientists run the computer test program again on a second sample searching for the next thirty-two most prominent Jewish sages listed in the encyclopædia. To the astonishment of the skeptical reviewers, the results on the second set of famous sages were equally successful. The staggering result of the combined test revealed that the names and dates of the birth or death of every one of the sixty-six most famous Jewish sages were coded in close proximity within the text of Genesis.

An article in *Bible Review* magazine by Dr. Jeffrey Satinover, in October 1995, reported that the mathematical probability of these sixty-six names of Jewish sages and their dates of birth or death occurring by chance in an ancient text like Genesis was less than one chance in two and a half billion! Interestingly, the researchers attempted to reproduce these results by running the computer program on other religious Hebrew texts outside the Bible, including the Samaritan Pentateuch. The Samaritans developed their own variant text of the five books of Moses, called the Samaritan Pentateuch, which differs in many very small textual changes from the Hebrew Bible, which is the basis of our modern Authorized King James Version. Despite the surface similarity of the two texts to the normal reader, the researchers could not detect word-pairs in the Samaritan Pentateuch or any other Hebrew text outside the Bible.

When you carefully think about the phenomenon you can see that even a minor change of spelling or choice of words would totally destroy the precise sequence of Hebrew letters that reveals these hidden words coded at evenly spaced distances throughout the text of the Torah. A reviewer insisted they attempt to find codes in a Hebrew translation of Tolstoy's famous novel *War and Peace,* because it was the same length as the Book of Genesis. However, the phenomenon was not present in *War and Peace,* nor any other modern Hebrew writing. In fact, an exhaustive analysis reveals that no other Hebrew text outside the Old Testament contains these mysterious codes, not even the Hebrew apocryphal books written during the four hundred years before the birth of Christ.

Naturally, following the appearance of this article on divine authority in *Bible Review,* there was a virtual onslaught of letters to the editor in the following monthly issues attacking the article in the strongest terms. Most of the critical letters dismissed the phenomenon out of hand without seriously considering the scientific data that was presented. Several critics attacked the author's argument and data in ways that revealed they either failed to grasp the actual statistical method used to detect the Hebrew codes or they didn't understand the rigorous methodology that eliminated the possibility that this phenomenon had occurred by pure random chance.

After his research was published in *Bible Review* in November 1995, the original researcher, Dr. Jeffrey Satinover, responded to his critics who had challenged his assertion that a pattern of elaborate and significant words was encoded within the text of the Torah. Dr. Satinover replied to his critics as follows: "The robustness of the Torah codes findings derives from the rigor of the research. To be published in a journal such as *Statistical Science,* it had to run, without stumbling, an unusually long gauntlet manned by some of the world's most eminent statisticians. The results were thus triply unusual: in the extraordinariness of what was found; in the strict scrutiny the findings had to hold up under; and in the unusually small odds (less than 1 in 62,500) that they were due to chance. Other amazing claims about the Bible, Shakespeare, etc., have never even remotely approached this kind of rigor, and have therefore never come at all close to publication in a peer-reviewed, hard-science venue. The editor of *Statistical Science,* himself a skeptic, has challenged readers to find a flaw: though many have tried, none has succeeded. All the 'First Crack' questions asked by *Bible Review* readers—and many more sophisticated ones—have therefore already been asked by professional critics and exhaustively answered by the research. Complete and convincing responses to even these initial criticisms can get fairly technical" *(Bible Review,* November 1995).

Some critics have suggested that the Israeli scientists simply played with the computer program long enough, that by chance alone, "they got lucky." This objection raises the relevant objection that there might be numerous unreported "hidden failures," a common problem in most scientific research today. To prevent this from occurring, editorial observers from *Statistical Sceince* demanded that the scientists analyze their data by examining a completely new group of personalities that were chosen solely by *Statistical Science* editorial judges, namely the sixty-six most famous Jewish sages. The results I quoted earlier in this chapter were based on this group of individuals chosen by these judges. In addition, the judges appointed by *Statistical Science* analyzed the computer programs to determine that they were both valid and neutral in their design.

We need to keep in mind that the standard text of the five books of the Torah was published years ago in widely available computer programs and printed texts. These texts cannot be modified. In fact, as a result of the production and sale of fascinating "Torah Codes" computer programs that are now available in North America, anyone with a computer and lots of time can personally verify the existence of these codes beneath the text of the Scriptures. I have personally verified the presence of these fascinating patterns of hidden codes during long hours of examination using the computer programs I acquired several years ago in Jerusalem when this research was just beginning.

Professor Harold Gans, a senior researcher who examined sophisticated foreign government intelligence codes for the U.S. Army, has publicly confirmed the existence of these codes as reported in *Statistical Science* through the use of advanced analytic techniques and his own sophisticated computer program. Dr. Gans is a brilliant mathematician who has published one hundred and eighty technical papers. Gans learned of this discovery by Professor Witztum of coded words hidden within the Torah. However, as a skeptic, he initially believed that the claims were "ridiculous." Unlike many readers, as an intelligence specialist dealing with complex codes and computers, Gans had the technical ability to test the claims and data for himself. In 1989 he created a complex and original computer program on his computer to check Witztum's data. For nineteen straight days and nights, Gans let his program examine all possible variations and combinations in the 78,064 Hebrew letters in the Book of Genesis. Dr. Gans's computer program checked through hundreds of thousands of possible letter combinations at many different spaced intervals. Finally, Gans concluded that these Torah codes actually existed and that they could not have occurred by chance or by human design. He had confirmed the absolute accuracy of Professor Witztum's conclusions. As a result of his discoveries, Professor Gans now teaches classes in synagogues throughout the world about the incredible evidence proving divine authorship of the Bible.

A follow-up study examined the data on the sixty-six Hebrew sages in the last two thousand years. Incredibly, Dr. Harold Gans's study found that the text of Genesis also revealed the encoded names of the actual cities where each of these sixty-six sages was born. Professor Witztum produced a new scientific paper on this new set of data about the cities of the sages, which proved that the odds against this occurring by chance were one chance in two hundred and fifty million.

In response to the claim that this phenomenon is a result of simple chance, the scientific team determined that the odds against even the simplest codes occurring by chance are only one chance in 62,500. However, when we examine the most complex patterns mentioned in this chapter, the odds are far in excess of billions to one against the possibility that this phenomenon has occurred by random chance. I can assure you that there are many additional examples of this phenomenon that have been discovered recently that will be revealed in the future. Careful investigations are now being conducted by many scientists from other universities and laboratories that confirm the supernatural nature of the phenomenon.

A Caution Regarding This Phenomenon of Hebrew Codes

There is an important caution we need to keep in mind regarding this phenomenal discovery. Remember that no one can search the Torah using these codes to foretell future events. The reason is that it is impossible to extract the encoded information unless you already know what the future facts are. The information about a future event cannot be pulled out of the text in code in advance of the event because you wouldn't know what to tell the computer to look for. It is only after the event has occurred that you could have the program look for the name of the person or event and check to see if the codes contained the information confirming the event. In other words, this method confirms that the Torah has encoded data about events that occurred centuries after it was written. However, the method cannot be used to foretell the future. The Bible prohibits us from engaging in foretelling the future.

The ability to prophesy future events is left to God alone. The Bible clearly forbids fortune telling. The prophet Isaiah warned against false prophets and declared that only God can prophesy future events accurately (Isaiah 46:9–10). When an event has occurred and we can verify that the codes within the text of the Bible accurately described it thousands of years ago, then God will receive the glory, not man. Although this discovery proves that some future events were encoded by God within the text of the Torah, we must wait until the future becomes the past before we can find it. It is also important to remember that, although the phenomenon of hidden codes is statistically powerful, it is still relatively weak. The proximity of the word-pairs in the Hebrew text is defined only statistically. In addition, the phenomenon of word-pairs appears only when we examine a large number of examples that reveal a much closer proximity than would be expected by chance occurrence alone.

Another important point to note is that these Hebrew codes do not contain any hidden theological or doctrinal messages. This phenomenon has nothing to do with numerology. There are no secret messages or theology. God's message to mankind is only found in the open words of the Scriptures. However, the discovery in our lifetime of these incredible codes reveals names and events that provide a wonderful proof to a skeptical humanity that God truly inspired the writers of the Bible to record His message to mankind.

The phenomenon of Torah codes is now being presented to Jewish groups and synagogues throughout North America and Israel by a group called the "Discovery Seminar," sponsored by the Aish HaTorah College of Jewish Studies. This group was created in Israel by a number of scientists, mathematicians, and Judaic scholars. In addition to presentations in Israel, Aish HaTorah have adapted the material to English enabling their teams to share this fascinating information with Jewish audiences throughout the world showing the divine inspiration and authority of the Torah. Many people have told me that numerous agnostic Jews have returned to their religious roots in Orthodox

Judaism as a result of their exposure to this incredible evidence of God's inspiration of the Scriptures as discussed in this chapter.

The Implications

Even those scholars who are philosophically opposed to God and the inspiration of the Bible are stunned by this research. Despite many arguments and challenges the data still stands uncontested. Secular scientific journals have declared that the phenomenon is real and not a result of fraud or computer error. The simple truth is that this phenomenon could not have occurred by chance alone. Nor could any group of brilliant human beings, even with super-computers at their disposal, produce this awesome result of encoding a huge number of significant names beneath the surface text of the Torah. The odds against these biblical codes occurring by random chance are one chance in several billion.

To those who would casually ignore these odds and suggest that they are not that impressive, consider this equivalent scenario. Imagine that someone blindfolded you and laid out before you a mountain of one billion pills loaded with cyanide. In the whole pile of pills there is only one pill that contains sugar. Would you blindly swallow one of these pills by chance if you knew that only one of the billion pills was sugar while all of the rest would result in instant death by cyanide poisoning? Obviously, no one in their right mind would casually accept the odds of one billion to one against you, that the one pill they chose would result in instant death. However, every day millions of men

and women risk their eternal souls as they reject this overwhelming evidence that the Bible is true and that we must
either accept Christ as our Savior or face an eternity in hell.

It would surpass the skills of any group of human writers
to encode these complex and prophetic messages within the
text of the Torah. Since the evidence is overwhelming that
the five books of Moses were written over three and a half
thousand years ago, we are left with the undeniable conclusion that this phenomenon is another clearly authenticated
signature of God upon the pages of His message to
mankind. The evidence in the next chapter will reveal that
God has encoded information throughout the text of the
Bible, not just the five books of the Torah. As you will discover in this fascinating chapter, God has also encoded a
special message to mankind hidden in the Messianic passages of the Old Testament. The Lord has encoded the name
of His Son, the Messiah, *Yeshua,* throughout the Hebrew
text of the Old Testament.

Special Addition:
Recent Discoveries in the Hidden Hebrew Codes

Researchers have found additional astonishing codes that
refer to the War in the Gulf and the tragic assassination of
Yitzchak Rabin. I have spent countless hours exploring the
Bible using the *Torah Codes* computer program. This computer program allows you to examine personally the Hebrew
text from Genesis to Deuteronomy to search for targeted
words. The *Torah Codes* program is available in both IBM-
compatible and Macintosh formats from Frontier Research
Publications, Inc.

The War in the Gulf

The researchers were amazed to find the following names that refer to the War in the Gulf in Genesis. I personally verified these discoveries with my computer and my Hebrew-English Interlinear Bible. First they found the name "Saddam" at a six-letter interval in Genesis 8:12. In Genesis 19:1–2 they found "Scud-B" and "Russian" clearly identifying the missiles Iraq fired at Israel. In Chapter 19 they discovered the phrase "they shut the door," which may refer to the sealing of rooms by Israelis to protect against chemical weapons. Genesis 19:29 contained the phrase "the missile will terrify" spelled out every second letter followed by "the 3rd of Shevat," the actual day in the Hebrew calendar the first missiles hit Israel. Incredibly, the Hebrew name "America – אמריקה" occurred every 100 letters starting with the letter *aleph* א in Genesis 29:2. The phrase, "in Iraq" and "in Saudi Arabia" appeared at equally spaced intervals in the same chapter. Possibly the most amazing codes reveal the names of the allied leaders "Schwarzkopf" and "George Bush." The researchers found the name "CNN" spelled out in Numbers together with the name of Peter Arnet, the famous CNN reporter who broadcast from Bagdad throughout the Gulf War. The name "Peter – פיטר" was spelled out every fourth letter left to right while his last name, "Arnet – ארנט" was spelled out right to left in Hebrew every second letter in Numbers 36:5.

The Tragic Assassination of Yitzchak Rabin

The world has been fascinated by the momentous Middle

East peace talks. Millions watched Yassir Arafat reach out to shake the hand of a reluctant Yitzchak Rabin during the signing of the Declaration of Principles on the White House lawn several years ago. Incredibly, this dramatic event was hidden in code in the Torah written by Moses thirty-five hundred years ago. Dr. Moshe Katz, one of the Israeli Hebrew codes scholars, reported in his book, *Computorah— Hidden Codes in the Torah,* that they discovered the names of Arafat and Rabin in Genesis 32:23-26. They were astonished to find the coded words spelled out "Arafat—shook the hand—of Rabin." The word *Arafat*—ערפאת was spelled out every twelve letters in reverse in Genesis 32:26 together with the phrase "shook the hand." The words *of Rabin*— לרבין appear in Genesis 32:23 counting every eighth letter. It is intriguing to note that the phrase "not a real peace" is spelled out in the same chapter every 196 letters beginning in Genesis 32:19. The name "Rabin" is found in another passage of the Torah spelling out "first-born son" together with "head" and "Israel." Yitzchak Rabin was the first prime minister who was born in Israel. The most startling of all the coded words refers to Yitzchak Rabin's tragic assassination. Following his assassination the scientists searched the Bible's text to see if there were any coded words hidden near the place where Rabin's name occurred. The computer found the eight Hebrew letters of "Yitzchak Rabin—רבין ירצחק" spelled out beginning in Deuteronomy 2:33 at an interval of every 4,772 letters. The researchers were shocked to discover the four-letter Hebrew word ירצח which spells "will be assassinated," actually incorporates the צ letter, the second letter in Yitzchak Rabin's Hebrew name. These codes displaying prophetic knowledge of events thousands of years in advance of their writing provide irrefutable evidence of the supernatural inspiration of the Bible.

New codes are being discovered every day by researchers in Israel and around the world. However, the next chapter will introduce you to the greatest code discovery yet—the name of God's Messiah Yeshua—ישוע—Jesus, revealed throughout the Old Testament passages written more than a thousand years before He was born in Bethlehem.

Eleven

The Name of Jesus Encoded in the Old Testament

Yeshua Is My Name
ישׁרע שׁמי

Of all the discoveries and information that I have researched for *The Signature of God,* the following material is the most thrilling revelation that I could share with my readers. Not only has God included thousands of hidden coded messages within the text of the Bible, but He has actually hidden the name *Yeshua,* which means "Jesus" in numerous passages from Genesis to Malachi throughout the Old Testament. Especially within the great Messianic prophetic passages, God has hidden at equally spaced intervals in the Hebrew text the incredible message that "Yeshua is My Name." This is one of the most astonishing and tremendous biblical discoveries in the last two thousand years.

    The research on the phenomenon of Hebrew codes hidden within the text of the Torah during the last several years has given us one of the strongest possible proofs that the Bible was truly inspired by God. Naturally, as a committed Christian, I realized that Jesus Christ appeared numerous times in the Old Testament narrative. However, as I pointed out in the previous chapter, once I fully appreciated that the hidden codes revealed an awesome amount of information about events such as Hitler's death camps and the French

Revolution, I naturally wondered if God had secretly encoded the name of Jesus Christ in the text of the Old Testament. Providentially, a while ago I received a request from Yacov Rambsel, a Jewish student of the Scriptures, asking if he could quote from the research material I had written on the Laws of Probability regarding the prophecies fulfilled in the life, death, and resurrection of Jesus from my earlier book, *Armageddon—Appointment with Destiny*. In discussing this material with Yacov I realized that he had a real passion for the study of the Scriptures and for Jesus Christ as his Messiah. After I completed my writing of the chapter on the "Mysterious Hebrew Codes" in April 1996, I asked Yacov to review it for accuracy because he had spent years studying the Hebrew Scriptures.

In the providence of God, I then learned that Yacov had just completed his own book that focused on a series of extraordinary discoveries, which he had made independently, that complemented my research. In addition, Yacov's research provided the answer to my question about whether God had placed the name of Jesus in code within the Hebrew Scriptures. With Yacov Rambsel's permission I want to share a small part of the phenomenal research that he had completed through thousands of hours of painstaking analysis of the hidden codes. As I mentioned earlier, the Israeli researchers used complex computer programs to explore these codes, and I purchased three computer pro- grams in Jerusalem several years ago that I used on my Power Macintosh computer to verify the research at Hebrew University. However, Yacov completed his detailed analysis by patiently examining the text of the Old Testament and individually counting the equally spaced intervals between the letters. The amount of work and dedication involved to complete this analysis is staggering. I highly recommend to anyone who is fascinated by this research that they acquire a copy of Yacov Rambsel's new book, *Yeshua—The Name of Jesus Revealed in the Old Testament.* His book is available through Frontier Research Publications or you can purchase it in Christian bookstores.

Incredibly, the original Hebrew name of Jesus, *Yeshua—*ישרע, was found encoded in the Book of Genesis beginning with the very first verse, Genesis 1:1, "In the beginning God created the heaven and the earth." Starting with the very first word in the Bible, *B'raisheet* בראשית "In the beginning," the name of Jesus, *Yeshua—*ישרע, is found encoded beginning with the fifth letter in the word בראשית, the Hebrew letter *yod* י. Counting forward every 521st letter we can read the letters of the words *Yeshua Yakhol,* which translates as "Jesus is able."

One of the most astonishing features is that the clearly Messianic passages of the Old Testament often contain the name *Yeshua—*Jesus—encoded beneath the text of the words of the prophecy about the coming of the Messiah Jesus. As an example, Yacov found the name *Yeshua* embedded in the text of Isaiah 53:10 that prophesied about the grief of our Lord and the atoning sacrifice that Christ made for our sins when He was offered as the Lamb of God, a perfect sacrifice, on the cross two thousand years ago. "Yet it pleased the LORD to bruise him; he hath put him to grief: when thou shalt make his soul an offering for sin, he shall see his seed, he shall prolong his days, and the pleasure of

the Lord shall prosper in his hand" (Isaiah 53:10). Beginning
with the second Hebrew letter *yod* י that appears in the
phrase "he shall prolong," *ya'arik* יאריך, Yacov counted
forward every 20th letter and discovered that the phrase
"ישרע שמי—*Yeshua—Shmi*," which means "Yeshua
[Jesus] is My name," was encoded in this verse that teaches
us about the suffering Messiah who died to atone for our
sins. Mathematical experts have calculated that the probability of this astonishing combination, "Yeshua [Jesus] is My
name," occurring by random chance in this Messianic
prophecy in Isaiah is only one chance in 50 quadrillion, an
inconceivable number!

A passage in the Book of Genesis declared that the Lord
provided "coats of skin" for Adam and Eve to cover their
nakedness after they sinned: "And Adam called his wife's
name Eve; because she was the mother of all living. Unto
Adam also and to his wife did the LORD God make coats of
skins, and clothed them" (Genesis 3:20–21). God was
forced to kill the first animal as a sin sacrifice to provide
their covering. This was a prophetic sign of the perfect sacrifice of the Lamb of God to cover the sins of all those who
would confess and ask Christ to forgive them. However, this
important passage also contains a hidden message about
Jesus. Beginning with the last Hebrew letter *heh* ה in Genesis
3:20 and counting forward every ninth letter we find the
word *Yoshiah* meaning "He will save." The word *Yoshiah* is a
Hebrew equivalent name for Yeshua (Jesus). This encoded
name Yoshiah, meaning "He will save," found in the first few
verses of the Old Testament reminds us of the parallel message given to the young virgin Mary by the angel that "thou

shalt call his name JESUS: for he shall save his people from their sins" (Matthew 1:21) as recorded in the first few verses of the New Testament. The sacred message in Genesis 3:20–21 containing a reference to Jesus is confirmed by the fact that another code revealing the name *Yeshua* is also hidden in this passage. Beginning with the letter *ayin* ע in the Hebrew word for "coats of skin" and counting forward every seventh letter spells out another form of the word *Yeshua*—יׁשע, which is spelled without using the letter *vav* ו.

One of the most well known of the Messianic prophecies in the Old Testament describes the exact price of Christ's betrayal, namely thirty pieces of silver. Over five hundred years before the birth of Jesus the prophet Zechariah gave this prediction: "And I said unto them, If ye think good, give me my price; and if not, forbear. So they weighed for my price thirty pieces of silver" (Zechariah 11:12). The phrase in the verse that reads "My price" is *se'kari*. Beginning with the letter *yod* י, Yacov counted forward every 24th letter and found the word *Yeshua* יׁשרע. In this astonishing hidden message, as He did throughout the Scriptures, the Lord inspired the writers of the Old Testament to choose specific Hebrew words and precise spelling to create this phenomenon. Here, in the exact prophecy that five hundred years earlier described the precise price of our Lord's betrayal, God chose to include a hidden encoded message to His chosen people that identified forever the name of the promised Messiah—"*Yeshua*—Jesus." In the prophetic passage that followed this first prediction of Christ's first coming, the prophet Zechariah looked forward over twenty-five centuries to describe the incredible emotional upheaval and mourning that will occur when the Jewish people have their spiritual eyes opened to see that the Messiah that they have longed for many centuries, is in fact, the Messiah Yeshua— Jesus Christ who was crucified two thousand years ago. Zechariah looks forward to His second coming to save Israel following Armageddon: "And I will pour upon the house of David, and upon the inhabitants of Jerusalem, the spirit of grace and of supplications: and they shall look upon me whom they have pierced, and they shall mourn for him, as one mourneth for his only son, and shall be in bitterness for him, as one that is in bitterness for his firstborn" (Zechariah 12:10). Beginning with the letter *chet* ח found in the phrase, "an only son" *ha'yachid*, Yacov discovered that the word *Mashiach*, which is "Messiah," was encoded by counting forward every 38th letter.

The Book of Leviticus reveals an astonishing hidden coded message about the blood of Jesus Christ being shed for our sins. In this passage Moses gave God's detailed instructions regarding the rules of the holy priesthood and the sacrifices for the sins of the chosen people. "And he that is the high priest among his brethren, upon whose head the anointing oil was poured, and that is consecrated to put on the garments, shall not uncover his head, nor rend his clothes; neither shall he go into any dead body, nor defile himself for his father, or for his mother; neither shall he go out of the sanctuary, nor profane the sanctuary of his God; for the crown of the anointing oil of his God is upon him: I am the LORD" (Leviticus 21:10–12). Yacov examined this passage and found that, beginning with the first *heh* ה in Leviticus 21:10 and counting forward every third letter, it spelled out the phrase *hain dam Yeshua,* which means "Behold! The blood of Yeshua." It is awesome to realize that God has secretly encoded these profound messages regarding His Son, Jesus, in these significant passages throughout the Old Testament.

One of the most startling of all the Messianic messages was found hidden within the passage in Psalm 41:7–10, which predicted the betrayal of Jesus by His disciple Judas Iscariot: "All who hate me whisper together against me; against me they devise my hurt. "An evil disease," they say, "clings to him. And now that he lies down, he will rise up no more." Even my own familiar friend in whom I trusted, who ate my bread, has lifted up his heel against me. But You, O LORD, be merciful to me, and raise me up, that I may repay them" (Psalm 41:7–10). Yacov noted that verse 8 contained the phrase "they plot evil," *yach' shvu rah'ah.* However, he noticed that, beginning with the letter *yod* ‫י‬, when he counted forward every second letter, he found it spelled out the word *Yeshua.*

The Book of Ruth contains a wonderful love story that reveals the ancestry of King David. It is fascinating to note that the name *Yeshua*—‫ישרע‬ is encoded in the very first verse, Ruth 1:1. Counting every fifth letter from right to left from the letter ‫י‬ spells out the name of *Yeshua*—‫ישרע‬.

The prophet Isaiah announced centuries before the birth of Christ that He would come as the great liberator to mankind. This prophecy of the Great Jubilee at the end of this age reminded Israel that their Messiah would finally cancel all their debts and proclaim liberty to all of those who were captives to sin. "The Spirit of the Lord GOD is upon

Me, because the LORD has anointed Me to preach the good
tidings to the poor. He has sent Me to heal the brokenhearted,
to proclaim liberty to the captives, and the opening of the
prison to those who are bound; to proclaim the acceptable
year of the LORD, and the day of vengeance of our God; to
comfort all who mourn" (Isaiah 61:1–2). Starting with the
yod ׳ in the phrase "the Spirit of the Lord GOD," *Ruach
Adonai Yehovah,* counting nine letters from left to right
spells *Yeshua.* In addition, Yacov discovered that the word
Oshiyah אֹושִׁיעַ, was also encoded beginning with the last letter *aleph* א in the second verse and counting every 36th letter from left to right. This word *Oshiyah* means, "I will save"
and is a variation on the word *Yeshua*—"Jesus" as we saw
earlier in Genesis 3:20.

Of the many incredible discoveries made by Yacov
Rambsel, one of my favorites concerns the great prophecy of
the Seventy Weeks given by the prophet Daniel in Daniel
9:25–27. "Know therefore and understand, that from the
going forth of the commandment to restore and to build
Jerusalem unto the Messiah the Prince shall be seven weeks,
and threescore and two weeks: the street shall be built again,
and the wall, even in troublous times. And after threescore
and two weeks shall Messiah be cut off, but not for himself:
and the people of the prince that shall come shall destroy
the city and the sanctuary; and the end thereof shall be with
a flood, and unto the end of the war desolations are determined. And he shall confirm the covenant with many for
one week: and in the midst of the week he shall cause the
sacrifice and the oblation to cease, and for the overspread-
ing of abominations he shall make it desolate, even until the
consummation, and that determined shall be poured upon

the desolate" (Daniel 9:25–27). Students of the Bible are familiar with the controversy over the last century about the correct identity of the "Messiah the Prince" that Daniel referred to in verse 25. Those who deny that the prophecy teaches about Jesus Christ's first coming have usually claimed that "Messiah the Prince" was Hezekiah or some other individual. However, Yacov made a wonderful discovery when he found that the name *Yeshua* was embedded in Daniel 9:26 starting with the letter *yod* ר in the phrase "the city," *v'ha'iry,* by counting left to right every 26th letter.

The significance of Yacov Rambsel's discovery is overwhelming. When added to the awesome research in Israel on the hidden codes of the Torah we can see the sovereign hand of God bringing about an incredible proclamation of His inspiration of the Word of God. Hundreds of thousands of people around the world, mostly Jews, have heard about the secret Torah codes. These people, who have reaffirmed their belief in God's inspiration of the Old Testament because of this phenomenon, will now learn that God has secretly encoded the actual name of His Son, the Messiah, *Yeshua,* within these numerous Messianic texts. For anyone who ever wondered about whether or not the Old and New Testaments were equally inspired, the overwhelming evidence now available proves the unity of both the message of redemption through God's Messiah and that *Yeshua*—Jesus is the central figure of both testaments that make up our Holy Scriptures.

This revelation of God's matchless wisdom and inspiration in this decade as we rapidly approach the new millennium reminds me of the angel's prophecy to Daniel: "But you, Daniel, shut up the words, and seal the book until the time of the end; many shall run to and fro, and knowledge shall increase. . . . Many shall be purified, made white, and refined, but the wicked shall do wickedly; and none of the wicked shall understand, but the wise shall understand" (Daniel 12:4, 10). Truly, the discovery of these codes revealing the name of God's Son, *Yeshua,* that were hidden within the text of the Bible for over three thousand years, is a fulfillment of the angel's prophecy to Daniel. Our knowledge of the Bible, its hidden code, and its divine prophecies is truly increasing at a phenomenal rate in these exciting last days as we approach the time of the Messiah's return to set up His kingdom on earth.

Over the course of my research on *The Signature of God,* Yacov Rambsel and I have had many conversations about the tremendous significance of his discovery of the *Yeshua* codes. There is much more exciting material in Yacov's book than I could cover in this chapter. As a result of these discussions, our ministry will be publishing Yacov's fascinating book *Yeshua* ישׁוע*—The Name of Jesus Revealed in Codes in the Old Testament.* If any reader is interested in studying this phenomenon and documentation in greater detail, they can order the book from any Christian bookstore or directly from our ministry, Frontier Research Publications, Inc. As Yacov wrote in his book, "Without a doubt, the Messiah's Name is *Yeshua—*ישׁוע, but in English, His Name is Jesus."

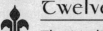

Twelve

The Mathematical Signature of God in the Words of Scripture

The Scriptures reveal God as the great mathematician who knows the smallest detail of His creation, and measures and numbers all things. This character of God is consistent with the revealed phenomenon of staggering complexity involving mathematical patterns within the text of the Scriptures. The Bible declares that God is so concerned with the details of His children's lives that He has numbered the hairs on our head. "But the very hairs of your head are all numbered" (Matthew 10:30). The prophet Isaiah speaks of His majesty and His concern for numbering and measuring all things: "Who has measured the waters in the hollow of His hand, measured heaven with a span and calculated the dust of the earth in a measure? Weighed the mountains in scales and the hills in a balance?" (Isaiah 40:12, NKJV). When you consider the Bible's declaration that God "measured the waters," "measured heaven with a span," and "calculated the dust of the earth in a measure," it does not seem unusual or out of character that this same Almighty God would inspire His writers to record His precise message to mankind in the Scriptures with a mathematical precision within the original text that surpasses our ability to understand fully.

Evidence of Divine Authorship of the Old Testament

Ivan Panin was one of the most remarkable Christians to live in this century. Almost one hundred years ago, this fascinating and famous mathematician left Russia to settle eventually in Canada in the town of Aldershot, Ontario, not far from where I live. Although he was a committed atheist in his early years, he discovered the reality of Jesus Christ later. In 1890, Panin embarked on an exciting journey of scientific exploration of the text of the Bible that would prove that the Bible is truly the inspired Word of God. This century has witnessed a progressive abandonment of the doctrine of verbal inspiration of the Scriptures by many biblical scholars and religious leaders. As the leaders of many mainline churches succumbed to the continuous assaults on fundamental doctrines and the authority of Scripture, many Christian laymen began to lose their confidence that they could absolutely trust that the Bible was truly the inspired Word of God. As Ivan Panin wrote, "In the early centuries Christianity suffered most from its avowed enemies; in the last, from its professed friends."

Panin completed an astonishing study during the course of fifty years that revealed the most amazing mathematical pattern beneath the surface layer of the text of the Bible. He worked diligently up to eighteen hours a day for half a century to illustrate the divine inspiration and authority of Scripture. As one small example, Panin discovered that the first verse of the Book of Genesis contains an astonishing number of mathematical patterns that illustrate divine inspiration. "In the beginning God created the heaven and the earth (Genesis 1:1).

The phenomenon of these mathematical patterns cannot be understood until we realize that the Bible was composed in alpha-numeric languages—Hebrew and Greek. These ancient languages did not possess Arabic numbers to express numeric data. Therefore, these languages used various letters of their alphabet to express numbers such as "1, 2, 3," etc. In addition, a small portion of the Bible was written in Aramaic, which is also alpha-numeric. Each letter in these languages stood for a number. In other words, each of the letters expressed both a letter and a number. When they wished to express a number, such as 22, they would choose two Hebrew letters—one letter כ stood for 20 and the second letter ב stood for 2.

The first letter of the Hebrew alphabet stood for 1, the second for 2, the third for 3, etc. When we come to the eleventh letter, it represented 20, the twelfth stood for 30, etc., all the way through to 800. Because each letter had a numeric value, every word can be given a *numeric* value by adding up the total value of each of the individual letters. In addition, every one of the Hebrew and Greek letters was given a *place* value as well. To help illustrate this phenomenon let's apply this system to the English language. It would look like this:

An Example Illustrated in the English Language

PLACE VALUE

1	2	3	4	5	6	7	8	9	10	11	12	13	14	15
A	B	C	D	E	F	G	H	I	J	K	L	M	N	O
1	2	3	4	5	6	7	8	9	10	20	30	40	50	60

NUMERIC VALUE

The Hebrew Language

PLACE VALUE

1	2	3	4	5	6	7	8	9	10	11	12	13	14	15
א	ב	ג	ד	ה	ו	ז	ח	ט	י	כ	ל	מ	נ	ס
1	2	3	4	5	6	7	8	9	10	20	30	40	50	60

NUMERIC VALUE

Note that in the above example using the English alphabet the first ten letters have the same *place* values and *numeric* values. However, when we get to the eleventh letter K, the numeric value begins to increase by ten with each additional letter until we reach the value of 100. From that point in the alphabet forward the *numeric* value of each letter will increase by 100.

Every single word in Hebrew contains a series of letters with individual numeric values. For example, the word *B'raisheet*, "beginning," is expressed in Genesis 1:1 in Hebrew as בראשית. If you add up the total value of the individual letters in *B'raisheet* the numeric value of the word is 913. Since each word has a numeric value, we can add up the value of each of the words in a biblical verse to determine the numerical value of the sentence.

The Astonishing Pattern of SEVENS in Genesis 1:1

Let us begin by examining the first verse of the Bible to explore Panin's discovery.

> *"In the beginning God created the heaven and the earth"*
> (Genesis 1:1)

בראשית ברא אלהים את השמים ואת הארץ:

(Genesis 1:1)

Ivan Panin carefully examined the Hebrew text of Genesis 1:1 and discovered an incredible phenomenon of multiples of 7 that could not be explained by chance. Genesis 1:1 was composed of 7 Hebrew words containing a total of 28 letters. Throughout the Bible, the number 7 appears repeatedly as a symbol of divine perfection—the 7 days of creation, God rested on the 7th day, the 7 churches, the 7 seals, the 7 trumpets, etc. In total, Panin discovered 30 separate codes involving the number 7 in this first verse of the Bible.

A Listing of the Phenomenal Features of Sevens Found in Genesis 1:

1. The number of Hebrew words   Seven
2. The number of letters equals 28 (28 ÷ 4 = 7)   Seven
3. The first three Hebrew words translated "In the beginning God created" contain 14 letters (14 ÷ 2 = 7)   Seven
4. The last four Hebrew words "the heavens and the earth" have 14 letters (14 ÷ 2 = 7)   Seven
5. The fourth and fifth words have 7 letters   Seven
6. The sixth and seventh words have 7 letters   Seven
7. The three key words: *God, heaven,* and *earth* have 14 letters (14 ÷ 2 = 7)   Seven
8. The number of letters in the four remaining words is also 14 (14 ÷ 2 = 7)   Seven
9. The middle word is the shortest with 2 letters.

However, in combination with the word to the
right or left it totals 7 letters   Seven
10. The numeric value of the first, middle,
     and last letters is 133 (133 ÷ 19 = 7)   Seven
11. The numeric value of the first and last letters
     of all seven words is 1,393 (1,393 ÷ 199 = 7) Seven

When professors on the mathematics faculty at Harvard
University were presented with this biblical phenomenon,
they naturally attempted to disprove its significance as a
proof of divine authorship. However, after valiant efforts
these professors were unable to duplicate this incredible
mathematical phenomenon. The Harvard scientists used the
English language and artificially assigned numeric values to
the English alphabet. They had a potential vocabulary of
over 400,000 available English words to choose from to construct a sentence about any topic they chose. Compare this to
the limitations of word choices in the biblical Hebrew language, which has only forty-five hundred available word
choices that the writers of the Old Testament could use.
Despite their advanced mathematical abilities and access to
computers the mathematicians were unable to come close to
incorporating 30 mathematical multiples of 7 as found in the
Hebrew words of Genesis 1:1.

If anyone doubts the difficulty of producing a passage
following such an intricate pattern of sevens, I challenge you
to try it yourself. I have tried, and it is impossible to complete
a paragraph on any topic and remain true to the system of
interlocking sevens. I doubt that anyone could complete a
paragraph of over one hundred and fifty words following

such a pattern of sevens, as found in Genesis 1:1 and Matthew, chapter 1, even if they were to devote several years to the effort. The problem is that with the addition of every single word and sentence the magnitude of the challenge to integrate the new phrase into the existing pattern grows geometrically. Each word and sentence must fit into the pattern existing within the preceding sentences. In light of this virtual impossibility we need to remember that the writers of the Bible were forty-four mostly common men who wrote their individual texts separated from one another over a period of sixteen centuries. How could these ordinary men contribute to this hidden pattern without consultation when most of them never met their fellow authors? The only logical explanation is that God directed their minds through supernatural inspiration to write His precise inspired words.

The number "seven" permeates the totality of Scripture because the number speaks of God's divine perfection and perfect order. The actual number 7 appears 287 times in the Old Testament ($287 \div 41 = 7$) while the word *seventh* occurs 98 times ($98 \div 14 = 7$). The word *seven-fold* appears seven times. In addition, the word *seventy* is used 56 times ($56 \div 8 = 7$).

Ivan Panin discovered literally thousands of such mathematical patterns underlying all of the books of the Old Testament before his death in 1942. I refer the interested reader to Panin's book, *The Inspiration of the Scriptures Scientifically Demonstrated,* which discusses these phenomena extensively. Panin and others have examined other Hebrew literature and have attempted to find such mathematical patterns, but they are not found anywhere outside the Bible.

Matthew 1:1-17—Evidence of Divine Authorship of the New Testament

Panin also examined the New Testament to discover whether or not the pattern continued. There were four hundred years of silence between the completion of the Old Testament around 396 B.C., and the writing of the New Testament following the resurrection of Jesus Christ. However, when God inspired the New Testament authors, including Matthew, to begin writing the Gospels, He again manifested His signature on the pages of Scripture by creating a marvelously complex pattern of sevens beneath the text of Matthew's Gospel.

The first section in Matthew's account consists of seventeen verses from Matthew 1:1 to 1:17 that describe in detail one particular subject, the genealogy of Jesus Christ. This seventeen-verse text contains 72 Greek Vocabulary words. A Vocabulary word is a particular word different from any other word that was used in a passage. In other words, a Greek word that appears 6 times in the passage would only be counted as 1 Vocabulary word. Obviously, the number of Vocabulary words will differ from the number of total words appearing in the passage. The same system of numeric and place values for letters exists in the Greek language used in the New Testament as we found in Hebrew of the Old Testament.

A Listing of the Phenomenal Features of Sevens Found in Matthew 1:1-17

1. The total numeric value of the 72 Vocabulary words is 43,364 (42,364 ÷ 6,052 = 7)   Seven

2. The number of Greek nouns in the passage
   is 56 (56 ÷ 8 = 7)   Seven
3. The Greek article for "the" occurs 56 times
   (56 ÷ 8 = 7)   Seven

In the first eleven verses of Matthew 1:1–11 we find these additional features:

4. The number of Greek vocabulary words is 49
   (49 ÷ 7 = 7)   Seven
5. Of these 49 words, 28 words begin with a vowel
   (28 ÷ 4 = 7)   Seven
6. Of these 49 words, 21 begin with a consonant
   (21 ÷ 3 = 7)   Seven
7. The number of letters in these 49 words equals
   266 (266 ÷ 38 = 7)   Seven
8. Of these 49 words, 35 words occur more than
   one time (35 ÷ 5 = 7)   Seven
9. Of these 49 words, 14 words occur
   only one time (14 ÷ 2 = 7)   Seven
10. The number of proper nouns is 35
    (35 ÷ 5 = 7)   Seven
11. The number of times these proper
    nouns occur is 63 (63 ÷ 9 = 7)   Seven
12. Of the 35 proper nouns, the number of
    male names is 28 (28 ÷ 4 = 7)   Seven
13. Three women, Tamar, Rahab, and Ruth, are named
    in this section. The number of Greek letters in
    these three names is 7 (14 ÷ 2 = 7)   Seven

Only a few of the numerical features that are found in this passage are listed in this analysis by Ivan Panin.

However, these features reveal an underlying profound mathematical design that reveals the signature of the true author of both the New Testament and the Old Testament—God Himself. However, to illustrate that this is not an unusual phenomenon occurring only in this one isolated passage, I will list some additional mathematical features that occur in the balance of Matthew 1:18–25 and describe the birth of Jesus Christ. In this seven-verse section God has placed an astonishing pattern of SEVENS that verify the signature of the original author.

The Pattern of SEVENS in Matthew 1:18–25—
The History of Christ's Birth

1. The number of letters in the seven word
   passage is 161 (161 ÷ 23 = 7)   Seven
2. The number of Vocabulary words is 77
   (77 ÷ 11 = 7)   Seven
3. Six Greek words occur only in this passage
   and never again in Matthew. These six
   Greek words contain precisely 56 letters
   (56 ÷ 8 = 7)   Seven
4. The number of distinct proper nouns in
   the passage is 7   Seven
5. The number of Greek letters in these seven
   proper nouns is 42 (42 ÷ 6 = 7)   Seven
6. The number of words spoken by the angel to
   Joseph is 28 (28 ÷ 4 = 7)   Seven
7. The number of Greek forms of words used in
   this passage is 161 (161 ÷ 23 = 7)   Seven
8. The number of Greek forms of words in the

angel's speech is 35 (35 ÷ 5 = 7)   Seven

9. The number of letters in the angel's 35 forms
    of words is 168 (168 ÷ 24 = 7)   Seven

This phenomenal discovery by Panin has been examined by numerous authorities and the figures have been verified. In total, Panin accumulated over forty thousand pages of detailed calculations covering most of the text of the Bible before his death. These incredible, mathematical patterns are not limited to the number seven. There are numerous other patterns. These amazing patterns appear in the vocabulary, grammatical forms, parts of speech, and particular forms of words. They occur throughout the whole text of the Bible containing 31,173 verses. When you consider the amazing details of this mathematical phenomenon you realize that the change of a single letter or word in the original languages of Hebrew or Greek would destroy the pattern. Now we can understand why Jesus Christ declared that the smallest letter and grammatical mark of the Scriptures were preserved by God's hand: "For verily I say unto you, Till heaven and earth pass, one jot or one tittle shall in no wise pass from the law, till all be fulfilled" (Matthew 5:18).

Naturally, the religious skeptics did not abandon their atheism in response to these incredible discoveries by Ivan Panin that revealed a staggering pattern of complexity hidden beneath the text of Scripture. After many skeptics had dismissed his research, Ivan Panin issued a public challenge through one of the major newspapers of the day, the *New York Sun,* in a letter to the editor on November 20, 1899, offering his detractors an opportunity to prove his research wrong if they could. Panin issued his public challenge to some of the greatest atheist scholars of the day. "I herewith respectfully invite any or all of the following to prove that my facts are not facts: namely Messrs. Lyman Abbott, Washington Gladden, Herber Newton, Minot J. Savage, Presidents Eliot of Harvard, White of Cornell, and Harper of the University of Chicago, Professor J. Henry Thayer of Harvard, and Dr. Briggs, and any other prominent higher critic so called. They may associate with themselves, if they choose, all the contributors to the ninth edition of the *Encyclopædia Britannica,* who wrote its articles on Biblical subjects, together with a dozen mathematicians of the calibre of Professor Simon Newcomb. The heavier the calibre of either scholar or mathematician, the more satisfactory to me. They will find that my facts are facts. And since they are facts, I am ready to take them to any three prominent lawyers, or, better still, to any judge of the superior or supreme court, and abide by his decision as to whether the conclusion is not necessary that Inspiration alone can account for the facts, if they are facts. All I should ask would be that the judge treat the case as he would any other case that comes before him."

Despite his public challenge in the *New York Sun,* not one of these prominent men attempted to refute Mr. Panin's undeniable facts or to deal with the unavoidable conclusion that the evidence produced by Panin proved that the Bible was truly inspired by a divine intelligence. The critics could not refute these facts. The only thing they could do was to ignore them. Were Mr. Panin's research and calculations wrong? If so, where? If they were correct, and they are, then the evidence exists for all to see that God did truly inspire the words of Scripture. One of Panin's last challenges consisted of this argument. He wrote to his detractors: "Lastly, my argument can also be refuted by showing that even though my facts be true, my arithmetic faultless, and my collocation of numerics honest, that men could have written thus without inspiration from above." However, any honest attempt to create a paragraph on any subject that will contain this astonishing pattern of mathematical features within the surface text will utterly fail. I doubt that even a modern Cray super-computer could produce a passage containing the "wheels within wheels" pattern of sevens as revealed in Genesis 1:1 or Matthew 1:1–25. To date, no one has succeeded in duplicating the phenomenon produced by the biblical writers in ancient times.

What was Panin's own view of the Scriptures after a lifetime of diligent study? He wrote the following statement in one of his essays after warning of the limitations of wisdom found in secular philosophy. "Not so, however, with The Book. For it tells of One who spake as men never spake, who was the true bread of life, that which cometh down from the heavens, of which if a man eat he shall never hunger." Ivan Panin's conclusion of the matter was the following challenge. "My friend of the world, whoso you are: Either Jesus Christ is mistaken or you are. The answer that neither might be is only evading the issue, not settling it. But the ages have decided that Jesus Christ was not mistaken. It is for you to decide whether you shall continue to be."

Why Did God Hide This Information Until This Century?

Possibly, the Lord hid this incredible revelation of His divine authority and authorship of the Scriptures until a generation would arise in the last days that would be primarily a generation of skeptics and unbelievers who would require such scientifically, verifiable evidence to convince men that the Bible is true. In addition, the prophet Daniel foretold that "knowledge shall be increased" in the last days and that the secrets of God would finally be unsealed. Daniel was told to "seal the vision until the end." As we approach the apocalyptic days when all of these prophecies will be fulfilled it is consistent that God would allow His servants to lift the veil and share His secrets to this final generation.

A careful examination of the evidence for divine inspiration demonstrated in the mathematical patterns and the words hidden beneath the text of Scriptures in this chapter reveals the true author of the Holy Scriptures. When comparing two documents or two devices a judge will look for similarities of design and pattern to determine if one creator is responsible for the creation of the two items. In a similar manner, the same mathematical patterns revealed in the Scriptures are also found in the rest of the physical creation proving that God is the author of both. The prophet Daniel reveals that one of the angelic messengers sent to him to prophesy about coming events of the last days is called "Palmoni" in the original Hebrew text, which means "the numberer of secrets" or "the wonderful numberer." In the English translation of Daniel 8:13–14 we find the angel's name was translated as "that certain saint." We are informed that Palmoni told Daniel the precise time of the duration of the defilement of the Temple sanctuary. "How long shall be the vision concerning the daily sacrifice, and the transgression of desolation, to give both the sanctuary and the host to be trodden under foot? And he said unto me, Unto two thousand and three hundred days; then shall the sanctuary be cleansed." As I showed in my earlier book, *Armageddon —Appointment with Destiny*, this prophecy points to the final cleansing of the Temple sanctuary in our generation. This same angel Palmoni, the "numberer of secrets" declares to the prophet Daniel, "For at the time appointed the end shall be" (Daniel 8:19).

Just as the number seven is found repeatedly hidden beneath the text of Scripture we find the same number used repeatedly by the Creator in His physical creation of the universe and its inhabitants. There are precisely seven colors in the light spectrum that merge together to form light. The study of music again reveals that there are exactly seven musically whole tones in the scale. Every eighth musical note creates a new higher octave repeating the pattern of seven tones. The seven colors correspond to the seven musical notes. In another manifestation of design, the whole human body is effectively renewed at the cellular level every seven years. By the end of seven years almost every single cell of our flesh, organs, and bones will be replaced with new cells manufactured according to an incredibly complex genetic program in our DNA. Our blood pulse rate slows down noticeably every seven days throughout our life. The gestation cycle to produce a baby takes 280 days (7 x 40). Our

lives are marked with the number seven as God commanded us to rest every seventh day and noted that our life
expectancy is seventy years (7 x 10). Almost all of the animals have gestation periods that are multiples of seven: lion
= 98 days; sheep = 147 days; hens = 21 days; ducks = 28
days; cats = 56 days; dogs = 63 days.

The number "seven" in Hebrew is derived from the root
word שבע meaning "to be full, satisfied, or have enough of"
while another meaning of the root is "to swear," or "to make an
oath." We find "seven" appearing on the surface of the biblical
text, as well as in prominent places, including the seven spirits
or manifestations of God (Isaiah 11:2); the seven-fold blessing
of Abraham (Genesis 12:2–3); God's seven-fold covenant with
Israel (Exodus 6:6–8); and the marvelous design of sevens
found in the Book of Revelation. John describes seven groups
of seven in his Apocalypse, including: 7 churches, 7 seals, 7
trumpets, 7 vials, 7 personages, 7 dooms, and 7 new things. A
profound and mysterious pattern of sevens runs through the
Scriptures from Genesis to Revelation both on its surface text
as well as hidden deep beneath the Hebrew and Greek letters.
The consistency of these remarkable patterns reveals the common authorship behind all sixty-six books of Holy Scripture.

Just as an expert's examination of a disputed document
can reveal the unmistakable signature and character of the
original writer, the mathematical and textual phenomenon
explored in this chapter prove conclusively to any open-
minded reader that the text of Scripture contains the genuine signature of its author—God. Four thousand years ago,
Moses wrote these words under the inspiration of God's
Holy Spirit: "The secret things belong unto the LORD our

God: but those things which are revealed belong unto us and to our children for ever, that we may do all the words of this law" (Deuteronomy 29:29). The evidence in this chapter reveals once more the signature of God revealed in the pages of the Scriptures.

Thirteen

The Phenomenon of "Undesigned Coincidences"

One of the strongest proofs that the Scriptures are absolutely reliable and inspired by God is revealed in the phenomenon called "undesigned coincidences" in the Bible, which cannot be explained unless these writings are absolutely true. The evidence of undesigned coincidences was first noted in 1738 by Dr. Philip Doddridge in his *Introduction to the First Epistle to the Thessalonians.* Doddridge wrote, "Whoever reads over St. Paul's epistles with attention . . . will discern such intrinsic characters of their genuineness, and the divine authority of the doctrines they contain, as will perhaps produce in him a stronger conviction than all the external evidence with which they are attended. To which we may add, that the exact coincidence observable between the many allusions to particular facts, in this as well as in other epistles, and the account of the facts themselves, as they are recorded in the history of the Acts, is a remarkable confirmation of the truth of each."

Dr. Paley, in his noteworthy book *Horæ Paulinæ,* was the first writer to develop this evidence regarding these coincidences in great detail as proof that no man could have created these Epistles of Paul without the divine aid of God Himself. However, the greatest evidence of this type was researched by Rev. J. J. Blunt as detailed in his book, *Undesigned Coincidences in the Writings of the Old and New Testament.* As Rev. Blunt declared in his fascinating manuscript, the evidence from "instances of coincidence without design" provides an incredibly strong proof that the Scriptures were inspired by God (London: John Murray, 1847). The evidence from coincidence is so strong in the mind of the average person that juries have often convicted people of capital crimes upon this kind of evidence. The value of this evidence is that it establishes a strong proof that the individual authors of the books of the Bible acted as independent witnesses to the facts that they observed and recorded in the Scriptures. Furthermore, these coincidences are such as could not possibly have arisen as a result of mutual understanding among the biblical writers or artificial arrangement. Often the facts and evidence that coincidentally prove the accuracy of the Bible's narrative are found in obscure passages unconnected with the main passage describing the story.

The Rebellion of Absalom Against King David

One of the saddest and most tragic stories found in the pages of the Scriptures concerns the revolt of David's son Prince Absalom toward the end of David's reign and the agony experienced by the king when his beloved and rebellious son was killed. Absalom was the third son born to David as a result of his marriage with Maacah, the daughter of Talmai, the king of Geshur. This story has often been preached from the pulpit to remind us of the consequences of pride and blind ambition in the inevitable judgment of God upon Absalom's rebellion and his ultimate death. Many preachers have reminded parents about David's complacency in failing to discipline his favorite son as he grew to manhood, full of pride and arrogance. The Scriptures record that "Absalom prepared him chariots and horses, and fifty men to run before him" (2 Samuel 15:1) and stirred rebellion against his father by promising the people that he would rule in their favor when he became king of Israel. David's unwillingness to deal with the growing rebellion of his son ultimately set the stage for Absalom's revolt against his father's throne, David's flight from Jerusalem, and the bitter war against the rebels. Finally, the tragic moment came when David heard of his loyal army's victory over the rebels. He cried out in anguish, "Is the young man Absalom safe?" (2 Samuel 18:29). When the servants of the king finally had the courage to tell the truth, they admitted that Absalom was dead. King David wept bitterly for the loss of his beloved son, crying out, "O my son Absalom, my son, my son Absalom! would God I had died for thee, O Absalom, my son, my son!" (2 Samuel 18:33).

In the midst of the rebellion the Bible records that, "Absalom sent for Ahithophel the Gilonite, David's counsellor, from his city, even from Giloh, while he offered sacrifices. And the conspiracy was strong; for the people increased continually with Absalom" (2 Samuel 15:12). Ahithophel had been King David's faithful counselor or prime minister for many decades, giving the king the benefit of his great wisdom. The Book of Samuel tells us that Ahithophel was considered a brilliant counselor. "And the counsel of Ahithophel, which he counselled in those days, was as if a man had enquired at the oracle of God: so was all the counsel of Ahithophel both with David and with Absalom" (2 Samuel 16:23). In fact, when David learned that his trusted friend and counselor had betrayed him, he was so afraid of the danger from Ahithophel that he prayed, "O LORD, I pray thee, turn the counsel of Ahithophel into foolishness" (2 Samuel 15:31). Years earlier King David had prophesied a double prophecy in his Book of Psalms that foresaw the betrayal by his friend Ahithophel. However, David's words also predicted the ultimate betrayal a thousand years later of Jesus of Nazareth by His friend and disciple Judas Iscariot. "Yea, mine own familiar friend, in whom I trusted, which did eat of my bread, hath lifted up his heel against me" (Psalm 41:9).

The question that has troubled many Bible students and writers of commentaries is this. Why did Ahithophel, David's trusted counselor, immediately join Absalom's rebellion against his father's throne after a lifetime of faithful service? Furthermore, why would Ahithophel ask the young prince to allow him personally to lead the army of rebels to attack and kill King David immediately before the king could escape? "Moreover Ahithophel said unto Absalom, Let me now choose out twelve thousand men, and I will arise and pursue after David this night . . . and I will smite the king only" (2 Samuel 17:1–2). Finally, why would Ahithophel advise Absalom to have sexual relations openly with his father's wives on the roof of the palace? "And Ahithophel said unto Absalom, Go in unto thy father's concubines, which he hath left to keep the house; and all Israel shall hear that thou art abhorred of thy father: then shall the hands of all that are with thee be strong. So they spread Absalom a tent upon the top of the house; and Absalom went in unto his father's concubines in the sight of all Israel" (2 Samuel 16:21–22). The Bible does not openly record the motivation for this incredible betrayal of King David as if the reason were so obvious to people living in that day that there was no need to comment on it.

The answer to this great mystery is found in several of the passages in the Old Testament that often cause readers to skip forward because the list of names recorded in the chapter seems to have little relevance to us. However, the solution to this puzzle about Ahithophel's motive does exist in the Word of God and it reveals a very important lesson that every single follower of Christ needs to learn. To find the solution to the mystery of the betrayal surrounding Absalom's rebellion, we need to go back almost thirty years to the incident when David committed adultery with Bathsheba, the beautiful wife of Uriah the Hittite. Most commentators and preachers have discussed the sin of David as if it were the result of a momentary weakness when he happened to observe the woman Bathsheba bathing. The truth is somewhat different. When David was supposed to be at war leading his troops against the enemy, the Scriptures record that he had stayed home in his palace in Jerusalem. "And it came to pass, after the year was expired, at the time when kings go forth to battle, that David sent Joab, and his servants with him, and all Israel; and they destroyed the children of Ammon, and besieged Rabbah. But David tarried still at Jerusalem" (2 Samuel 11:1). David's first mistake was that he was not in the place God had called him to be, leading his nation against their enemies as their king. As the evidence unfolds about this biblical mystery, we will also find that Bathsheba was no stranger to the king.

When you read the Scriptures carefully you will note that the passage describing Bathsheba tells us that she was the "daughter of Eliam" and "the wife of Uriah the Hittite" (2 Samuel 11:3). Another significant passage in the Book of Samuel lists the great military heroes that guarded King David throughout his many battles against Saul, the Philistines, and many enemy nations. This list of the thirty-seven "mighty men" of David records that "Uriah the Hittite" and "Eliam the son of Ahithophel the Gilonite" were part of this elite force that fought for the king (2 Samuel 23:34, 39). Now we can begin to understand what was occurring behind the scenes in this famous biblical story. Uriah the Hittite, the husband of Bathsheba, and Eliam, the father of Bathsheba, are not strangers to David. They are friends who had fought back-to-back against their enemies over many years. They had sat together around the campfire at night during many military campaigns. Bathsheba is the wife of Uriah, David's loyal bodyguard, and the daughter of Eliam, another faithful bodyguard. David viewed Bathsheba while she was bathing because Uriah and his wife had a house close to King David's palace as a probable reward for his years of loyal service. It is very likely that Bathsheba, Uriah, and her father, Eliam, had attended royal banquets in David's palace.

The story of David's sin with Bathsheba takes on a very different complexion in light of these scriptural facts that have been unnoticed for centuries. When David committed adultery with Bathsheba, he took the wife of Uriah, a loyal friend, and the daughter of another friend. Then when she became pregnant, David tried to get Uriah to visit his wife to provide confusion about when and how she became pregnant. When Uriah refused to visit his wife, David conspired with his general Joab to murder Uriah to cover up his shameful betrayal and adultery. Later, the prophet Nathan came to David and proclaimed God's anger against David's sins of adultery and the murder of Uriah. Nathan warned that David would be afflicted by warfare the rest of his life in punishment for his sins. Furthermore, the prophet foretold that "by this deed thou hast given great occasion to the enemies of the LORD to blaspheme, the child also that is born unto thee shall surely die" (2 Samuel 12:14). Throughout history this prophecy was fulfilled as the skeptics and critics attacked the Bible and King David's character by referring to his great sin with Bathsheba.

Yet, there is still more to the story. Note carefully that 2 Samuel 23:34 told us that Eliam, the father of Bathsheba, was also the son of Ahithophel, David's counselor. Therefore, Ahithophel, David's prime minister, was the grandfather of Bathsheba. After David sinned with Bathsheba and killed Uriah, many people in the palace and the army would have realized that David was the father of the child born to Bathsheba after the death of her husband. People living at that time knew the length of a woman's pregnancy was nine months and therefore knew that the king must be the father of the child of the widow Bathsheba, whom he later married. As David's counselor in the palace, Ahithophel must have burned with rage to know his king had betrayed his granddaughter's honor and killed Uriah, her husband, who was a fellow soldier with his son Eliam, Bathsheba's father. However, there was nothing he could do at that time to exact his revenge. If he had risen in anger against the king, he would have lost his life. So he remained silent, keeping his thoughts of revenge secretly to himself all of the years that followed until he saw an opportunity to destroy King David. The Arabs have an expression, "That man who seeks his revenge before forty years has past, has moved in haste."

Finally, after decades of waiting, King David's rebellious son Absalom revolted against his aged father. This was Ahithophel's chance to get revenge for the wrongs committed years earlier against his family. He joined Absalom's conspiracy and offered to kill David personally. Finally, we can understand Ahithophel's strange advice to Absalom to have sexual relations with David's wives "in the sight of all Israel." He was attempting to get his revenge by encouraging Absalom to do the same thing to David's wives as the king had done to his granddaughter. Significantly, as David fled from Jerusalem, a man named Shimei cursed the king and cast stones at him, saying, "Behold, thou art taken in thy mischief, because thou art a bloody man" (2 Samuel 16:8). When David's men wanted to kill this man, the king stopped them, and stated that the man was right and that God had told him to curse the king. Obviously, King David knew very well, as did the people around him, why Ahithophel had joined Absalom's revolt.

These verses provided clues and evidence that finally allowed us to solve the mystery of Ahithophel's betrayal of David. More important, these clues scattered in passages throughout the Old Testament provide an overwhelming evidence for the truthfulness of the Bible's report about the life of King David. No one writing a story like this as fiction would hide the clues so well that the mystery of Ahithophel's motive for betrayal could not be discovered for thousands of years. However, someone truthfully recording a contemporary series of events will often pass over in silence the motive for a person's actions because that motive is so obvious and well known to the writer and those who were living at the time of the events. The presence of coincidental evidence such as we find in this analysis provides very strong proof that the biblical record is a faithful and reliable account of the events in question. As Paul Harvey often says when he completes his fascinating radio program, "Now you know the rest of the story!"

There is one further detail that should not be overlooked. Consider how David responded to his sin and God's punishment in the death of his child born to Bathsheba. While the baby was sick, King David fasted and prayed that God would allow the child to live. However, after his child died, David stopped fasting and said, "But now he is dead, wherefore should I fast? can I bring him back again? I shall go to him, but he shall not return to me" (2 Samuel 12:23). In this touching scene, where the Bible assures us that children who die will go to heaven, we can see the difference between the way a man thinks about his sin and the way God deals with our sins. King David had sinned in his weakness. He sincerely repented of his sins as witnessed by his touching words of deep repentance in his Psalms. His son had died as God warned through His prophet Nathan's words. David stopped fasting and prepared to carry on with the rest of his life, believing that his sin and its consequences were over forever.

This is the way most Christians think about their sins. When convicted of our sin, we sincerely repent and ask God to forgive us. The Lord forgives our sin and we believe, like King David, that the consequences of our sins are removed. We believe that it's all over. However, although God truly forgives our sins, it's not over. God will not stop the natural consequences of our sin from affecting our lives and the lives of those around us. When we sin, it is similar to throwing a pebble on a pond. The ripples on the pond are like the effects of our sinful actions that will affect many things in our lives and those we know. Often the consequences will cause great problems many years later. King David thought his sin with Bathsheba was dealt with forever, but the tragic consequences caught up with him years later and almost caused him to lose his life and throne. At a time in his life when David should have been enjoying his victories and honors, the consequences of his sin from years before almost destroyed him. David was forced to flee from his royal city, up the side of the Mount of Olives in fear after the betrayal of his son and his closest counselor. It was the worst moment in his long life.

The true and lasting consequences of our sins are often underestimated by Christians. Sometimes Christians, when they are tempted to sin, begin to think like King David. They feel that they can sin, then ask God to forgive their sin and that He will make everything perfect as if their sin had never occurred. But our sins have consequences that will continue to destroy our bodies, our friendships, our families, and our careers, years after God has forgiven us if we truly repent of our rebellion. We need to realize that, when we choose to sin against God, the effects of our choice will continue to affect our life as long as we live. While God does forgive He does not change the law of cause and effect that will inevitably produce the consequences of our sins.

David and Goliath

The story of David and Goliath is one of the most well known of the Bible stories. During that time the Jews were under the brutal domination of the Philistines. Finally, the Lord raised up a hero to stand against the Philistines and defeat their great champion, Goliath. The army of Israel faced the army of the Philistines, but King Saul could not find an Israelite brave enough to engage the Philistine's giant warrior in hand-to-hand combat that would determine who would dominate the land. There are a number of small details or coincidences in this biblical story that provide very strong proof that it is a genuine account. Consider that the Bible mentions that Goliath comes from the village of Gath. "And there went out a champion out of the camp of the Philistines, named Goliath, of Gath, whose height was six cubits and a span" (1 Samuel 17:4). This is significant because Gath was one of the villages where the giant race of Anakims lived. When the twelve spies entered Canaan they were fearful of the giant races that lived in the land. "And they brought up an evil report of the land which they had searched unto the children of Israel, saying, The land, through which we have gone to search it, is a land that eateth up the inhabitants thereof; and all the people that we saw in it are men of a great stature" (Numbers 13:32).

Another passage in the Book of Joshua tells us that Gath was one of the few places where the giant race of Anakim still survived. "And at that time came Joshua, and cut off the Anakims from the mountains, from Hebron, from Debir, from Anab, and from all the mountains of Judah, and from all the mountains of Israel: Joshua destroyed them utterly with their cities. There was none of the Anakims left in the land of the children of Israel: only in Gaza, in Gath, and in Ashdod, there remained" (Joshua 11:21–22). There were only three cities in Israel where the remnants of the giants survived. This coincidence that, four hundred years after the conquest of Canaan, we find Goliath living in Gath, one of those three villages, is a marvelous confirmation of the truthfulness of the biblical record about David and Goliath. In this coincidence we find that three separate biblical books, Numbers, Joshua, and Samuel, confirm the accuracy of one of the elements in this famous biblical account.

One other feature in the story of David and Goliath always fascinated me as a young boy. Why did David pick up five smooth stones for his sling when he knew that God would guide his aim to kill the Philistine giant with only one stone? Did David lack faith in God's supernatural power to destroy Israel's great enemy? The answer to this mystery appeared to me one night when I was reading the Book of 2 Samuel, chapter 21. To my surprise I found that Goliath was not the only giant in his family. The father of Goliath was a giant who had five sons, all of whom fought for the Philistines. Every one of these four brothers was also a giant who ultimately died in combat with the brave soldiers of David. Summarizing the story of their death in combat with David's men, the prophet Samuel recorded: "These four were born to the giant in Gath, and fell by the hand of David, and by the hand of his servants" (2 Samuel 21:22). When David picked up five smooth stones for his sling he was simply being prudent in preparing for the possibility that Goliath's four brothers might have joined the battle when Goliath was killed. He might have needed the additional four stones to defeat the four other giants.

Why Did Israel Not Use Horses?

I believe the horse is the most noble and beautiful animal on earth. I grew up on a ranch in Canada where my family ran a western-style Christian summer camp for young people, Frontier Ranch, where we raised over a hundred quarter horses. Some of my fondest memories are those when I would ride my horse along old abandoned logging trails and camp out overnight in the forest. As one who loves horses I always thought it strange that the Israelites never used horses in their many battles against the pagan armies in their conquest of the Holy Land prior to the reign of King Solomon.

Why did Israel never use horses to defend themselves against the cavalry and war-horses of their enemies? There are one hundred and eighty-eight references to horses throughout the Old Testament, proving that the horse was well known to the Jews. The Book of Job describes the glory and bravery of the horse in the following passages: "Hast thou given the horse strength? hast thou clothed his neck with thunder? Canst thou make him afraid as a grasshopper? the glory of his nostrils is terrible. He paweth in the valley, and rejoiceth in his strength: he goeth on to meet the armed men. He mocketh at fear, and is not affrighted; neither turneth he back from the sword. The quiver rattleth against him, the glittering spear and the shield. He swalloweth the ground with fierceness and rage: neither believeth he that it is the sound of the trumpet" (Job 39:19-24).

Archeology has revealed that horses were commonly used in the armies and societies of all of the ancient nations of the Middle East, with the exception of Israel, until the reign of King Solomon approximately 970 B.C. For example, the Ten Commandments prohibited the Jews from coveting an ox or ass, but there was no mention of horses. "Thou shalt not covet thy neighbour's house, thou shalt not covet thy neighbour's wife, nor his manservant, nor his maid-servant, nor his ox, nor his ass, nor any thing that is thy neighbour's" (Exodus 20:17). In the Book of Judges we find evidence that donkeys were the normal mode of trans-portation for Israel rather than horses. As an example, according to Joshua 15:18, when the daughter of Caleb, a leader of Israel, came to visit Othniel she used an ass, or donkey, not a horse. The Book of Judges revealed that the governors of Israel rode upon white asses. Later, we read of Saul searching for the lost asses of his father. In the passages of the Old Testament dealing with this period before the reign of King Solomon, although the Jewish state trained very effective armies and won numerous wars in their con-quest of Canaan, they never used horses for cavalry nor for their war chariots. The only horses mentioned were those of the enemies of Israel such as the nine hundred chariots of the cavalry of King Jabin of Canaan. In the Bible's description of the battle with the Philistines, when they seized the Ark of God, Israel lost thirty thousand infantry, but there was no mention of horsemen, proving they had no cavalry. The Scriptures describe the battle against King David, when his son Absalom was killed by riding his mule under the branches of a tree, proving that even royal princes did not ride horses in that time.

Why did Israel refuse to use horses for their cavalry when the foreign armies had the advantage of horses in their cavalry and war chariots? The answer is found in a single command of God forbidding the use of horses as recorded in Deuteronomy 17:16. "But he shall not multiply horses to himself, nor cause the people to return to Egypt, to the end that he should multiply horses: forasmuch as the LORD hath said unto you, Ye shall henceforth return no more that way."

The primary reason for God's prohibition of horses for Israel was the fact that Egypt was the world's premier source of breeding farms to produce war-horses. God knew that Israel would be tempted to enter into alliances with Egypt to acquire horses for their army. Therefore, the Lord gave a prohibition against the use of horses to ensure that Israel would not depend on an alliance with Egypt to obtain war-horses. Egypt used its virtual monopoly on war-horses to enforce a series of alliances. Just as America and Russia use the supply of advanced weapons they offer to client states to lock them into defensive treaties, nations could only purchase Egyptian war-horses if they entered into defensive treaties with Egypt. Therefore, if Israel had acquired horses from Egypt, she would have been entangled in foreign alliances rather than trust in the power of God to save her.

However, there is another reason. Israel was a nation of valiant soldiers who won astonishing battles against the overwhelming armies of her pagan enemies, through the supernatural power of God. When they won such battles against the more powerful armies of her pagan enemies, they knew that it was only through the supernatural power of their God. When they acknowledged that they won such battles through God's miraculous intervention, the Lord received the glory. War chariots with horses and cavalry were the equivalent of modern tanks in terms of warfare. By forbidding the Jewish state to acquire horses, God assured that the Israelites would be forced to fight defensive battles to protect the territory of the Holy Land that the Lord had given to them. If the aggressive armies of Israel had access to highly mobile horses, they would have been tempted to use their increased mobility with horses and war chariots to conquer foreign lands and nations far beyond the borders of the Promised Land. The coincidence that Israel never used horses in its many battles until the apostasy that followed King Solomon's reign, without the writers ever explaining their motive, provides a strong indication that the narrative is genuine and accurate.

The coincidences discussed in this chapter form a subtle kind of proof for the inspiration of the Scriptures. I have just touched the tip of the iceberg of those that we could examine. However, if you think about this evidence carefully, you will appreciate that these undesigned coincidences are absolutely consistent with God's direct inspiration of the Bible.

Fourteen

The Evidence of the Men Who Wrote the New Testament

"The Bible itself is a standing and an astonishing miracle. Written, fragment by fragment, throughout the course of fifteen centuries, under all different states of society, and in different languages, by persons of the most opposite tempers, talents, and conditions, learned and unlearned, prince and peasant, bond and free: cast into every form of instructive composition and good writing, history, prophecy, poetry, allegory, emblematic representation. Judicious interpretation, literal statement, precept, example, proverbs, disquisition, epistle, sermon, prayer—in short all rational shapes of human discourse; and treating, moreover, of subjects not obvious, but most difficult—its authors are not found, like other writers, contradicting one another upon the most ordinary matters of fact and opinion, but are at harmony upon the whole of their sublime and momentous scheme" (Professor Maclagan).

Aside from the pages of the Scriptures, we know almost nothing about the lives of the Jewish patriarchs, priests, and prophets who were chosen by God to record His revelations to mankind in the Old Testament. However, one of the unusual features of the Scriptures that proves it was inspired by God is that the writers of the Bible wrote as no other men have ever written, before or since. The normal tendency of writers in literature is to protect their reputations by disguising or minimizing their weaknesses and failures. In total contrast to normal human motivations, the writers of the Bible reveal themselves "warts and all" throughout their manuscripts. Rather than minimize their mistakes and weaknesses, these writers revealed their total character; both weaknesses and strengths. This is one of the strongest proofs that these men were inspired by God to record these words for eternity in the Word of God. The apostles who wrote the Gospels admit that they hid in fear when their leader was arrested and crucified. They admit to many human weaknesses and failures, yet they changed their world through the supernatural power of God's Holy Spirit.

The Lives of the Apostles

On the other hand, when we examine the lives of the writers of the New Testament, we find that there is a considerable amount of historical evidence about the lives of the disciples and apostles revealed within the writings of the early Church. Jesus Christ chose the twelve apostles whose role was to confirm by their words and their lives the reality of the life, death, and resurrection of Jesus Christ. As a new faith, Christianity needed reliable eyewitness accounts of those who would personally verify the facts regarding the life of Jesus of Nazareth. He commanded these fishermen and tax collectors to abandon their previous lives and follow Him to a destiny beyond that of any other man in the history of mankind. To this day, two thousand years later, millions of parents still name their sons by the names of the apostles who followed Jesus Christ and turned their world upside down. Certainly, Christ's choice of disciples was not based on their previous character or accomplishments because none of them had risen to prominence in the society of Israel in the first century. It is interesting to note that Jesus did not choose the type of men most modern leaders would choose for such an overwhelming task of preaching a revolutionary message to the world. None of the twelve disciples were religious scholars or professional men of distinction before Christ chose them. None of the disciples were wealthy; none were professionals or natural leaders within the Jewish society during that first century. None of the revealed personal qualities of the disciples at the time Jesus chose them suggested that they would ultimately prove to be great men of faith who would stand the test of time. However, after only three and a half years in the daily presence of Jesus, these men were transformed into great men of God who would stand unflinchingly against the imperial power of Rome, the greatest power on earth in their lifetime.

Jesus apparently chose His disciples in the same manner that the sculptor Michelangelo chose the rough marble for his projects—because he saw the possibilities hidden within the uncut stone. A story about Michelangelo tells about a young girl who watched the sculptor as he produced his masterpiece in his workshop in Rome. As she watched him chisel into the huge block of marble, she asked Michelangelo how he knew that the figure of David lay hidden within the huge block of uncut marble. The answer, of course, was that Michelangelo, the master sculptor, saw in his imagination the possibility of what the marble could reveal if he removed the unnecessary material that surrounded and hid the potentially beautiful sculpture from the eyes of anyone but the master sculptor. Jesus Christ chose His band of disciples, not for what they were in themselves before He met them, but for what they could become after the touch of the Master's hand. The truth of this statement is found in the Gospel of John, which recorded Christ's words: "And when Jesus beheld him, he said, *Thou art Simon* the son of Jona: *thou shalt be called* Cephas, which is by interpretation, A stone" (John 1:42, italics added). The transformation of the character of the apostles was possibly the greatest miracle performed by Jesus Christ during His years of ministry. These simple disciples, after living in the presence of Jesus Christ, turned the world upside down. The result of their teaching the words of Jesus Christ was to turn their world right side up.

When Jesus entered history two thousand years ago, the Roman Empire held over half of the population of the known world as slaves, subject to the vilest abuse of their masters. Most of humanity lived as slaves or serfs under the cruel brutality of Rome's mighty legions. Yet the life and teaching of Jesus, as expressed in the lives of these twelve men and those who took up the cross to follow Him, would ultimately transform this wicked Roman Empire into the first society in history that would proclaim and uphold the rights of men and women to live in freedom and liberty. In a similar manner, Jesus is still transforming the lives and characters of countless men and women who are still turning their world right side up. When we encounter Jesus Christ, the most important thing is not our previous personal history of sinful rebellion, but the transformation that Jesus Christ will produce in us when we surrender our lives to His power and authority. Through His grace and power He can transform every one of us into someone who can make a true difference in our world as witnesses of His power to save and transform the lives of His followers.

One of the criteria by which we can judge the trustworthiness of the testimony of the apostles is whether or not they held firmly and consistently throughout their lives to their testimony about Christ's miracles, His claims to be God, and His death and resurrection. The combined testimony of their teachings, the history of their lives, and their martyrdom provides the strongest witness to the truthfulness of their story. After the arrest, trial, and death of Jesus, these men initially fled in fear. However, these same men were totally transformed in their characters by the power of the Holy Spirit in the days following the resurrection of Christ. The historical records of the first century clearly prove that every one of these men later faced a martyr's death without denying their faith in Jesus Christ as their Savior. What could possibly account for their transformation from defeated cowards to mighty men of God within a few days of the death of their leader? Obviously, the only answer that makes sense is that these men were transformed in their character and motivation by their personal knowledge of the facts surrounding the resurrection of Jesus Christ.

Some atheists have suggested that the disciples, during the decades following His death, simply invented their accounts of Jesus. These Bible critics say that the disciples, in an attempt to enhance His authority, then published the story that Jesus claimed to be God and was resurrected. Any fair-minded reader should consider the historical evidence. First, the apostles were continually threatened and pressured to deny their Lord during their ministry; especially as they faced torture and martyrdom. However, none of these men who spent time with Jesus chose to save their lives by denying their faith in Him. Consider this hypothetical situation: Suppose these men had conspired to form a new religion based on their imagination. How long would anyone continue to proclaim something they knew was a lie when faced with lengthy torture and an inescapable, painful death? All they had to do to escape martyrdom was to admit they had concocted a lie and simply deny their faith and claims about Jesus as God. It defies both common sense and the evidence of history that anyone, let alone a group of twelve men, would persist in proclaiming a lie when they could walk away by admitting that it was a fraud.

Yet, history reveals that not one of these men, who knew Jesus personally, ever denied their testimony about Him despite the threat and reality of imminent death. This proves to any fair-minded observer that these men possessed an absolute, unshakable personal knowledge about the truth of the life, death, and resurrection of Jesus. Each of the apostles was called upon to pay the ultimate price to prove their faith in Jesus, affirming with their life's blood that Jesus was the true Messiah, the Son of God, and the only hope of salvation for a sinful humanity.

The Martyrdom of the Apostles

Most of our information about the deaths of the apostles is derived from early Church traditions. While tradition is unreliable as to small details, it very seldom contains outright inventions. Eusebius, the most important of the early Church historians, wrote his history of the early Church in A.D. 325. He wrote, "The apostles and disciples of the Savior scattered over the whole world, preached the Gospel everywhere." The Church historian Schumacher researched the lives of the apostles and recounted the history of their martyrdoms.

Matthew suffered martyrdom in Ethiopia, killed by a sword wound.

Mark died in Alexandria, Egypt, after being dragged by horses through the streets until he was dead.

Luke was hanged in Greece as a result of his tremendous preaching to the lost.

John faced martyrdom when he was boiled in a huge basin of boiling oil during a wave of persecution in Rome. However, he was miraculously delivered from death. John was then sentenced to the mines on the prison island of Patmos. He wrote his prophetic Book of Revelation on Patmos. The apostle John was later freed and returned to serve as Bishop of Edessa in modern Turkey. He died as an old man, the only apostle to die peacefully.

Peter was crucified upside down on an x-shaped cross, according to Church tradition, because he told his tormentors that he felt unworthy to die in the same way that Jesus Christ had died.

James the Just, the leader of the church in Jerusalem, was thrown over a hundred feet down from the southeast pinnacle of the Temple when he refused to deny his faith in Christ. When they discovered that he survived the fall, his enemies beat James to death with a fuller's club. This was the same pinnacle where Satan had taken Jesus during the Temptation.

James the Greater, a son of Zebedee, was a fisherman by trade when Jesus called him to a lifetime of ministry. As a strong leader of the Church, James was ultimately beheaded at Jerusalem. The Roman officer who guarded James watched amazed as James defended his faith at his trial. Later, the officer walked beside James to the place of execution. Overcome by conviction, he declared his new faith to the judge and knelt beside James to accept beheading as a Christian.

Bartholomew, also known as Nathanael, was a missionary to Asia. He witnessed to our Lord in present-day Turkey. Bartholomew was martyred for his preaching in Armenia when he was flayed to death by a whip.

Andrew was crucified on an x-shaped cross in Patras, Greece. After being whipped severely by seven soldiers, he was tied to the cross with cords to prolong his agony. His followers reported that, when he was led toward the cross, Andrew saluted it in these words: "I have long desired and expected this happy hour. The cross has been consecrated by the body of Christ hanging on it." He continued to preach to his tormentors for two days until he expired.

The apostle Thomas was stabbed with a spear in India during one of his missionary trips to establish the Church in the sub-continent.

Jude, the brother of Jesus, was killed with arrows when he refused to deny his faith in Christ.

Matthias, the apostle chosen to replace the traitor Judas Iscariot, was stoned and then beheaded.

Barnabas, one of the group of seventy disciples, wrote the *Epistle of Barnabas*. He preached throughout Italy and

Cyprus. Barnabas was stoned to death at Salonica.

The apostle Paul was tortured and then beheaded by the evil emperor Nero at Rome in A.D. 67. Paul endured a lengthy imprisonment, which allowed him to write his many Epistles to the churches he had formed throughout the Roman Empire. These letters, which taught many of the foundational doctrines of Christianity, form a large portion of the New Testament.

The details of the martyrdoms of the disciples and apostles are found in traditional early Church sources. These traditions were recounted in the writings of the Church fathers and the first official Church history written by the historian Eusebius in A.D. 325. Although we cannot at this time verify every detail historically, the universal belief of the early Christian writers was that each of the apostles had faced martyrdom faithfully without denying his faith in the resurrection of Jesus Christ.

The Transformed Lives of Men and Women

"The study of God's Word for the purpose of discovering God's will, is the secret discipline which has formed the greatest characters" (J. W. Alexander, quoted in *Leaves of Gold*).

One of the greatest and most convincing bodies of evidence proving the truth of the Bible is found in the transformed lives of men and women who placed their faith and trust in Jesus Christ. An abiding faith in the revealed truth of God in the Scriptures strengthens people to rely on God in the face of the greatest trials and tribulations of their life. An unshakable faith in the Bible's revelation will enable us to stand against the greatest persecutions as

Hebrews 11 records how great heroes of the Bible stood against the opposition of Satan.

The Scriptures have fascinated and held the undying attention of the most brilliant men of each age. An anonymous writer once wrote, "He who teaches the Bible is never a scholar; he is always a student." An early Church father living in the second century, Tertullian, devoted his life to the study of Scripture each day and night. By the end of his life Tertullian had memorized most of the Bible, including the punctuation! A profound love of the Scriptures motivated the Christians in those early centuries of persecution to walk in obedience to their Savior, Jesus Christ. Eusebius, the greatest historian of the early Church, wrote about one persecuted Christian whose eyes were burned out during one of the ten great waves of persecution against the early Church. Despite the loss of his eyes, this Christian saint could repeat to assembled Christians large portions of the Bible from memory. Thomas Beza, the brilliant translator of the Scriptures in A.D. 1585, had such a profound love of the words of his Savior that, at the age of eighty, he could still repeat from memory in the Greek language all of the New Testament Epistles. Two of the leading reformers during the Protestant Reformation, Cranmer and Ridley, found their faith immeasurably strengthened as both memorized the entire New Testament during the time of their persecution. Those who love the Bible will never find themselves without a faithful friend, a wholesome and wise counselor, the most cheerful companion, and the most effectual comforter of their soul.

Dr. A. T. Pierson suggested in one of his books about

the Scriptures that we should approach spiritual discovery much as the ancient Jews approached the Temple in Jerusalem. The Outer Court of the Gentiles is analogous to the letter of Scripture. The Inner Court of the Israelites, a much holier place, is similar to the inner truth of Scripture; the Holy of Holies, the most holy place in the Temple, is equivalent to the person of Jesus Christ Himself. It is only when we pass through the veil into the innermost Holy of Holies that we come to meet Him face to face.

The great men who founded the United States of America, including George Washington, were strongly influenced by their faith in the Word of God. President Washington once declared, "It is impossible to rightly govern the world without God and the Bible." The great writer Charles Dickens stated that the Bible is the Word of God. "The New Testament is the very best book that ever was or ever will be known in the world." Another great writer, Lord Francis Bacon, was the finest scientist in England in the sixteenth century and contributed much to the scientific study of nature. Bacon wrote a pivotal book, *The Advancement of Learning*, in which he called for a study to be made of Bible prophecy to show systematically how God had precisely fulfilled the predictions made over thousands of years. Filled with wonder at the creation of the world, Francis Bacon wrote: "Thy creatures, O Lord, have been my books, but thy Holy Scriptures much more. I have sought thee in the courts, fields and gardens; but I have found thee, O God, in thy sanctuary, thy temples." Although Bacon acknowledged the awesome evidence about God revealed by science and nature, he discovered that the most profound knowledge of God was found in his detailed study of the inspired Word of God.

Many Christians have personally studied the Scofield Reference Bible. However, very few are aware of the spiritual motivation that encouraged C. I. Scofield to embark upon the production of a study Bible complete with cross references and study notes to help the student explore the biblical text. When he was a young Christian, Scofield met a friend, C. E. Paxson, in his office and noted that his friend had marked his Bible with notes and underlined related passages. Scofield was initially angry at the idea that his friend had defaced his Bible with these personal markings. However, he soon realized that these markings were extremely helpful to his friend and assisted in his understanding of the relation between various passages. In his later life Scofield would declare that the inspiration of his friend's Bible markings would lead him to prepare the exhaustive study notes and research presented in the now-famous Scofield Reference Bible with its helpful footnotes, maps, and cross-references. Truly, the Bible is a deep well that can never be exhausted by a student of the Scriptures. Those who preach constantly from the depths of God's Word will always have something fresh and meaningful to say to their hearers.

The Seven Wonders of the Word of God

We have all heard of the Seven Wonders of the World that have fascinated mankind throughout history. Yet, for those who will examine the evidence, the Scriptures should hold an equal fascination. The Bible also manifests Seven Wonders of the Word of God.

1.   The wonder of its formation.

The marvelous manner in which the Scriptures grew from the first five books of Moses to include all thirty-nine books of the Old Testament and, then, the addition of the twenty-seven books of the New Testament in the first century of our era, is one of the greatest mysteries of the ages.

2.   The wonder of its unity.

The Bible is a complete library composed of sixty-six books written by forty-four different authors over a period of sixteen hundred years. The authors came from different backgrounds—including kings of Israel, warriors, shepherds, poets, a physician, and fishermen. However, the Bible is the most unified book in the world, containing a progressive revelation of the message of God without any real contradictions.

3.   The wonder of its age.

The Bible is without doubt the oldest and most ancient book in the world, beginning with its first section of five books written by Moses thirty-five centuries ago. What other ancient writing is read daily by hundreds of millions of people who find answers to their most immediate problems and concerns?

4.   The wonder of its sales.

Despite the fact that it is the oldest and most popular book in the world, its continuing sales year after year are the greatest wonder in the field of book publishing. Scholars have estimated that there are far more than two billion Bibles published throughout the globe. Incredibly, the American Bible Society printed its two-billionth Bible in 1976 and presented it to President Ford. Despite the phenomenal number of Bibles that exist, it continues to outsell every other book with several hundred million in annual sales worldwide.

5.   The wonder of its popularity.

Despite the fact that the Bible was written over two thousand years ago by ancient inhabitants of the Middle East in an oriental form of literature, the Bible remains the most fascinating and intriguing book on earth. Every year the Bible is read by over a billion adults and young people representing every nation and class of people on the planet.

6.   The wonder of its language.

The Scriptures were written in three languages, Hebrew, Aramaic, and Greek, by forty-four writers. Most of these writers were not well educated, nor did most of them know one another. Yet the wisest men of every age have acknowledged the Bible as the world's greatest literary masterpiece.

7.   The wonder of its preservation.

There is no other book in history that has suffered more opposition, hatred, persecution, and outright burning. Yet, after thousands of years of opposition, the Bible has not only survived, it has triumphed over emperors, kings, and dictators who sought to silence its message of salvation through the blood of Jesus Christ.

The Bible's Transformation of Society

Did the Bible actually change society? The answer is *Yes!* The early Christians startled the pagan world of Rome by their altruism and unselfish care for the poor, the sick, and the dispossessed. Despite the overwhelming wealth of the powerful Roman Empire and other pagan empires of

Egypt, Babylon, and Assyria, there is no evidence from inscriptions or archeology that these societies ever developed hospitals, housing for the poor, or any other provision for the unfortunate people in great need. However, early Christians manifested the love of Christ by caring for both the sick and the needy out of a pure altruism that shocked the jaded Romans.

Let us examine the social situation in England before the Evangelical Revival led by John and Charles Wesley that saved England from a moral abyss. The situation faced by England in the early 1700s was virtually the same as the current moral collapse we see in North America every day. Bishop George Berkeley wrote in his 1738 book, *Discourse Addressed to Magistrates and Men in Authority,* that the level of public morality and religion had collapsed in Britain "to a degree that has never been known in any Christian country. . . . Our prospect is very terrible and the symptoms grow worse from day to day." Berkeley spoke of a torrent of evil in the land, "which threatens a general inundation and destruction of these realms. . . . The youth born and brought up in wicked times without any bias to good from early principle, or instilled opinion, when they grow ripe, must be monsters indeed. And it is to be feared that the age of monsters is not far off." Many different writers and observers, including Daniel Defoe, Alexander Pope, and Samuel Johnson confirm that England was on the point of moral collapse in the early part of the 1700s. In the previous century the official Church of England had severely suppressed other Christians through strict laws, such as the Act of Conformity, forbidding Nonconformists (independent pastors who were not endorsed by the Church of England) to teach or preach. Many of the greatest preachers in England were driven out of their churches for refusing to accept these laws.

When the Great Plague of 1665 killed one of every five people in London, everyone who could fled London, including most of the leaders of the official Church of England and the government. Many of the Nonconformist pastors ignored the laws and returned to help their dying congregations by preaching that the only hope for mankind was trusting in Jesus Christ. Then the apostate government of England passed the infamous Five Mile Act, which prohibited any of the expelled clergy from approaching within five miles of their former church. As a result of this continuing persecution, the Puritans and other Nonconformist pastors were driven from their churches and from society. Over four thousand pastors were thrown into prison. Finally, in 1714, the Schism Act prohibited anyone from teaching anywhere without a special license from his bishop. The result of the suppression of the free preaching of the Word of God was the descent of England into a morass of immorality, perversion, and a widespread moral collapse. The writer Thomas Carlyle wrote his verdict on this society, which could easily fit the condition of North America today, "Stomach well alive, soul extinct." The writer Mark Pattison wrote about the state of morals in this period as follows, "Decay of religion, licentiousness of morals, public corruption, profaneness of language—a day of rebuke and blasphemy." As the moral code broke down, with the teaching of the Gospel repressed, and the crime rate rising, the ruling classes naturally responded by fearfully demanding severe laws to restrain criminals. The moral debasement of England in this century can be illustrated by its savage laws that showed no mercy to those who violated them.

At a time when the writer William E. Blackstone was proudly writing about the glory of England's "unmatched Constitution," both adults and children were subject to one hundred and sixty different laws that resulted in hanging. If anyone shoplifted more than one shilling, stole one sheep, harmed a tree, gathered fruit from someone's property, or snared a rabbit on someone's estate, they would be hanged until dead. The evangelist Charles Wesley reported in his *Journal* that he preached in one jail to fifty-two people on death row including one child of ten years. Public drunkenness was so widespread that many adults and children died as alcoholics. Millions of children and women were working in appalling conditions in factories and mines with unbelievably low wages and no safety rules whatsoever. In other words, England was a moral and spiritual wasteland. Truly, the name *Ichabod,* "the glory of the Lord hath departed," was the epitaph that should be written over this tragic and most shameful century of England's history.

Yet, into this cesspool, God sent the only hope for England; His Holy Scriptures as preached by the greatest evangelists of that age, John and Charles Wesley. In 1769 John Wesley began the Sunday School movement that ultimately flourished throughout England teaching the Bible to millions of young English children. The preaching of the Wesley brothers brought about a spiritual revolution in England and the return to a true faith in the Word of God and its laws. John Wesley's preaching of the whole Bible transformed an immoral state into a reformed nation based to a great extent on the Word of God. As Wesley addressed three thousand people on one occasion, he declared these words from the prophet Isaiah (61:1-2): "The spirit of the Lord is upon me, because he hath appointed me to preach the Gospel to the poor; he hath sent me to heal the broken-hearted; to preach deliverance to the captive, and recovery of sight to the blind; to set at liberty them that are bruised, to proclaim the acceptable year of the Lord" (Wesley's *Journal*, March 31, 1739).

The incredible spiritual energy of this renewed preaching of the Gospel of Christ produced a remarkable series of Christians, including John Milton and John Bunyan, who collectively transformed the soul of that nation. Their faithful preaching of the Word of God produced a marvelous passion for righteousness and freedom that became the central principle of the Evangelical Renewal that saved England from moral corruption. John Wesley preached, "We know no Gospel without salvation from sin.... Christianity is essentially a social religion; to turn it into a solitary religion is indeed to destroy it." The revival of Christianity under the Wesleys and other great preachers of the Gospel produced a practical religion that transformed every aspect of their world. Wesley declared that "a doctrine to save sinning men, with no aim to transform them into crusaders against social sin, was equally unthinkable" (Henry Carter, *The Methodist*, p. 174). The Christian revival in England spread across the English-speaking world-causing innumerable souls to turn to personal faith in Jesus Christ. The brilliant writer Thomas

Macaulay wrote about the Scriptures in the *Edinburgh Review* (January 1828), "The English Bible, a book which, if everything else in our language should perish, would alone suffice to show the whole extent of its beauty and power."

In addition to the personal transformations, this evangelical revival based on the Word of God transformed all of society. Many features of modern Western society that we take for granted today are the result of the great move of God produced by the Wesleyan Revival. The imprisonment of debtors and children was made illegal. Schools were opened to every child who wanted to learn in every parish in the nation. Harsh penal laws and child labor in mines and factories ended as a result of new laws based on the Scriptures. The evangelical movement created the first hope for prosperity and self-respect that the forgotten masses of England had ever known. Finally, the return to the Bible brought about the greatest religious transformation known to mankind. England was restored to greatness. Universal free schools, charities, and free hospitals were formed by Christians who found their motivation in following the Savior, who said, "And ye shall know the truth, and the truth shall make you free" (John 8:32).

Bishop Davidson declared that Wesley was "one of the greatest Englishmen who ever lived" and stated that "Wesley practically changed the outlook and even the character of the English nation." In truth, it was the return to the Bible, the Word of God, that transformed England from a moral wasteland into a land based on the Bible and the faith of Jesus Christ. The only hope for North America today is a similar spiritual revival based on a return to the unchanging Word of God.

Fifteen

The Decision Is Yours

In the final analysis the evidence presented in this book regarding the authority and inspiration of Scripture should prove to any fair-minded reader that the Bible was truly inspired by God. This fact brings us to the place where there is one basic choice that each of us must make. For those who still reject the Bible, there are only two possibilities: either Jesus Christ is wrong or you are. The suggestion that neither is wrong or that it doesn't really matter is untenable because you are simply avoiding the real issue. The evidence presented in this book and the history of the last two thousand years prove that Jesus Christ is not mistaken about the truths He articulated. Each of us must decide if we will personally accept or reject the truth about Jesus Christ expressed in the inspired Word of God. Our answer to this question will determine our happiness in this life and our eternal destiny in either heaven or hell in the next life.

Our personal determination about whether or not the Bible is the inspired Word of God will depend on our evaluation of the Scriptures and the evidence we have explored in this book, *The Signature of God*. However, God never told us, "Believe in the Bible and you shall be saved." The demons of hell know that the Scriptures are true, but this knowledge does not save them. It is significant that the Bible tells us: "Believe on the Lord Jesus Christ, and thou shalt be saved, and thy house" (Acts 16:31). The clear message of the

Scriptures is that our personal relationship to Jesus Christ will determine our eternal destiny—heaven or hell.

The Coming Kingdom of God

The ancient Scriptures tell us that there will be a generation of men at the end of this age living in the Tribulation period who will endure the greatest evil ever unleashed by Satan. The wrath of God will be poured out on unrepentant sinners during that unprecedented seven-year period. Satan himself will be unleashed to attempt his final rebellion against Almighty God in his relentless campaign to establish his satanic kingdom throughout the earth under the rule of his personal representative, the Antichrist. However, these same Scriptures assure us that Jesus Christ will return from heaven at the moment the earth faces its final crisis to defeat the armies of the Antichrist and save mankind from certain destruction. The Lord will defeat Satan after a terrible seven-year period of trial known as the Tribulation. The prophets reveal that two-thirds of mankind will die in horrific judgments, wars, famines, and plagues during this terrible seven-year period. However, this final trial of mankind in this age will end triumphantly with the glorious return of Jesus Christ from heaven with an army of powerful angels and the saints of all the ages. When Christ finally defeats the evil leaders of the world, He will establish His righteous government throughout the world from His throne in Jerusalem. Ultimately, the sound of gunfire will be silenced forever, the terror of torture chambers will be destroyed, the horror of starvation and plague will be removed, the fear of violence and abuse will be lifted from the hearts of men and women. Mankind will finally experience true peace under the kingdom of the Messiah, Jesus Christ.

The Nature of God

What is the nature of God who inspired the writers of the Bible? For thousands of years men have attempted in every culture and society to imagine the nature of God. They have created God in their own image, in the image of the sun, the moon, the stars, the earth, and a hundred other objects. Regardless of their philosophical speculations about the divine intelligence that created our universe, man will never be able to find the truth about God unless he is willing to accept God's written revelation regarding His nature and commands to mankind. The Bible, from Genesis to Revelation, reveals the nature of God as a loving, holy, powerful personality who is vitally interested in the lives and destiny of men.

Years ago, philosophers assigned the name *First Cause* to describe the intelligent supernatural power that must have created our universe. Someone once analyzed the nature of the First Cause by comparing the nature of the First Cause to the Creator, and to the nature of the universe.

The First Cause of limitless Space must be infinite in extent.

The First Cause of endless Time must be eternal in duration.

The First Cause of perpetual Motion must be omnipotent in power.

The First Cause of unbounded Variety must be omnipresent in phenomena.

The First Cause of infinite Complexity must be omniscient in intelligence.

The First Cause of Consciousness must be personal.

The First Cause of Feeling must be emotional.

The First Cause of Will must be volitional.

The First Cause of Ethical values must be moral.

The First Cause of Religious values must be spiritual.

The First Cause of Beauty values must be aesthetic.

The First Cause of Righteousness must be holy.

The First Cause of Justice must be just.

The First Cause of Love must be loving.

The First Cause of Life must be alive.

This analysis reveals that the First Cause of all things, the Creator, must be infinite, eternal, omnipotent, omnipresent, omniscient, personal, emotional, volitional, moral, spiritual, aesthetic, holy, just, loving, and alive. However, when we examine the nature of God as revealed throughout the Holy Scriptures, we discover that the Holy nature of God is precisely that as described above.

Your Final Decision

The decision as to whether or not the Bible is truly the inspired Word of God is vital for every person because it will affect every other area of his or her life. If the Bible is true, then we are accountable to Jesus Christ who will judge each of us at the end of our life. However, if the Bible is not the inspired Word of God, we can safely ignore its commands and warnings about heaven and hell. In the absence of the Word of God those who search for ultimate truth are like a man searching in a strange country for a hidden treasure without the assistance of a map or a guide.

In light of the overwhelming evidence presented in this book for the inspiration and authority of the Bible, any fair-minded reader can see that only a supernatural intelligence could have produced the Scriptures. *The Signature of God* proves that the Bible contains scientific, archeological, and historical information that could not have been produced by human beings unless God directed their writing. However, there are many people, including some readers of this book, who will still claim they can't accept that the Bible is the inspired Word of God. The problem with those readers who still refuse to acknowledge the evidence for inspiration is not a problem of belief; rather, it is their lack of willingness to accept information that challenges long-held positions. While such people can see the strong evidence supporting the Bible, they cannot bring themselves to accept the inevitable conclusion because they would have to abandon their previously held agnostic position to which they are emotionally and intellectually committed. In other words, the problem is not that they *cannot* believe the evidence before their eyes; the problem is that they *will not* believe the evidence pointing to the Bible's divine inspiration, no matter how powerfully the evidence points to the authorship of the Scriptures by God Himself.

Many individuals who have rejected God and the Bible have a huge "investment" in their declared position of rejection of the Scriptures. When they are faced with the evidence that proves the Bible is inspired by God, they are threatened by this information because it requires them to think seriously about God and their responsibility to Him. Many people have avoided thinking seriously about Jesus Christ and eternity by hiding behind their denials of the authority of the Bible and its demands for a decision about Jesus Christ. However, in light of the fascinating evidence provided in this book, every one of us needs to consider the implications carefully. If the Bible is truly the Word of God, then every one of us will stand before Jesus Christ at the end of our life to answer for our sins. On that day, Christians, who accepted Christ's payment of our debt to God through His sacrifice on the cross, will know that their sins have been forgiven by God. Their destiny will be to live with God forever in heaven. However, those who rejected Christ's salvation and the hope of heaven as presented in the Scriptures will have to bear their own punishment for their sinful rebellion when they are exiled to hell forever.

The powerful evidence in this book that proves the Bible is truly the Word of God provides us with a confidence that we can believe the words of the apostle Peter when he spoke about the necessity of faith in Jesus Christ: "Neither is there salvation in any other: for there is none other name under heaven given among men, whereby we must be saved" (Acts 4:12). This declaration of Paul runs counter to the natural inclination of mankind to believe that all religions are equally true and that all roads lead to Rome. Many in our society today believe that, if a person is sincere, God will allow him or her to enter heaven. However, the Word of God declares that sincerity is not enough. If you are sincere in

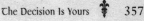

your faith, but have chosen to place your faith in a false religion, then you are sincerely wrong.

There is only one way to reconcile ourselves as sinners to a holy God. The true path to salvation according to the Bible is through personal repentance of our sins and placing our total faith in Christ's sacrificial death on the cross. Every one of us has rebelled against God through our personal sins: "For all have sinned, and come short of the glory of God" (Romans 3:23). The Scriptures declare that our sinful rebellion has alienated each of us from the holiness of God and prevents us from ever entering heaven unless our sins are forgiven by God. "For the wages of sin is death; but the gift of God is eternal life through Jesus Christ our Lord" (Romans 6:23). The death of Jesus Christ on the cross is the key to bringing us to a place of true peace in our heart. The death of our old nature when we identify with Christ's death is the key to finding true peace with God. The only way we can be filled with the grace of God is to approach Him as we would bring a container to a well. It must be empty. It is only then that God can begin to fill us with His grace and spirit.

God cannot simply ignore our sin and allow unrepentant sinners into heaven despite their rejection of God. God's absolute justice makes it impossible for Him to ignore our sins. God's holiness demands that "death," as the "wages of sin," must be paid for our sins in order for His justice to be satisfied (Romans 6:23). If unrepentant sinners actually entered heaven without repenting of their sins, their presence in the Holy New Jerusalem would actually turn that portion of heaven into hell. If you think carefully about it, sinners who reject the forgiveness and worship of Christ would not want to live in heaven. They would despise the holy living and glorious worship of God. The sacred nature of a holy heaven and the evil nature of sin make it absolutely impossible for God to forgive men's sins unless they whole-heartedly repent and turn from them. Only then can God forgive and transform us into sinners saved by the grace of Jesus Christ who cleanses us from our sinful rebellion against His laws. Although we can cleanse our bodies with water, the cleansing of our souls requires the spiritual application of the blood of Christ to our heart.

The Gospel of John records the answers Jesus gave to Nicodemus, one of the religious leaders of Israel, who asked Him about salvation. He told him that "ye must be born again" (John 3:7). Jesus explained to Nicodemus, "whoever believes in him should not perish, but have eternal life. For God so loved the world, that He gave His only begotten Son, that whoever believes in him should not perish, but have everlasting life" (John 3:15–16, NKJV). Every sinner stands condemned by God because of our sinful rebellion against His commandments as revealed in the Scriptures. Jesus said, "He that believeth on him is not condemned: but he that believeth not is condemned already, because he hath not believed in the name of the only begotten Son of God" (John 3:18).

The decision to accept Christ as your personal Savior is the most important one you will ever make. It will cost you a great deal to live as a committed Christian today. Many people will challenge your new faith in the Bible and in Christ. The British writer John Stuart Mill wrote about the importance of our belief in Christ: "One person with a belief is equal to ninety-nine people who only have opinions." However, the Lord Jesus Christ asks His disciples to "follow Me." That decision and commitment will change your life forever. Your commitment to Christ will unleash His supernatural grace and power to transform your life into one of joy and peace beyond anything you have ever experienced. While the commitment to follow Christ will cost a lot, it will cost you everything if you are not a Christian at the moment when you die. Jesus challenges us with these words, "For what shall it profit a man, if he shall gain the whole world, and lose his own soul?" (Mark 8:36).

If you are a Christian, I challenge you to use the evidence in this book when you witness to your friends about your faith in Christ. The proof that the Bible is inspired by God will not convince anyone to place their faith in Jesus Christ. Nevertheless, this evidence proving the Bible's inspiration may remove the intellectual barriers that many people in modern society have raised against seriously considering the claims of Jesus Christ. Once they acknowledge the Scripture's authority, they can begin to consider whether or not they want to accept Christ as their Savior.

If you have never accepted Christ as your Savior, the evidence in *The Signature of God* provides proof that God inspired the writers of the Bible to record His message to mankind. The Scriptures reveal that every one of us will be judged by God as to what we have done with His Son, Jesus Christ. Will you accept Him as your personal Savior and find peace with God throughout eternity; or will you reject Him forever?

You have seen the evidence. The decision is yours.

Selected Bibliography

Anderson, Sir Robert. *Human Destiny.* London: Pickering & Inglish, 1913.

Aviezer, Nathan. *In the Beginning . . . Biblical Creation and Science.* Hoboken: KTAV Publishing House, Inc., 1990.

Ball, Rev. C. J. *Light from the East.* London: Eyre and Spottiswoode, 1899.

Bentwich, Norman. *Fulfillment in the Promised Land.* London: The Soncino Press, 1938.

Blomberg, Craig. *The Historical Reliability of the Gospels.* Leicester: Inter-Varsity Press, 1987.

Blunt, Rev. J. J. *Undesigned Coincidences in the Old and New Testaments.* London: John Murray, 1876.

Bready, J. Wesley. *England: Before and After Wesley.* London: Hodder and Stoughton, Ltd., 1939.

Bright, John. *The Authority of the Old Testament.* Grand Rapids: Baker Book House, 1967.

Burrows, Millar. *The Dead Sea Scrolls of St. Marks Monastery.* New Haven: The American Schools of Oriental Research, 1950.

Canton, William. *The Bible and the Anglo-Saxon People.* London: J. M. Dent & Sons, Ltd., 1914.

Cobern, Camden M. *The New Archeological Discoveries.* London: Funk & Wagnalls Co., 1929.

De Haan, M. R. *The Chemistry of the Blood.* Grand Rapids: Zondervan Publishing House, 1943.

Duncan, J. Garrow. *Digging Up Biblical History, Vol. I & II*. London: Society for Promoting Christian Knowledge, 1931.

Ebers, Georg. *Egypt: Descriptive, Historical, and Picturesque, Vol. I & II*. London: Cassell, Petter, Galpin & Co., 1878.

Finegan, Jack. *Archeological History of the Ancient Middle East*. New York: Dorsett Press, 1979.

————.*Light from the Ancient Past*. Princeton: Princeton University Press, 1946.

Forster, Rev. Charles. *Sinai Photographed*. London: Richard Bentley, 1862.

Gaussen, L. *The Divine Inspiration of the Bible*. Grand Rapids: Kregel Publications, 1971.

Geikie, Cunningham. *The Holy Land and the Bible*. New York: James Pott & Co. Publishers, 1891.

Greenblatt, Robert B. *Search the Scriptures*. Toronto: J. B. Lippincott Co., 1968.

Josephus, Flavius. *Antiquities of the Jews*. Grand Rapids: Kregal Publications, 1960.

Keith, Alexander. *Christian Evidences: Fulfilled Bible Prophecy*. Minneapolis: Klock & Klock Christian Publishers, Inc., 1984.

————.*Evidence of the Truth of the Christian Religion*. London: T. Nelson and Sons, 1846.

Layard, Austen H. *Discoveries Among the Ruins of Nineveh and Babylon*. New York: Harper & Brothers, 1853.

Little, Paul. *Know Why You Believe*. Downers Grove: Inter-Varsity Press, 1988.

Loftus, William Kennett. *Travels and Researches in Chaldea and Susiana.* London: James Nisbet & Co., 1857.

Manniche, Lise. *An Ancient Egyptian Herbal.* London: British Museum Press, 1993.

Maspero, G. *History of Egypt.* London: The Grolier Society, 1900.

McDowell, Josh. *Evidence That Demands a Verdict.* Arrowhead Springs: Campus Crusade for Christ, 1972.

McMillen, S.I. *None of These Diseases.* Grand Rapids: Fleming H. Revell, 1984.

Morris, Henry M. *The Bible and Modern Science.* Chicago: Moody Press, 1968.

————.*The Biblical Basis for Modern Science.* Grand Rapids: Baker Book House, 1984.

————.*Many Infallible Proofs.* El Cajon: Master Books, 1974.

————.*Remarkable Record of Job.* Santee: Master Books, 1988.

————.*Scientific Creationism.* El Cajon: Master Books, 1985.

Morris, Herbert W. *Testimony of the Ages.* St. Louis: William Garretson & Co., 1884.

Panin, Ivan. *The Writings of Ivan Panin.* Agincourt: The Book Society of Canada, Ltd., 1972.

Petrie, Flinders. *Seventy Years in Archeology.* New York: Henry Holt and Co., 1932.

Ragozin, Zenaide A. *Chaldea from the Earliest Times to the Rise of Assyria.* London: T. Fisher Unwin, 1886.

Rambsel, Yacov A. *Yeshua—The Hebrew Factor.* San Antonio: Messianic Ministries, Inc., 1996.

Rappaport, S. *History of Egypt.* London: The Grolier Society, 1904.

Rawlinson, George. *History of Herodotus,* 4 vol. London: John Murray, 1875.

Richards, Lawrence O. *It Couldn't Just Happen.* Fort Worth: Word, Inc., 1989.

Robinson, Gershon. *The Obvious Proof.* London: CIS Publishers, 1993.

Rosner, Fred. *Medicine in the Bible and the Talmud.* Hoboken: KTAV Publishing House, Inc., 1995.

Rule, William Harris. *Biblical Monuments.* Croydon: Werteimer, Lea, and Co., 1873.

Sayce, A. H. *Records of the Past,* 5 vol. London: Samuel Bagster & Sons, Ltd., 1889.

Sheppard, Lancelot C. *Prophecy Fulfilled—The Old Testament Realized in the New.* New York: David McKay Co., Inc., 1958.

Siculus, Diodorus. *Library of History.* Cambridge: Harvard University Press, 1989.

Smith, George Adam. *The Historical Geography of the Holy Land.* London: Hodder and Stoughton, 1894.

Smith, William. *A Dictionary of the Bible.* Boston: D. Lothrop & Co., 1878.

Stanley, Arthur Penrhyn. *Sinai and Palestine.* London: John Murray, 1905.

Stone, Michael. *The Armenian Inscriptions From the Sinai.* Cambridge: Harvard University Press, 1982.

Stoner, Peter W. *Science Speaks.* Chicago: Moody Books, 1963.

Thompson, J. A. *The Bible and Archeology.* Grand Rapids: Eerdmans Publishing Co. 1972.

Thompson, William M. *The Land and the Book.* Hartford: The S. S. Scranton Co., 1910.

Tiffany, Osmond. *Sacred Biography and History.* Chicago: Hugh Heron, 1874.

Unger, Merrill, F. *Archeology and the Old Testament.* Grand Rapids: Zondervan Publishing Co., 1954.

Varghese, Roy Abraham. *The Intellectuals Speak Out About God.* Chicago: Regnery Gateway, 1984.

Vermes, Geza. *The Dead Sea Scrolls in English.* London: Penguin Books, 1988.

———.*Discovery in the Judean Desert.* New York: Desclee Co., 1956.

Vincent, Rev. J. H. *Curiosities of the Bible.* Chicago: R. C. Treat., 1885.

Vos, Howard. *Can I Trust the Bible?* Chicago: Moody Press, 1963.

Wilson, Bill. *A Ready Defense—The Best of Josh McDowell.* San Bernardino: Here's Life Publishers, Inc., 1990.

Wood, Percival. *Moses—The Founder of Preventative Medicine.* London: Society for Promoting Christian Knowledge, 1920.